Masters and Miracles

By
Sam Podany

Published in the United States of America by
Ariadne Publishers, Brookfield, WI, U.S.A.
© 2017 Sam Podany. All rights reserved.
ISBN: 9781548073664

Cover photo credits:

- Swami Rama: psychicregister.com

- Sai Baba: sathyasai-se.org

- Yogananda: Self-Realization Fellowship

- Dr. George Gaye: unknown

Contents

Friends: I have been on the Spiritual Path and meditating since age 17.

What has it done for me? No matter what happens in the outer, no matter what trials, defeats, tribulations, insults, problems, et. al., that have befallen me in this life, I AM HAPPY!

Down deep within, I have steady reliable joy.

My teacher, Master George, said to me: "You may never be rich, you may never be famous, but you WILL be happy." He spoke truth.

The great Yogi Master Swami Sri Yukteswar said "God is ever-new, ever-increasing joy and bliss."

Integrating Statement

This entire effort can be summed up in one paragraph: *It is quite remarkable that nearly all advanced beings and great spiritual teachers in history came forth with wisdom and teachings that were so VERY SIMILAR in their essence and so very similar in areas which their sources obviously thought were the most important.... that despite great variance in times, places, customs, etc.*

I found out another similarity: All organized religions are the offspring of a specific major spiritual teacher, whose remarkable, mystical, and miracle-filled lives inspired many followers. These followers codified the teachings of these original founders and formed "religions" to propagate or perpetuate these teachings and reverence for the lives of these founders. Thereupon, these "religions" often changed, modified, and transmuted into shadows of their initial reality. However, even in the shadows, there is light. For example, despite the horrible cruel and corrupt history of the Catholic Church, it has spawned great saints of majestic spiritual heights, such as St. Theresa of Avila, Padre Pia, St. John of the Cross, and others. Throughout history, spiritual giants have walked with us, playing various human roles, but ascended to the infinite.

I have been extremely lucky as to have walked with, studied with, been blessed by, purified by, and known close up a number of these Great Beings, right here in the 20th and 21st centuries, in the U.S., Europe, and India.

In this book, I am studying in greater depth the mystical, miraculous, and metaphysical teachings of five contemporary teachers, Master George, Swami Vishwananda, Swami Rama, Sathya Sai Baba, and Paramahansa Yogananda, with the leaven of the metaphysical teachings of Jesus. With the exception of Master George, these teachers are of such significance that their followers have or may implement "organized religions."

Because of time and common-sense limitations, I am only giving cursory mention to Buddhism and Islam. Buddhism is extremely complex and I could write ten books but still not do it justice. While I greatly respect Buddhism and I have personally meditated often in Buddhist temples, and while I go specifically to the Great Stupa in Red Feather Lakes, Colorado once a month, and while I recommend every reader have that experience sometime; nonetheless, I have not studied Buddhism and my attempts at any legitimate discussion of same would be ineffectual.

Likewise, with Islam, given all the circumstances in the world today, and given my significant lack of experience and knowledge with this tradition (with the exception of the Sufi branch), and given the limitations of this book, I will not investigate Islam and its complexities therein.

I have given information on a number of major spiritual teachers. There are many more that I have not discussed. For that, I apologize. I could easily add many other great souls and great teachers. I have tried to include as wide a variety of teachers as possible. As stated, I am diving deeper into the teachings of five major spiritual teachers, namely Sathya Sai Baba, Paramahansa Yogananda, Swami Vishwananda, Master George, and Swami Rama, with leavening by a metaphysical view of the words of Jesus. The reasons for focusing on these teachers are as follows: 1) Other than Jesus, these are all contemporary teachers and more relevant today, 2) I have known personally four of them: Master George, Sai Baba, Swami Rama, and Swami Vishwananda, 3) I have studied the life of Jesus for years and have alternative views of same, 4) Paramahansa Yogananda is the guru of my teacher, Master George, and 5) I feel that I can do the best job possible dealing with these teachers.

The way I am organizing this book is to include major topics connected to the Spiritual path and the teachings of the aforementioned six major spiritual teachers related to those topics, as well as brief mention of others.

On each topic, I add commentary of my own personal experiences related thereto.

In doing this work, I have learned much. The foremost thing I have learned is a tremendous respect for the great hearts and souls of these masters. They have unconditional love. In my opinion, this is the highest and best ideal to which we can all aspire. It was difficult to fathom the amazing state of consciousness of these men and women in human form who could love so greatly and so wonderfully.

In the world of sports, there are certain athletes who rise to quite unique and remarkable levels. For example, Michael Jordan rose to the top of basketball and is regarded as the greatest player of all times. Relative to their contemporaries, there have been three athletes in other sports who were almost supermen, namely Babe Ruth in baseball, Wayne Gretzky in hockey, and Tiger Woods in golf. When you study someone like Sai Baba, and compare him to a normal "spiritual" person, it is like comparing a weekend golfer to Tiger Woods. Just as Tiger inspires all of us weekend golfers to improve and play better, so does a being like Sai Baba inspire us to rise to the divinity within ourselves.

That is the main purpose of their lives, to inspire, cajole, teach, and lead us to find and realize our own divinity within ourselves.

I am mightily inspired to rededicate myself to this effort.

Master George

Most real spiritual Masters are secret. They do not make themselves public. They do not advertise, charge money, take huge donations, or appear on television.

These secret Masters generally quietly teach and work with a select small group of disciples. They gradually help their disciples evolve quickly and work out their past karma, so that the disciples can experience God within. They also work quietly, uplifting the vibrations of mankind.

Most of these masters are in India and most of those are in the Himalayas.

4

Master George Gaye was one such secret Master. He brought a beautiful light and joy to this bleak world, and raised the spiritual consciousness of many, yet, he was an American.

He worked quietly, in obscurity, and never charged a dime, never advertised, never made himself a public figure; yet, he was a giant of a being. He was a fully-realized Master who lived continuously in omnipresent, God-consciousness right here in America, in the years 1900-1978.

I was one of his disciples. I bless the day that I met Master George. He was a great, great yogi!

Because I have been inwardly guided by him, I am writing this book to tell his story.

Biography of Master George

Born in Chicago around the turn of the century, young George was soon an orphan. He did not know his father and his mother died soon after his birth.

An older half-sister took care of him until he was five. At that time, he lived with a farmer outside of West Bend, Wisconsin.

Master George was probably the only Yogi Master in many ages who worked his way through grade school!

The first farmer he lived with worked him very hard and fed him very poorly. For a number of years, at ages five through nine, young George worked hard on the farm for his board and room, as well as going to school. He had to milk all the cows every morning and every night. Dr. George mentioned to me that this was fortunate, in a way, because the cruel farmer would only feed him oatmeal for breakfast, lunch, and dinner. Jokingly, he told me that milking the cows had it ancillary benefits because he was able to drink some good, fresh milk regularly to supplement his diet. Living on a farm, he also could garner raw apples, carrots, and other fruits and vegetables once in a while.

Finally, George got a break in the outer world. A kindly, old childless couple took him in on their farm nearby to the mean farmer's farm. He had far less chores to do and they fed him well. They were kind to him in many ways and he lived with them through high school. Unbeknownst to them, they were extremely blessed, spiritually, by their kindness to a Great One like Master George.

The cruel farmer, however, had a different fate. Soon after young Master George left his farm, it was totally destroyed by fire. The cruel farmer was out of business as there were no insurance policies in those days.

Lest you think that Master George had a hand in this stroke of Divine Justice, have no fear. Master explained to me one time about this incident: "I didn't do that to him. His own thoughts and selfishness created that. In the long run, it helped him awaken his soul consciousness. I loved him and sent him love always. I felt bad for his soul that he was so mean." Master spoke of that cruel farmer with no condemnation, no anger, only love, forgiveness, and understanding.

Also, lest you feel sad that Master George had such a tough time of it as a young boy, remember that he was visited by some of the Great Ones, spiritually and physically. Dr. George told me that he was visited in physical manifestation by more than one of the Great Beings who guide man's evolution, including Paramahansa Yogananda, Jesus, Babaji, and Moses.

Also, he always stayed in that high consciousness of God. He was in touch with the Great Ones on the inner plane, even as a young boy. He told me in later years, "I knew who I was, even while I was being born."

After high school, he obtained his teacher's certificate and taught school for a while. He was briefly in the army, but got in just as America's involvement in World War I was winding down and the war ended. Technically, he was a veteran.

In the 1920's, he built his amazing house in Milwaukee by himself, out of used lumber and materials. (See "Twentieth Street" below.)

In 1924, a great yogi master, one of the few real ones who ever came to America, Paramahansa Yogananda, was traveling around the U. S. giving classes and teaching folks to meditate. He gave classes at the old Schroeder Hotel (now the Hilton) in downtown Milwaukee, Wisconsin.

One day, he was out walking on Wisconsin Avenue near the hotel when a young man, George Gaye, came walking the other direction. As they passed each other, much to George's total shock, this long-haired, orange-robed swami said in his customary firm voice, "George! Come to my meeting tonight." Since they had never met before and since George had no knowledge of Yogananda whatsoever until Yogananda said those words, George was pretty shocked. He found out who that fellow was and attended his class that night, and continued with the remainder of Yogananda's classes. He was initiated into Kriya yoga[*] and started practicing Master Yogananda's teachings.

Master George was a loyal disciple the rest of his life and traveled regularly to California to see Yogananda. In those days, the trip took two-three weeks in a Model T or Model A Ford. Sometimes it took even longer if the weather washed out the roads. One time, Dr. George told me that he had trouble with the transmission and had to go up the mountains in reverse! Finally, in 1938, Yogananda sent a letter to Dr. George saying that he was a Master of Yoga and should be addressed with a title of respect, like Master or Dr. (Note: Others called him "Dr." George because he had done so many miraculous healings over the years.)

Dr. George had most of the miraculous powers associated with advanced saints, masters, or yogis. He did countless healings and did little subtle "miracles" to let his students know who he was and that he was with them all the time.

In the 1930's, Dr. George switched occupations and was the head of the tool and die department of a major manufacturer in Milwaukee. Under Yogananda's auspices, he ran the SRF (Self-Realization Fellowship, Yogananda's organization) centers in Chicago and Milwaukee for many years.

---

[*] A psycho-physiological yoga technique Yogananda brought to the West that helps the practitioner achieve rapid spiritual advancement.

He often worked two shifts, sleeping only two hours per night, if that. One of the significant yogi powers is the ability to go into the "breathless state" at will, evidence that they are, in fact "masters" of themselves and masters of death. Dr. George used to go into this state every morning from 3-5 a.m., like his guru and lineage before him.

Yogananda wrote in his book, *The Autobiography of a Yogi*, the following on this subject, on page 125, quoting his guru, Sri Yukteswar:

"So long as you breathe the free air of earth, you are under obligation to render grateful service. He alone who has fully mastered the breathless state is freed from cosmic imperatives. I will not fail to let you know when you have attained the final perfection"; and on page 212 Yogananda says "Numerous bewildered seekers in the West erroneously think that an eloquent speaker or writer on metaphysics must be a Master. The rishis [†] have pointed out that the acid test of a Master is the person's ability to enter <u>at will</u> the breathless state and to maintain the unbroken *samadhi* (highest spiritual state of consciousness humans can attain on earth) of *nirbikalpa*.

I, myself, have had the true good fortune to actually meet and be with four Masters who could attain this state, namely Dr. George, Swami Rama,

---

[†] *Rishis* are the ancient sages in the Himalayas who developed the Vedas, the scriptures of India. The rishis proved through their own internal and external spiritual due diligence the metaphysical truths which carry on today. Their teachings are, directly or indirectly, the basis of all religions.

Sathya Sai Baba, and Swami Vishwananda. They have another thing in common: they emanate a continual aura of bliss. If you are receptive, you can feel a great ocean of bliss coming from these Great Beings. It makes you work hard inwardly to feel that same bliss all the time, no matter what circumstances befall you.

Dr. George stared a Center in Milwaukee in the 1920's connected to Yogananda. He never charged a dime, never took a collection, and never tried to convert anybody.

Starting in the 1920's, he built an amazing set of buildings on his land in Milwaukee at 5000 So. 20th St. He built this remarkable monstrosity out of used lumber, used blocks, used everything. Nothing was square or level, except a lot of the nails, which were square (which tells you how old the nails were!). Roofs, walls, interiors, floors, etc., were all made of totally mismatching salvaged materials. During the depression, he had as many as 19 families living there (which gives you some idea of the size of this incredible structure).

This artifice violated every building code in the city. It was condemned by the city of Milwaukee in 1934. It was still there when I joined Dr. George in 1969. I personally witnessed Milwaukee cops tack up condemned notices twice. Knowing the absolute power that building inspectors have, I do consider Dr. George's continued residence there for all those years one of his best miracles. I asked him how this could happen. His simple and child-like response (with his unique gleam in his eyes) was: "Master wants me to live here" (referring to Yogananda). I thought to myself, "If Masters George and Yogananda are on one side of an issue, you can pretty well kiss goodbye the other side."

While Yogananda was still in the body, Dr. George donated this Milwaukee property to Yogananda's organization, Self-Realization Fellowship, in Los Angeles, maintaining a life estate. Years later, in 1970, he released the property to SRF, even though Dr. George and the organization parted company in 1957. Dr. George formed his own church, called Self-Realization of Friendship Church of Wisconsin.

Dr. George had many wonderful stories about his guru, Paramahansa Yogananda. Here are a few of them:

Dr. George told me this story at The Farm (Dr. George's yoga retreat in northern Wisconsin) in September, 1970. One night in the late 1930's at the SRF ocean retreat in Encinitas, California, Yogananda led a long chanting session. George said they were nearly floating out of the place. Afterwards, Yogananda said, "Come with me, George." They went down to the ocean and Yogananda *walked on the water.* He beckoned for George to come out and do the same. At this point in the story, Dr. George looked at me sheepishly and said, "I did not go because I was afraid." Well, I enjoyed the story, but I pondered it for quite a while because I knew that fear was not in the lexicon of Dr. George. I didn't believe that Dr. George would be afraid of going out and walking on the water; something didn't make sense to me. I meditated on it for a number of weeks. Then the answer came: "Oh yes," I realized. "Yogananda had always told Dr. George to remain secret and not demonstrate his yogi powers. This was a test of Dr. George." The very hour after this came to me, I saw Dr. George and he smiled very big and confirmed outwardly what I had realized. He wanted me to know that he was a very secret saint this lifetime. He went on to tell me that Yogananda had done many public miracles from 1920 to 1931 as he traveled around the United States, personally initiating thousands of people into Kriya yoga. Then, George said, Yogananda told his close devotees that he would do no more public miracles in the United States.

I had a good friend in Dr. George's church named Waldo Moe. When Moe was in college, he met Yogananda in Pittsburgh, PA in 1926. He took Yogananda's classes and became a lifelong disciple. Moe worked for International Harvester out of Chicago his whole life and was a member of George's church for 30 years when I met him. A delightful, joy-filled fellow, I used to help him take his dock out in the Fall at his place in Lake Geneva, Wisconsin. Moe told me the following story about Yogananda's presentation in Pittsburgh in 1927: "Master stood on stage and said in his customary strong voice, 'You people have weak thoughts. Your bad thoughts make you sick, but good thoughts can make you healthy. I will show you. I will form a boil on my arm and then I will remove it.' Master thereupon rolled up his sleeve, formed a

12

boil mentally on his arm, showed everybody in the audience, and then *mentally removed it!* He showed it to the stunned audience. Then, he said 'You people have weak wills. You need to develop more willpower. I will demonstrate.' Then he asked five of the biggest men in the audience to come up and hold the other end of a rope. Master was only 5 feet, 4 inches tall and pudgy. However, he instructed those men to try to move him pulling on the other end of the rope he casually held in his hands. He said, 'I am setting my will and you will not move me!' The men yanked and yanked and pulled and absolutely could not move him!"

A long-time Yogananda disciple, A. M. Keith, a noted attorney in Minneapolis, Minnesota, told about this experience with Yogananda in 1928 when Yogananda gave classes in Minneapolis. I summarize the story as follows:

"I was enthralled with these amazing teachings of this remarkable Master form mysterious India. I told one of my law partners all about it. This partner was very skeptical and asked how this person could discuss these eternal verities and talk so glibly about realizing God within, life after death, and reincarnation. So, I invited Master to come and speak with us during the day in our offices. He came into our conference room, sitting down on the leather couch. My partner started grilling him. Master chuckled and said, 'You are a good attorney and I see that you are cross-examining me to establish my bonafides. Let me demonstrate.' Thereupon, Yogananda lay down on the couch and proceeded to go into the breathless state. There he was, lying on the couch, with no breath and no heartbeat! We checked carefully. He was not breathing. We checked his pulse. There was none. We were screaming, 'come back, please come back!' We were totally scared about the implications of having the corpse of a well-known foreigner in our law offices! For over 45 minutes, we debated about calling the police. We prayed. We didn't know what to do. Then, Yogananda came back into his body! He sat up and cheerfully said, 'See, it's very easy if you know what you are doing!'

"Then, the Master said to me, 'Mr. Keith, you have had many Christian lifetimes. I am giving you a special meditation technique. If you practice it faithfully, the Spirit will descend on you with a dove, just like the Spirit descended on Jesus at the River Jordan.' Mr. Keith went on to attest that he faithfully practiced Master's teachings for two years and was, indeed, blessed with a great spiritual initiation of the Spirit descending on him like a dove. He practiced Kriya yoga his entire life.

Railroad

At age twelve, Master George traveled the entire summer out in the American West, working as a water boy on a large railroad construction crew. It was a rough and primitive time, in many ways. He had a lot of help from many kind men. However, as you might surmise, there were a lot of bad men and very rough men, as well. George told me about some remarkable events in which he was protected by his spiritual guides from many bad experiences, including possible death.

One time, two very big and bad men were going to rob him. He was warned inwardly in advance. He managed to get away before they could complete their nefarious mission. On other occasions, his *chi* (spiritual energy) blocked physical abuse and actually knocked villains down or out, as required.

During high school, he worked at a job in a factory, as well as doing his farm chores and maintaining excellent grades. The school officials singled him out as the outstanding graduate of his class.

Rattlesnake

Dr. George showed me a big scar on his hand. I asked him what it was. He told me the following very unusual story: "One year, on a trip back from seeing Master (Yogananda) in California, I stopped in New Mexico. I stayed up in the mountains by myself, outdoors. I fasted on water for 40 days and 40 nights like Jesus did. Master told me to do this." I asked him if he had visions. He said, "Oh, yes. You, too, should fast one day a week on liquids only. It will be good for your inner organs and give them a rest." I did do that for many years. (Come to think of it, I need to get back doing that again, I reminded myself!) He continued: "I slept each night right on the side of a ledge, with a big drop. Master told me I needed to do that to 'train my subconscious.' It was there that one morning, I woke up and a rattlesnake bit me right here. I used a knife and sucked out the poison. I felt bad for the poor fellow (the snake). I think I scared him." I asked him if he was affected by this. He said, "Just a little. I slept a bit longer for a few days, but Master helped me in the unseen."

Slugger George (1)

Master George told me one time with great solemnity, "The only thing that ever tempted me in this life was baseball." Well, as a lifelong baseball fan, I was really impressed. I thought it was great that God sent me to the only guru in the world who was actually "tempted by baseball." To me, that was cool. However, I truly did not ever connect the dots related to this statement. He said this to me a number of times over the years. I mentioned this to other students of Dr. George but they looked at me askance, never having heard anything like this. I still did not get the clue.

Many years passed, and long after Dr. George had passed from the body, I was reminiscing about this statement of his. I thought about it for some time and then literally broke out laughing, because this was a characteristically indirect teaching from Master George! Think for a second: Do you really believe that a Real Yogi Master would be tempted by baseball, of all things? Of course not; however, a student of a Real Yogi Master (such as me!) would and certainly could be tempted by baseball!

Master George was so tactful and kind, and so respectful of his students' free will that he rarely made any direct, stern pronouncements, or commandments. He would rather make indirect hints and off-hand suggestions, such as in this case actually transferring this "temptation" to himself.

Thus, a wise devotee will try to apply truth to himself rather than others. In this case, I have to say honestly that I would still trade all my lands and money to have played major league baseball. However, thanks to Master George, I certainly would not trade my soul, my meditations, my relationship with the Great Ones, or the joy, bliss and love of God.

Slugger George (2)

Master George did, however, play baseball. His compatriots called him "Slugger George." He was quite a hitter and became a player-coach of a town team in West Bend.

He told me of one case where his squad traveled to play a pretty tough team. This team, besides being good, was also downright mean, i.e., they verbally badgered the opposing team's pitcher and batters mercilessly. They hurled obscenities and crudities, and were supported by the ornery fans that threw objects at the players. Further, the pitchers routinely targeted at the opposition hitters, sometimes injuring them. They also used their spikes liberally while in the field and running the bases.

As the game progressed, the villainous team used their normal nasty tactics. They were ahead, 4-2 and appeared to be on their way to an easy victory. However, enter Dr. George:

Master George told me (albeit somewhat sheepishly) that he did something to these tough opponents that really wasn't fair, i.e., he concentrated! Master George smiled and pointed at his head, and told me, "I concentrated real hard and hit one <u>way</u> out there! That quieted them all down real quick, and we won the game!"

God help the baseball pitcher who has to face an athlete like Master George, who, besides a good batting stroke, has supernatural yogic powers!

Twentieth Street

Master George lived for many years at 5000 South 20th Street in Milwaukee, Wisconsin. He had large acreage there, 50 blocks south of downtown Milwaukee, 30 blocks or so from what is now General Mitchell International Airport, the main airport of Milwaukee.

Over the years, he donated land to the city for a road and sold some other parcels here and there. On the remaining heavily wooded twenty-seven acres, he built the most amazing set of buildings you ever saw in American civilization. He built them one on top of the other, adding room after room after room, all out of <u>used</u> building materials, which he salvaged from all over the place. He cared not a whit for artistry or architecture, but the building conglomeration was cool in the summer, warm in the winter, and solid as a building could be.

The City of Milwaukee did not appreciate these buildings. They violated nearly every code there ever was. They condemned the whole complex in 1934, and tried for 33 years to evict him, without success.

During the 1930's, he had a goat named, of course, "Billy." This goat was one tough, ornery goat! Among the goat's greatest pleasures was eating flowers from outraged neighbors' gardens when he could escape from his pen or tether.

Considering the fact that it was an urban area surrounding Master George's 13 acres, this goat was a real pain to civilization.

However, one must remember that in those days, these same outraged people had dogs that roamed the streets at will, defecating and biting whatever and whomever they wanted. So, in my mind, Billy wasn't that harmful relative to the surroundings of the day, particularly since Master George made a sincere effort to keep him penned or tied up, doing his milky duty for his female herd.

Billy, however, earned his final passport to the country, i.e., Master George took him far out of town and gave him to a farmer after Billy.... Well, first let me tell you that Master George's buildings had irritated the building inspectors once again. Thus, they sent a police officer out to serve papers on Master George. The officer arrived on his motorcycle and officially served Master the papers. Master George was gracious to the officer and politely accepted the papers, knowing that Divine Mother and Yogananda were going to allow him to stay there no matter what municipal authority said what!

The officer came out and got back on his motorcycle and (you probably guessed it) was unceremoniously dumped on his posterior by Billy, who had charged the unfortunate cop and motorcycle at full speed and butted the cop and the cycle head over teakettle.

Master George told me with a chuckle, "The city made me get rid of Billy, then."

That was one tough goat!

Work

Master George always worked. He worked inwardly and outwardly and he put us, his disciples, to work. Our biggest jobs were:

Building Buildings

We built buildings out of used lumber, used blocks, dead oak trees, used nails, wood shavings for insulation, used roofing, etc.

We would use any solid and thick wood or steel entity as joists. One of my specialties was cutting dead oak trees, stripping them, hauling them from the woods over to the building site. Thereupon, I would dig a 4-foot hole with a posthole digger. (The frost line was three feet in those days in Wisconsin). Then, I would put the log down into the hole, where it would be a joist. Every few feet, around the perimeter of the building we were creating, I would dig more holes and put more logs in same. Then, we would board up the exterior with used boards.

Thereupon, we would use 2 x 6's or whatever and make roof joists and beams. We would attach those to the tops of the logs (now joists) and board up the exterior of the roof with used lumber and used nails. We would use any roofing material we could find, both used and new.

Having completed the exterior, we would start on the interior. We started to board up the inside walls. Now, it got interesting. Dr. George had a very clever methodology: wood shavings. There was a sawmill nearby, and we would take our trucks and trailers over there. The sawmills had great piles of shavings. We loaded up trucks and trailer loads and brought the shavings back to The Farm. We stored the shavings in a dry place so they would not get soaked by rain or snow.

As we boarded up the interior walls, we would wrap up units of wood shavings with old newspapers. As we added a level of inside wall boards, we would stuff these paper-wrapped shavings down into the wall. The walls were at least 4-6 inches thick. This was a remarkable insulation. Our buildings were cool in the summer and kept heat real well in the winter.

Sometimes, when we had used cement blocks from salvaging a building, we would do it a little different. In cases where we had cement blocks, we would first dig a basement with a dredge and a bulldozer. Many times, I would "ride" the dredge and scoop out the dirt while Dr. George drove the bulldozer. Using that method, we dug one basement that was about 40 feet long, 30 feet wide, and 13 feet deep. We implemented used blocks and built a basement (with new cement). For the floor of the basement, we used the method I described in the section below "D" called "Concrete."

We would not use logs, obviously in such a case. We would use regular used lumber for joists. We would connect them in the normal manner to the above-established foundation. Then, we would complete them in the procedures already described.

Taking Down Buildings (To Get Used Materials)

When I first joined Dr. George, I found that the students had been engaged in taking down the 5000 So. 20th St. complex, board by board, block by block, miscellaneous part by part. I joined in that effort for a few years. We gradually took down every board, nail, etc., and transported the material up to The Farm, 160 miles away. Much of what we used at The Farm for the buildings there we salvaged from 20th Street. Note: these materials were ALREADY used, when Dr. George built the entire complex in the 1920's and 1930's! I must have straightened a billion nails in my career alone.

We took down other buildings as they came along as well. One time, there was a fast food restaurant being torn down. I made a deal with the owners and told them we would have it down and out of there in two weeks. We did it and got a whole lot of very nice concrete blocks for our efforts.

Moving Used Articles (Junk) from One Building to Another

This aspect of our works was an example of the "Zen" quality of Dr. George. There was no objective or outer reason for doing these things. We all laughed a lot about it and always wondered why.

First, we collected and saved every conceivable type of article that ever existed on earth. We would transport them up to The Farm every week in our trucks and trailers. We would unload them and store them in one building that we had built after another. Then, once stored in one building, Dr. George would order us to move the stuff to another building!

Having no *objective* reason why we did this stuff, there had to be a *spiritual* reason. We meditated and thought about it and discussed it for many years. Here are our conclusions: 1) We really worked out a lot of karma from past lives. I think this was the main purpose for all this effort; 2) After doing this for a day, we had unbelievably good meditations and dreams! We got high as kites, you might say; and 3) We learned to control out thoughts and have the consciousness that whatever job we did was for God and was good.

To my knowledge, Dr. George never explained to anyone why we did these things, in the outer, that is.

Concrete

When it came to concrete, think jigsaw puzzle. Dr. George was at his creative best. We used salvaged concrete.

We would pick up the used chunks of concrete from a road or a sidewalk that had been torn up for renovation or expansion, and we would power winch them onto our truck. We would take those concrete chunks and place them together like a jigsaw puzzle for a floor of a garage or basement.

(We would fill in the cracks with cement.) We used big steel bars as levers. We also used rollers to move the concrete along the ground. Dr. George and two people could easily do a basement or garage or building floor this way. It was solid as a rock and did not cost anything except for the cement.

Firewood

We were often in the woods cutting and dragging out dead trees for firewood. Then we would cut them into logs and store them in the basement. One funny thing: I got a great respect for maple trees when I tried to split a large maple log. It was about two feet in diameter and was about two feet high. I thought I could split it with wedges like I split oak and other large logs. By the time I got done and finally got the darn thing apart, I had used every wedge we had and other things besides. Dr. George really laughed at that miscalculation on my part.

Cesspools, Wells, Garbage Pits, Outhouses, etc.

We certainly dug enough of them and got real acquainted with Mother Earth.

Out standard method for cesspools and garbage pits was using the old bulldozer and scoop routine. As stated before, I "rode" the scoop many times as Dr. George drove the bulldozer.

For wells and outhouses, it was the shovel deeper and deeper method, no subtlety here.

Roofs and Chimneys

We sure did enough roofs and chimneys. We got up on the roofs near the eves and started boarding up. As we got a couple of rows of boards across, then we could sit on the beginning of the roof and keep adding rows of boards. Fortunately, I never had a fear of heights and I was thin and agile in my younger days.

We used *used* cement blocks to make chimneys. It was pretty simple: we just kept adding blocks around the central open area until we got it as high as we needed it. Our chimneys always worked real well. They were solid, too.

I have seen nearly every major miracle done by a saint or holy person on this earth, except one: Levitation. I never saw it, nor did I know any case of it except for one. Just recently, I heard from a man who had lived at The Farm in Dr. George's last few years in the body. This was during a time when my mother became paralyzed and I was spending more time in Minnesota with her. This man's name was Tom Trend. He and his brother Bobby were very nice fellows and good workers. This story came from Tom just recently, and I am paraphrasing his words: "Dr. George and I were up on the roof, finishing off some stuff up there. It was hot and near the end of the day. We were standing near the eve at the end of the roof. I stood up and paused for a minute. Dr. George was over to my right and said, 'Tommy, maybe we should go get some supper.' And then I realized that I was standing at the edge of the roof and he was over to my right, which meant that he was standing on

<u>nothing! i.e., levitating.</u> Then he chuckled and said, 'I better get back on the roof. Everyone will do too much talking otherwise.' He got back on the roof and we went down and had supper. I was in shock for a long time over that one."

When you worked with Master George, you were <u>immensely</u> spiritually blessed. Your entire system was oxygenated, and spiritualized, and you worked off and purified ages of past karma. It was truly magnificent.

Master George's Disciples

Master George had an unusual group of people as disciples. Except for a few quiet and mellow ones, I don't believe I ever saw a more stubborn and strong-minded lot in my life, myself included.

Nobody in the group really had much in common outwardly. In fact, there were numerous souls who had completely different needs and paths. However, we had two characteristics that were the same: 1) a complete dedication to Self-Realization, and 2) a complete love and trust of Master George.

Thus, the Spiritual Light in the church was intense and beautiful, and despite outer differences, everyone connected with Master George made tremendous inner progress. When we meditated and chanted as a group, with Dr. George, the energies would literally rise up like a spiritual fire filled with bliss and joy and love.

There were few if any of us who would be regarded as saintly. We certainly made every mistake in the book. I wonder to this day how and why that particular group of souls got together and why Dr. George even put up with us.

Somehow, we had achieved merit in past lives and deserved the blessing of being with him this lifetime.

Dr. George humorously said that he was a "Metaphysical Garbage Man." I asked him what he meant and he said that his big job was holding people's hands as they worked out their bad past karma.

Observations of Master George

Master George knew that I was very interested in history. He knew that I had a sympathy for soldiers. He told me that I had been a soldier in many past incarnations. He told me that this lifetime I had to come "unarmed" and do no fighting. He told me that this lifetime I had to learn to do it with love, kindness, and forgiveness. He told me one time, "You must learn to take it on the chin and forgive." I have tried my best to do just that. Fortunately, forgiveness is freeing for me and makes *me* happy, so it has become a lot easier over the years. My sense of humor has helped regarding this issue, not to mention my candid view of my own faults and stupidity, which makes it pretty dumb to be mad at someone else.

George noted a difference between Generals Eisenhower and Patton. He told me that Eisenhower dreamed and thought often of the men he had ordered into battle, sending many of them to their deaths. Eisenhower, he said, was very tired of war and deep in his soul, would not ever like to fight a war again. He had done his duty for the country and the world, but realized in doing it, a higher calling for future lifetimes. He told me that Eisenhower could have gone into Viet Nam after Dien Bien Phu fell to the communists in 1954, but that he prayed all night and decided not to.

General George Patton, on the other hand, according to Dr. George, <u>liked</u> war. He had a <u>desire</u> for war, and it would apparently take many lifetimes to release that desire. Dr. George told me that Patton had been the younger brother of Hannibal. Dr. George said that Hannibal was the greatest general of all time. He described to me in vivid detail Hannibal taking 25,000 men and 29 elephants through the Alps into Italy to fight the Romans. The Romans sent an army of 80,000 men to face him but they were obliterated.

Dr. George said that Hannibal later reincarnated as General Erwin Rommel, the famous Desert Fox of the German Army in World War Two. Dr. George said that the reason Rommel and Patton never faced each other on the battlefield was because of their past brotherhood closeness. They had great respect for each other.

Patton believed in reincarnation. Many times, he could tell folks things about a place he had been before. Dr. George said that he also had been a powerful American Indian chief in another lifetime.

Dr. George said that both Abraham Lincoln and Martin Luther King were yogis in the Himalayan Mountains in previous lives. Both had trained for a long time to enter Western bodies and accomplish their missions. He said that Lincoln, in particular, had spent two lifetimes in the Himalayas as a yogi acetic, meditating and gaining strength for the horrible job he had to do. Dr. George went on to say that rarely was anyone happier to leave the human body than Lincoln; Dr. George said that Lincoln was real grateful to be able to leave. What really hurt him, according to Dr. George, was the evil backbiting, jealousy, greedy money-making, and treachery of Lincoln's supposed allies in government and business.

He also said that James Earl Ray who supposedly killed Martin Luther King was nowhere near the event and could not have done it. He said that very high-up people in the government had a lot to do with it.

Dr. George surprised me one day by talking about Billy Graham and Oral Roberts in depth. He explained to me that they were both "old and good souls," doing hard jobs dealing with narrow-minded people with limited views of truth. He said that each had agreed to serve this lifetime in the manner in which they did. He said that their spiritual guides were "blocking them off" in consciousness so that they would stick to the very straight and narrow of the theology and help those who needed that particular brand of religion. Dr. George reminded me that just because I felt and lived in one manner, that it was not necessarily true for everyone. I said, "But Dr. George, these fundamentalist Christians are so narrow-minded, they do not accept anybody who differs with them even a little." He chuckled and said, "Well, that gives you a chance to expand your love and your forgiveness."

Dr. George said to me that of all the presidents, Jack Kennedy was the President "closest to the Light," and was able to receive the guidance of the Great Ones most easily. He said that both Jack and his brother Bobby had been great Romans during the days of the Roman empire. I did not get any specific identities.

Dr. George stated that Lyndon Johnson and Hubert Humphrey had strong desires in their hearts to help the poor and African Americans in the U.S., and rectify social injustice. Johnson and Humphrey got the Civil Rights Act passed. They also implemented rural electrification and passed legislation to help the poor and downtrodden in this country.

Dr. George said that Richard Nixon's mother was a strong influence on him, and he had a vision of world peace. He said that Nixon could have been one of the best presidents of all, but was undone by personal flaws. He said that he carried too much anger and resentment.

Dr. George stated that India would slowly and gradually rise into greater influence and prosperity. He said that America and India were each half of the whole. They both needed the good things of the other.

Dr. George stated that Europe has a cloud of karma from so many wars and battles. He said that all the European nations needed to be increasingly humanitarian and avoid war and conflict.

Regularly, he said to me, "Watch out for China." When I asked him what he meant, he would not say but would smile enigmatically and repeat, "Watch out for China."

In 1969, he said that there would be "no end of problems in the Middle East" because of the greed, anger, and stubbornness of all the participants, the United States included. He said that it was a "very mis-named place," i.e. calling it the "Holy Land," because it was one of the most unholy places on earth, with its history of war, killing, violence, and lack of forgiveness.

I almost laughed out loud when he told me that mosquitoes are the product of man's bad thoughts.

He said, "America would be spared much of its karma if there were enough people of self-realization."

He said one time when someone asked him about prophecies of earth changes, epic disasters, shifting of continents, California falling into the ocean, etc., "The work of the yogis and the Great Ones is to make sure that the prophecies do *not* come true."

He told me that Jesus had come back in human form at least one time. He would not tell me who or when.

He said that Jesus was in Divine Bliss on the cross. He said that Jesus was always immersed in divine joy.

He said that Jesus had definitely lived in India.

He said that the Three Wise Men were from India and the Himalayas.

He told me that he had a number of lifetimes in China.

He said that he had been on Venus and actually came from there. I truly did not understand this. I asked him quite frequently to explain further and he told me that this knowledge would come to me later when I was ready to receive it.

He used to chuckle about the Viet Nam War. He said, "Apparently they think those 'Viet Nans' are going to swim over and take us over." He added, "It is very bad karma for us to do what we are doing over there," and "They (American leaders) think they can kill anyone they want as long as they are not wealthy white people but it is all written in the Akashic Record. All these men (i.e., political leaders) will have to answer for their thoughts and deeds one day."

Yogi Powers of Master George

As I have stated throughout this work, Masters, saints, and sages exhibit "miraculous" powers routinely. My friend and teacher, Dr. George had no shortage of these powers. The interesting thing about Dr. George was that he had been specifically instructed by his guru, Paramahansa Yogananda, to be secret. Dr. George told me that Yogananda had said to him one day in California, "George, you must never let them know who you are." Dr. George explained to me that Yogananda had gone on to say that in America of contemporary times, it was not wise to be too open with miracles or yogic powers because of the rigid narrow-mindedness of the fundamentalist Christians.

However, when there was a need by his devotees or when he just wanted to encourage us, some amazing things happened. I describe a few of them in this section:

Saving My Life

It was September 1, 1968. I was 24 years old. I was at The Farm in Friendship, Wisconsin, and working on the side of a building. The scaffold broke and I fell from 12 feet and landed on my head on concrete. I was ostensibly dead.

The sheriff came and drove me at more than 100 miles per hour to a hospital in Marshfield, Wisconsin, over 50 miles away. The sheriff later told me, "You were dead!" and he walked away and wouldn't even look at me; he was spooked. Then, after he calmed down, I spoke with him and he stated that he had seen many accident victims in his day and that he felt he was just going through the legal motions delivering me to the hospital as required by his procedures.

When he got to the hospital, the surgeon, Dr. Salibi, a Moslem from Lebanon, told those present that there was no hope, that I was a goner. Then, Dr. George arrived. Against all established medical procedure, he entered the emergency room and told Dr. Salibi, "Patch him up the best you can and I will do the rest."

Thereupon, Dr. Salibi sort of patched me up and I regained life signs. Dr. Salibi told my parents when they arrived from Minnesota later in the evening that there was absolutely no hope, that even if I had somehow managed to have stayed alive temporarily, that I would be merely a vegetable. My head was irretrievably crushed.

My mom said for years, that she asked Dr. George, "Will Sam live?" Dr. George closed his eyes for about ten long minutes and opened them and said firmly, "Yes."

Well, I stayed alive. They moved me after a few days from the emergency room to a regular room. Dr. George told my mom to stay there and to keep praying. They allowed her to stay in the room with me, unheard of. Dr. Salibi ordered it and whatever doctors want, they get, so my mom stayed in the room against all regulations.

I kept staying alive. Thirty-five days passed. One day, I woke up in this strange hospital bed. I was lying there, knowing nothing after the time I climbed up on the scaffold and was working, listening to the Chicago Cubs play the St. Louis Cardinals on the radio.

Now, here I was in that bed. I had tubes in me and a bandage on my head. I was wondering what the heck I was doing there, when I looked over and saw my mom and dad sitting there watching a baseball game on television, and I started watching. Bob Gibson, future Hall of Famer, was pitching for the St. Louis Cardinals. Then, the announcer said, "The next batter for the Detroit Tigers will be Norm Cash." I thought to myself, "Wait a minute. How come Detroit is playing St. Louis? They're in different leagues." I said to my dad, "Hey Pop, how come Detroit's playing St. Louis?" My dad and mom almost fell over backwards from their chairs in surprise! My mom started crying tears of joy. My dad had tears in his eyes. They couldn't believe it. They looked at me like I was from outer space. I assured them that my mind was clear as a bell. They told me that I had fallen and had been in a coma for 35 days and that the game on television was the first game of the 1968 World Series! (I have always said in later years that God was not going to let me miss the 1968 World Series, which was a real good one.)

I convinced my mom and dad that I was in good shape by telling them from my memory that this world series was a replay of the 1934 Series when St. Louis and Dizzy Dean beat the Tigers in seven games. This was a good test of my mental capacities because I was a baseball trivia expert when I was young. They were ecstatic.

The next day, Dr. George came to visit. He said to me, "You're just fine," and got me unhooked from different tubes and helped me get up out of the bed. He walked me down the hall to where there was a pool table in the visitors' area. He got the cues and the ball and we started playing pool.

Nurses suddenly appeared from every direction and were shocked. They grabbed a wheelchair, and slapping me into it said that I should not be moving around. I looked at Dr. George. He had that gleam in his eyes and was chuckling. The nurses glared at him as they wheeled me away.

They slapped me back in bed. Soon a large, officious nurse showed up with a long needle in her hands. She told me to roll over. Foolishly, I did, and she gave me a real hard shot of some medicine in my backside. Whooh, it hurt. The next day, she came again, and I said, with much greater determination that she ever figured that I could muster, "No way." I absolutely refused to get shot in the backside again. I said, "If you think I need this medicine, then you can give it to me orally." She sniffed in surprise and said she would have to consult with the doctor. The doctor finally came by. Dr. Salibi had a hard time truly believing that I was well. He knew my medical record and had seen me dead or close to it. I told him with great vigor that he could certainly give me an oral medicine if he really deemed it necessary. He looked at me for a few minutes, then, he gave the approval for the oral version of the medicine.

All the staff there at St. Joseph's Hospital said that my survival was a miracle of the Virgin Mary. Dr. Salibi told me that my survival was a miracle of Allah. Many Christian preachers in town took credit or gave it to Jesus. We all knew, however, that Dr. George and God had saved my life. Period.

There is one more little detail. Dr. Salibi was real reticent about letting me leave the hospital. After all, he had seen, right in front of his nose, a seemingly dead person keep living. He had then seen the "vegetable" he had diagnosed walking around the hospital talking with the staff and going down to the chapel to meditate. Finally, he gave me the approval to leave. He armed me with a large box of medicines and prescriptions. Dr. George came and drove me to The Farm, which was about an hour away. I asked him what to do with the medicines, and he said, "They will make good firewood." So, I took them downstairs to the wood-burning furnace and pitched them in. I never took a medication and was fine for many years, until a month after Dr. George passed. Then, I had a seizure. The doctors told me that it was customary for an injury like mine; the scar tissue would expand over time and put pressure on the brain. Since then, I have taken a medication called Dilantin which solves the problem. Interesting note: the doctors could not believe that I had not been taking any such medication for ten years since the fall. They said that normally it would start happening fairly soon. I figured that the medications I threw away were supposed to be part of that process, but as long as Dr. George was in the body, I was covered.

People ask me if I remember anything about where I was during my coma. Even now, as I write about this, I remember an infinite white searing light of awesome Joy, Joy beyond description. Since I woke up in that hospital, I have had that Joy with me ever since. Sometimes it takes an hour or two of meditation to get it back after tough times in life, but it is always there.

Healing My Thumb

I have a big scar on my left thumb, back near where the thumb meets the hand. This scar goes nearly all around the thumb. It happened in 1964. I am not the most mechanically inclined person on earth. In fact, I probably have a learning disability when it comes to mechanical things. I am very good at math, science, music, communication, etc. but I have zero aptitude for art and mechanical things.

I never was around tools much as a kid. My dad wasn't that interested in building things and we didn't have a workshop in the basement or the garage like a lot of folks. However, when I joined Dr. George, I had a crash course in building everything. Also, I had little money and so all my cars were old and cranky for many years and I was forced to learn how to deal with a lot of issues thereof. I learned how to use many tools and many applications.

One such tool was a common saw. I found myself using a saw regularly as we built buildings. Unfortunately for doing such tasks, I am very absent-minded and my mind just doesn't get interested in this type of work. I did it and do it basically for God and I did it then because my teacher wanted me to do it. One day, I was thinking about something else, and Wham! I nearly cut my thumb off with the saw, it leaped right out of the board and I had almost cut through my thumb. It was bleeding profusely. Fortunately, Dr. George was nearby. He came over and motioned for me to show him. He took the thumb and hand in his fingers and held both hands over it. His eyes gleamed; I could feel the energy and my thumb got hot. The bleeding stopped. He said, "There. It will be fine. Go put a band aid on it." I went in and got a band aid and attached same. It did not bleed anymore and soon healed over. To this day, I can show you the scar which goes around 2/3 of my thumb. I showed it to a medical doctor one day who absolutely couldn't believe it. The doctor looked at me like I was speaking Chinese.

Thanks, Dr. George.

Broken Neck

Building all those buildings, roofs, chimneys, etc., over the years had its hazards. We had a rule: no kids on the roofs. We had many families with many different kids over the years and we disciplined the kids to stay off the roofs and stay away from chain saws, holes, etc.

However, there was one rambunctious young boy, named Greg, nine years old at the time, who later was a real good high school football player and a pretty strong man.

Greg was always into something, but he was so likeable that no one really minded too much. One day, he got up onto a roof. His mother, some other folks, and I were working nearby. Suddenly, we heard a noise and looked up. We saw Greg fall face forward off the roof. His mom screamed. He hit the ground like a rock, face first. His mother knelt down and held him; he looked dead but I couldn't tell for sure. Then, Dr. George came over and picked him up out of her arms and told us to stay where we were and he walked into the house. Both his mom and another person said they felt sure that his neck was broken. I could certainly see from my perspective that he may have broken his neck. About a half hour later, Dr. George came out on the porch and summoned us in. There was Greg with his face all scuffed sipping juice at the table. His mom cried and cried. She was so grateful. She thought she had lost a son.

Fortunately, this scared the other kids over the years from going on any roofs.

Dr. George's Driving

Earlier, I described how Dr. George "trained his subconscious." Well, I experienced this in spades a number of times as life went on. It had to do with his driving.

Dear reader, I can assure you, as can many of Dr. George's surviving students, that we rode many, many miles in his truck or car with him driving *with his eyes shut.* This was one of the more unusual of his "miracles." I can attest that I sat in the passenger seat of the car or truck as Dr. George drove many hundreds of miles of highways and freeways with his eyes shut. I cannot explain it. I have no idea why he did this, other than to instill faith in us, which it sure did!

Windshield Wipers

In April of 1975, I had completed a singing job in Steamboat Springs, Colorado. I was making my way back to Los Angeles. Dr. George was flying into Los Angeles for one of his speaking tours there, sponsored by his early student, Bob Raymer (see section, on Bob Raymer).

Although I am not much of a gambler, I love to play cards and my dad was a professional gambler in his day. He taught me how to play all the card games and I enjoy the competition.

I stopped in Las Vegas at the Circus Casino and had a salad bar. I went to the casino and won $220 in about a half hour playing blackjack and had that cash in my billfold when I picked Dr. George up at LAX the next day. We went to get something to eat and I pulled out my billfold to pay. Dr. George raised his eyebrows and asked where I got all the money (as if he didn't know). When I told him that I had won it in Vegas, he looked sternly at me and said, "The Lord doesn't want you to gamble. It doesn't affect you, but you will be a minister some day and you need to set an example for others." I felt about two inches tall and apologized to God within and vowed never to gamble again.

The trip went well for Dr. George, and I drove him back to LAX some days later. I had to wend my way to San Francisco immediately thereafter and decided to take the long scenic way up Hwy. 1 through Big Sur and Santa Cruz. I was in no hurry and that drive is one of the most beautiful in America.

Now, dear reader, I was driving a good car, i.e., a Mercedes. Also, in that coastline area of California, it rarely rains. The trees and the greenery get their moisture from the fog that covers the ground nearly every day. Ask any scientist, unlike the Midwest where the root system brings in the water from the ground, along the coast the trees bring it in from the foggy air.

Well, it was raining cats and dogs by the time I rolled into Santa Cruz, I mean really raining and, my windshield wiper motor went out. I will bet that there are few if any readers hereto who have ever had a windshield wiper motor go out on any kind of a car.

I had no choice but to stop and get it fixed. It cost me $218.54, almost exactly the $220 I won in Vegas. I laughed and felt better that I had evened my karma.

Sometime later, I was telling that story to my mom and dad. They reacted to this story as follows: 1) My mom said, "Oh yes, the Lord does not want you to gamble. You should listen to Dr. George." and 2) My dad said, "On the other hand, maybe the Lord saw that problem coming and gave you the means to solve it." In my mind, both potentially theologically sound doctrines.

The Passing of Master George

Master George passed away May 25, 1978. As usual, with Master George, there were entertaining and unusual events regarding his passing.

A) His body died of (twelve) fatal diseases, including jaundice.

He did not have a stomach! He hadn't had one for years, apparently. We all remembered that he would sip a little soup or a root beer float, and spit a lot of it out.

He lived without digesting the minimal amount of food he ingested for years! He never made a big production out of doing that.

It is my intuitive understanding that Master George took on much karma from many of his disciples.

B) On February 25, 1978, I was with him. I knew that his time to leave the earth was coming. I asked him aimlessly how he was. He chuckled, his eyes gleamed with Cosmic Consciousness, and said, "Three months, three months. Everything will be fine in three months." Sure enough, three months to the day, he passed away.

I asked him at that time when I had been in the body with him last, and he said in India, 300 B.C. or so. I asked if I was an Indian and he said no, that I was a Greek, which meant that I was in Alexander the Great's army, which invaded India, but was repulsed.

He chuckled, and told me that, "You got your face full," meaning I was definitely in on some of the defeats inflicted on Alexander's otherwise unbeaten armies by the Hindus.

He was a Hindu holy man who touched me spiritually and from whom I began to learn inner wisdom.

C) On May 19, 1978, I was meditating, deep into the night, in Kansas City where I was living. Master George came to me spiritually, in great joy, and he looked at me and stated clearly, "Come and see me!"

I emplaned on May 21 to Milwaukee, and was able to see him for a couple of days in the hospital, before he passed away. He was his jolly, chuckling self, always cheering everyone else up. It was so nice to see him, even under those circumstances. For that I was always grateful, very grateful!

D) One of the women in the church was with him, in the hospital, when he passed away. He lay there, almost dying, and she started to cry.

He suddenly sat bolt upright in the bed and look at her sternly, and said, "Becky, Christ is Light!" Needless to say, that stopped her sorrow and crying!

Then he lay back down and passed away.

My Sister Gail

My sister Gail was born on March 16, 1942. I was born on July 16, 1944. She was two years older than me and we were very close growing up.

Gail was totally deaf from birth. She was stone deaf. They called it a nerve injury at birth. Today, we would probably call it medical malfeasance and have a major lawsuit; who knows.

When she was about three years old, she went to a residential school for the deaf in a town called Faribault, Minnesota, and hour south of Minneapolis. It was a private school run by two dedicated ladies, Faye and Dena Allen. There were 25 to 30 kids there of various ages at a given time.

Faye and Dena were way ahead of their time. They taught an oral tradition for many years and pioneered the techniques of same, i.e., Gail learned to speak and read lips, which was unheard of for deaf people in those days. The huge state school across the road in Faribault taught sign language only for many, many years.

Gail was beautiful and smart. I respected her so much. I pondered all the time, "Why was I so lucky and why was she born deaf?"

When I was nine years old, I got the shock of my life. My mom and dad brought Gail back from the Mayo Clinic in Rochester, Minnesota. The doctors there had diagnosed her with Retinitis Pigmentosis, i.e., "Tunnel Vision," which meant that she was going blind. Her radius of vision decreased slowly every year. I saw my strong and tough dad cry like a baby. I asked my mom what I could do, and she said I should pray every day for Gail.

No preacher could ever answer the question why? I could not buy "Oh, it's God's will." What a load of falsehood. That would make the universe like a lottery. It did not make logical sense. Somewhere, there had to be an answer.

This is what spurred me onto the spiritual path and into meditation. It is the only thing that makes any logical sense.

Gail often spoke to us these some mysterious words: *"Whenever I am lonely at the Allen School, a very kind man comes and talks with me at night. I feel so much better after he talks with me."*

I pondered this often. For one thing, how did he talk with her at night? In the dark? How did she hear? Who was this? I asked my mom and she had no answers.

Many years passed. Gail graduated from high school, went to two years of college, all with hearing kids, but her vision got too bad so she truly couldn't study and keep going.

In the meantime, I found Dr. George and moved to Milwaukee to join Dr. George's church. A few weeks later, Gail and my mom drove down to Milwaukee to visit, see the church, and meet Master George. We went to church when they arrived and after the service, I will never forget as long as I live what Gail said. She came over to my mother's car where my mom and I were standing, pointed to Dr. George and said, "That's the man!" (i.e., the man who spoke with her at the Allen School).

Soon thereafter, Gail moved to Milwaukee to join the church. My dad helped me buy a house across the street from the church, where she and I lived. She was very happy for a number of years.

In 1966, I got a job running a computer midnight to eight and went to college full time during the day. On February 2, 1967, my boss called me at about 4:00 a.m. He told me to shut off the computer and some folks were coming to pick me up. It was two Milwaukee police officers. They were very solemn and didn't say a word as they drove me home. My house had burned down and my sister passed away in the fire. She never woke up. The Fire Dept. Captain told me and showed me scientifically that if I had been there and had been asleep, I would never have awakened either. He explained how fast the oxygen goes and that it is just a matter of seconds before you cannot wake up.

I somehow made it through that. I made a vow to the Divine Mother. I said, from the depths of my soul, "Divine Mother, every day, I will be meditating morning and night. I want to know why. I will be waiting for an answer. I do not want to hear some platitude. I do not want to read anything about it. I want to see and know like a real mystic can know. I <u>will</u> be waiting."

For thirty months, over two years, I meditated twice per day and waited. I kept asking, asking, asking why? Then, one day, I was in the woods at The Farm, cutting dead oak trees for joists and firewood. I sat down to rest, with my back up against a tree. Suddenly, a deer ran right by me, about six feet away. Then, the *shakti* (*kundalini*) surged up my spine and my crown chakra opened up. I saw! I saw and had a remarkable vision. I saw clearly that Gail had *chosen* to come to this lifetime in that manner and had *chosen* to leave in that manner. I saw that she had worked out the last visages of her karma and that this was her last compulsory lifetime on this earth. She could come back to help in God's plan or work on another level. I saw that she had been a queen, royalty in a past life. I saw that it was good. I saw that from the vision of God, from the Divine level, it was perfect. I had total peace and saw other things I cannot discuss and some I didn't understand until much later."

Since her passing, Gail has come to me many, many times. She sends me love and smiles and she is always standing by me when I am in tough times. She is still one of my best friends.

How I Got to Master George

I met Master George on May 29, 1964. I started meditating when I was 16 years old (1960). I did it on and off for a few years, but got real serious when I was 19.

47

My sister, Gail, was two years older than I was. She was totally deaf from birth and had an incurable eye disease, diagnosed by the Mayo Clinic when she was 10 as leading to irrevocable blindness.

As she grew older, her radius of vision grew less and less. My mother, Eleanore Podany, sought help from spiritual healers, mostly to no avail.

One healer, Ed Jennings, lived near our home in suburban St. Paul, Minnesota in White Bear Lake.

Ed had received the healing touch from a unique spiritual experience he had while on his deathbed in St. Joseph's Hospital in St. Paul, at the age of 54.

He was in a coma and was declared terminal by the doctors. However, suddenly Ed was looking down at his body and the Lord said, "Ed! You are not the body! You are Spirit!" He was then back in his body, regained consciousness, and walked out of the hospital, completely healed, shortly thereafter.

God sometimes has had a flair for the dramatic when He performs His "miracles" through his children, and this case was definitely one of those.

In succeeding years, people would come to Ed asking for help. He would pray for them. He said that most of the time nothing much happened. Sometimes the people felt good and peaceful. Sometimes, they even got better over a period of time. Once in a while, however, whammmm! They'd be healed, instantaneously.

This is the type of healing we prayed would come to my sister.

Gail, however, had a different path in store for herself. She was such a great soul, she had chosen a life of great outer sacrifice in order to maximize growth on the inner planes.

There is no doubt she could have been healed on the physical had her Divine Self wished it.

While in prayer and meditation with Ed and my mother one night, she received a deep spiritual experience, going into sabikalpa samadhi or what Christians would call complete Oneness with God.

We, in our limited view at the time, felt she had been healed <u>physically</u>, because, amazingly enough, later hearing tests showed her having substantial hearing, when every year from 2 to 20, she had tested out as *none* or tone deaf, with a "nerve injury at birth," according to the doctors.

However, when we tried to work with her to understand sounds, it didn't work! Her soul had made a choice to remain deaf to complete her <u>inner</u> mission.

Normal worldly people cannot grasp such a thing, because they seek only comforts here on this earth. To them, to willingly forego any pleasurable thing here on this earth for "spiritual" gain is absolutely dumb.

However, "…the wisdom of man is foolishness to God" and vice versa, sometimes.

Looking at life realistically, I've never seen anyone, anywhere, who didn't have a whole bushel of troubles, trials, and tribulations of one sort or another. How could anyone want to stay on this earth forever? How dull! Thank God we are kicked and booted and cajoled and loved into finally seeking God, and finally attaining joy and bliss beyond anything this earth can offer.

Finding God, alone, will give us the fulfillment our hearts yearn for! Seeking God with all our strength is the wisest and highest path we can take on this earth. Back to Ed, Gail, and my mother.

I was considerably moved by these experiences with my sister. I started to really seek God with all my heart.

I reread a great book, *The Autobiography of a Yogi*, by Paramahansa Yogananda. I realized that Yogananda was my guru, or close to it, but this was 1963, and he passed away in 1952. I was very frustrated about that and resolved to find a real guru on this earth. To do this, I figured I had to go to India.

Thus, I applied for a scholarship to spend my junior year in college at the University of Benares, Bengal, India, the Holy City of India, where Lord Krishna and Lahiri Mahasaya, Param-Guru of Yogananda, had walked.

I told all my friends in Minnesota that I was going to India to find a real yogi. They, of course, thought I was royally daft.

I got my passport, shots, visa, etc. I was primed and ready to go and even bought a very good pair of hiking boots so that I could trek through the Himalayas, if necessary, to find my guru, my real yogi.

Paramahansa Yogananda stated in his beautiful book, *The Autobiography of a Yogi*, an old Hindu aphorism: "When you are willing to go to the ends of the earth to find your guru, he appears nearby."

This was certainly true in my case, thank God.

I was five days away from leaving for India when I visited Ed Jennings. I thanked him for the help he had given my family and wished him well. He questioned me as to why I was going to India. I replied with my stock answer, "To find a real yogi."

Amazingly, he told me about Doctor George, a disciple of Yogananda, residing in Milwaukee, Wisconsin, of all places.

I could literally *feel* this Doctor George right then and there. Hope and faith rose up in my heart, and I knew intuitively that this mysterious Master George would lead me to God-realization.

I asked Ed to tell me about Doctor (Master) George. He told me the following remarkable story:

Ed's wife was an alcoholic, a serious closet drinker. They tried everything to change and solve this, but nothing worked. Finally, in desperation, Ed decided to take the train to Milwaukee, Wisconsin from St. Paul, Minnesota, to see Doctor George. (He had heard about Doctor George from some S.R.F. [Self-Realization Fellowship, Yogananda's organization] yogis in Minneapolis.)

Arriving at Master George's place, he was greeted warmly and seated on a couch. Master George told him, "Ed, I'm very happy that you came asking for help for another." Whereupon, they meditated for over two hours. Finally Master George said abruptly, "OK, everything will be fine," and blessed Ed on the forehead.

As Ed rode the train back to Minnesota, every time he closed his eyes, he saw a <u>white cross</u> in his spiritual eye.

Moreover, when he arrived back in Minnesota, his wife was healed from the booze, and she remained healed.

Naturally, I was pretty moved by that story, and was now really fired up about meeting Master George.

I left that very evening and drove straight through the warm spring night to Milwaukee. I slept a bit in my car on the way and got into Milwaukee about 6:00 a.m.

By pay phone, I reached Jerry Neal, Master George's assistant. He told me that Master George had driven up to the Church Retreat near a town called Friendship, Wisconsin.

He gave me directions there. I thanked him and away I went. I arrived there early and waited and waited and waited, until 6:00 p.m. when finally Master George showed up. He was pulling a trailer loaded with huge concrete sewer main pipe, seven or eight feet in diameter. The truck was full of all kinds of stuff tied down with many ropes.

Out came a graying older gentleman with a twinkle in his eye. I approached him and asked, "Are you Master George?"

For the first time in my life I could feel divinity — both within him and within me.

He abruptly had me climb in the truck. We drove back behind the main building through the woods, past some other strange looking buildings and stopped.

Somehow, with ropes and long steel crowbars, just he and I maneuvered the big sewer pipe off the trailer to the spot he wanted.

This was my first experience "working" with Master George.

He was a real craftsman, very strong for over 64 years old and it was marvelous to work with him. He had quite a style.

We reloaded the truck. I had never seen so much junk in one truck in my life. Boxes, bottles, wires, used lumber, battered items of all shapes and descriptions came off that truck and were stored in one of those aforementioned buildings. (I soon discovered that those very buildings were made from *used* lumber, *used* cement blocks, etc.)

After that, Master George invited me into the main house. I cleaned up and sat in the living room. He cooked supper for us — a vegetarian supper.

That night when I meditated with him was the first time I truly felt the beginnings of what I was looking for.

The next morning, I had breakfast with Master George and we drove to town (Wisconsin Rapids) to get some hardware-related items.

Funny thing: Master George, for being a spiritual giant, never *talked* much about "spiritual" things. Instead, boards, hammers, nails, screws, pipes, roofs, basements, concrete, cesspools, used lumber, used nails, window frames, power saws, chain saws, posthole diggers, etc., were the subject of conversation.

Later that day, I asked him if he would be my teacher and waited eagerly for his reply. I hope you (the reader) remember what I had been telling all my friends about my upcoming trip to India, i.e., "I want to find a *real* yogi." When I asked him if he would be my teacher, he replied, "No, I think you should go to India and find a *real* yogi." I was flabbergasted that he would paraphrase my own words like that, not having known me or heard me say that.

I blustered out from the deepest part of my heart, "No! I want to stay with you! You are my guru!"

Much to my relief, after a little more arguing and testing on his part, he relented, and said, *yes,* that he was my guru.

What a relief! I still dream about that moment today. It fills me with joy beyond description.

Later that day, he told me something which I treasure most deeply of all; he said very straightforwardly and looked me in the eye, "Yogananda sent you to me."

Praise God and Hallelujah! A deep aching in my heart was healed with those words and the vibration that came with it.

Now after many years have passed, I still thank God every day for sending me to Master George, because, as God is my witness, *He* was the *real* yogi I longed to meet! He was (is) *real* and will touch each one who reads this book. I promise you that if you have gotten this far in this book and are reading these words, that Master George is *yours*, just as much as he is *mine*, no more, no less. I sign my name below on that promise to you.

Look at his picture, *feel* his vibration. He is your friend, your helper, your guide, your teacher, and your guru, if you wish. His only interest is to help *you* realize *God* within yourself and to feel the majesty of the Divine within you, and feel the love, peace, and bliss that is your true being, that is *us*.

There are only a few beings I have actually met on this earth in whom you could see were fully God-realized. Dr. George, Sai Baba, Yogananda and his lineage of gurus, Swami Rama and his lineage, and Swami Vishwananda. I also believe that Mother Meera is, but I have never met her. There are many great teachers, but I have to know that they can "go into the breathless state at will." If they can do that, they are real.

Politics

Early on in my relationship with Dr. George, he looked at me very seriously, and said: "Master (Yogananda) always said that it was not wise to get involved in politics if you were on the spiritual path."

I thought to myself, "Yes, that's obvious enough and I certainly don't have any such ideas."

However, as time went on, periodically Dr. George would look at me very seriously and state again: "Yes, Master said to not get involved in politics."

This went on for years. Interestingly, Dr. George, to my knowledge, never said that to anyone else, just me. He said it quite often and I began to wonder why he was saying this so regularly. He never did anything without a reason.

Then, one day in 1975, eleven years after he started with the "no politics" routine, at the farm he looked at me very, very seriously and said again, but with extreme emphasis, the old line of no politics. I took it with aplomb and went out to continue working on the building. As I was walking down the path, I felt a huge force push up my spine, out my crown chakra, and a big dark bird spiritually flew away from my soul!

We sang a song by Yogananda, "Who is in my temple? Who is in my temple? All the doors do open themselves, all the lights do light themselves. Darkness like a dark bird, flies away, oh, flies away."

As I stood there enjoying the beautiful energy rising up my spine, liberating my crown chakra, I felt a release of something deep within me and then I realized what happened. Over a long period of time, patiently, patiently, subtly working away, Dr. George had helped me release a desire so deep-seated that even my conscious mind could not recognize that I had this desire. I felt a beautiful light in that part of my soul where that clod of darkness had once resided.

I thanked Dr. George in spirit and in person. As usual, he just smiled and put his finger to his lips and shushed me.

As life went on, I found that I had a much more detached and objective view of politics. I now began to see it as part of the drama of this earthly pageant, not to my fixed truths, but a ceaseless flow of mixed vibrations, good and bad, round and round. I realized that politics wasn't going to save mankind, only an act of God transforming the souls and motives of people could do this.

I increased my resolve to work on my own liberation, my own spiritual path, and to continue to dive deep within to feel the joy and bliss of God.

Cockroaches

To set the stage for this chapter, I must first talk about one of the most unique and remarkable aspects of Master George; building buildings out of *used* lumber, *used* nails, *used* everything!

These buildings were really off-the-wall, yet highly practical constructions. They manifested in the physical the remarkable, irrepressible bliss of God that was Master George.

God's life is not confined, no matter how man tries to shut it off. Weeds grow in cracks in the sidewalk, wildflowers grow out of almost solid rock, and Master George's buildings grew up in the middle of the city of Milwaukee. They followed no official building codes nor any architectural rules. What they followed was human need, i.e., the Depression had hit America, and families needed places to stay, people with no jobs in from small dusty towns, and Master George allowed them to stay in his ramshackle multi-storied, multi-faceted, spontaneous creations, adding on rooms and suites as needed, until as many as 20 families lived at 5000 South 20th Street, Milwaukee, Wisconsin.

I don't believe a single one of them knew that they were living on the premises of a great saint. Master George certainly never mentioned it! He never preached to them. But their souls' evolution was blessed immeasurably by their presence there. How could you not sit within range of Master's aura and not be blessed, consciously or not?

As the 1930's and 40's rolled on and life rolled into the 1950's, prosperity returned.

Master still helped some strugglers here and there, giving shelter now and then. One of these families was downright ornery. The patron of this family started to take advantage of Master George's good nature. He told Master George that he was going to stay there as long as he felt like it and also bring his ne'er-do-well friends and relatives in. In other words, he was just basically coming in and taking the place over. He also stated that he knew that Master George was some kind of minister, so he wouldn't use force on him, plus he knew that he couldn't appeal too much to the authorities since the place had been condemned by the city building inspectors since 1934! (See next section, "Building Inspectors.")

Master George didn't argue with this man. He just smiled when night came and the family went to sleep. Master went into meditation.

In the middle of the night, that aforementioned patron of the family left so fast, he barely got his family out with him. Neither they nor any of their friends or relatives, ever returned to Master George's place again.

The reason: Thousands of cockroaches literally came out of the walls! They flooded this unfortunate villain's apartment and drove his family and him out quicker than any attorney or Sheriff's department. Best of all, these cockroaches all conveniently died by morning so that Master George could sweep them up and scoop them into the fireplace for additional kindling wood!

Additional note: One of the members of Master George's church took a few of these dead cockroaches to the University. There, it was determined it was a "rare Asian cockroach, never seen in the United States"!

Building Inspectors

As I mentioned in the preceding chapter, Master George did have a few difficulties with building inspectors.

Anyone who has ever dealt with any municipal government in this country on any kind of real estate matter, knows they (the municipal governments) consider themselves to have absolute power in these areas. You might say that even Joseph Stalin would have liked to have similar inexorable authority.

That is why I consider Master George's greatest demonstration of Divine Power in his earthly life (my healing not withstanding) to be his ability to live peacefully and stubbornly at 5000 South 20th Street, Milwaukee, Wisconsin, in a building complex effectively condemned for over

30 years! Even while I was there in 1966, I saw a continuing series of notices put up by city authorities on one or another part of the buildings.

It was truly funny! There was not a single aspect of the buildings that *did* follow the prescribed codes!

How could this happen? I asked Master George how. He said simply, "Master (Yogananda) wanted me to live there."

Moral 1 of this chapter: There is no power on Earth than can disrupt the collective will of two great saints!

Moral 2 of this story: Accept no limitation on the power of God, on the love and mercy of the Divine Mother! I know Yogananda and Master George were visible manifestations of the Divine Mother. There was no way *She* would let them down!

During the period (1934-66) when Master George kept his residence at 20th Street rolling, a certain individual, whom we shall call "John," became the head of the department in the city of Milwaukee whose job it was, among other things, to eliminate Master's offensive property.

"John" did his level best, using every means at his disposal, but wound up being defeated by Master, Yogananda, et al.

He was so soundly defeated, in fact, that he wound up losing his job!

Amazingly enough, some years later, "John" came to see Master George. He said, "Thanks for your help. I know you are a true holy man and I know it was wrong of us to try to push you out of your property. What I'm thanking you about is that after losing my job, I went back to my hometown of Portage, Wisconsin, where I have had incredibly good fortune in business with my brother. I also am extremely happy being out of the big city and back where I belong in a wonderful small town. I know that your prayers have helped me."

When Master George told me this story, I asked him if he had prayed for "John." He smiled sheepishly, nodded, and said, "He's a good boy."

The Cap

In 1965, the Milwaukee school system, in their inimitable wisdom, built a large junior high school on 20th Street, right across from Master's property.

We were in the middle of a seven-year program of gradually dismantling the entire complex and bringing it board-by-board up to Friendship, Wisconsin, to our church retreat. There were open cellars around, there were countless boards with old rusty nails sticking out, there were roofs easy to climb up on that could collapse, a real danger zone for a bunch of 13-14 year-old kids. The kids were roaming in and out of this incredibly curious "haunted house" when we were not around.

Master George was concerned about this. Thus, one day Master and I were walking around the property discussing this issue. Suddenly, he got a gleam in his eye and he said, "Sammy, find me a hammer." I went over and found a hammer for him to use, and wondered what he had in mind. I gave him the hammer and watched as he dug around in a pile of old junk. Wallah! He found an old massacred baseball cap, which looked like it had survived the Thirty Years War, as well as being the recipient of much of the dirt on the South Side of Milwaukee. What on earth, I thought to myself, is he doing with that cap?

Well, he took it, a nail, and hammer, and went over to a big tree. Looking at it carefully with that gleam in his eye (which I later learned was him tuning into his cosmic consciousness), and with his characteristic good-humored flourish, nailed the cap to the tree. He said, "That'll do it," and *it did* it!

As I live and breathe on this earth, to my knowledge, *no* other junior high kid ever set foot on that property! They stopped using the 13 acres as a short cut. They stopped breaking what windows were left.

I asked Master George exactly what he did with that cap routine. He just smiled, enigmatically, *very* enigmatically.

Quite frankly, even though I saw it right before my eyes, I truly can't figure out that miracle of Master George's to this day.

Master George – His Path

After meeting Paramahansa Yogananda, Master George had a rugged inner and outer path to attain full God-Realization.

He once went 40 days and 40 nights without food or water.

He worked two jobs and still meditated four to six hours a night, for many years.

He went into the wilderness in the Southwest to work alone, in the Spirit.

He had a big scar on his hand where he was nailed by a rattlesnake in the mountains of New Mexico. He did first aid on himself and thereupon immediately went into his higher consciousness, and negated the poison with spiritual healing.

There in the mountains, he slept nightly, alone, on the edge of a precipice. One move, and he would have fallen a thousand feet. I asked him why he did that. He replied, "To train my subconscious."

He came into full God-Realization after twelve years of rigorous, deep spiritual *sadhana* (practices).

Yogananda gave him the title, "Doctor" or "Master" of Yoga. He said, "George, you are a Master and Yoga and should be addressed with respect" (from a letter to Dr. George in 1938).

Minister

One day in 1976, after I had been with Master George for over 12 years, I came in off the road to visit him. We laughed and talked. He surprised the daylights out of me by handing me a certificate. It stated that I was a minister of his church! He told me: "You're a minister." I said, "That's it?" He said, "Yes." He had always said that he would make me a minister, now he had.

On the inner plane, I realized that I had a deep joy and bliss of God that could not be affected, no matter what happened. (As I was to find out that "no matter what" got pretty hard later on in my life, but the joy and bliss and inner God consciousness never was affected.) I was so grateful to Master for his life and his guidance.

Later in life, his last words to me in 1978 were: "I want you to start a center in Minneapolis."

I can tell you that the last thing on earth I ever intended was to be a spiritual teacher. I know myself too well and know most of my own flaws, which, in my mind, would preclude me from being one. However, maybe George's purpose was to show other people that *anyone* could become spiritual and find God within, something like Geico's ad, "So simple a caveman can do it."

He authorized me to teach the Kriya Yoga. He told me to make folks promise that they would not eat meat, would not smoke, and not do dope, before I teach them Kriya.

Jerry Neal

Jerry Neal was a brother disciple of mine with Master George. He helped me out a whole lot over a number of years and is a very wise and advanced person and soul. Jerry was in the Navy, and had big tattoos on his arms, and was a very strong fellow. In his life, he played football at Nebraska, was an assistant lion tamer, and had many wild jobs. One day, he received a hand-written postcard in pencil in the mail, which said "SRF, come and see me, Dr. George, 5000 So. 20th St., Milwaukee, WI." To this day, Jerry has no idea other than George's omniscience how he could have received that postcard. He went to see Dr. George and became his student for life.

In some of his past lifetimes, Jerry had been in the Crusades and other armies of that sort. He fought with the broadsword, axe, sling, spear, etc. Jerry had memories and dreams about this awful fighting. He realized that Dr. George was helping him work through all that karma. After Dr. George passed away, Jerry never had any bad feelings/memories and realized that Dr. George had cleared it for him. He knew that Dr. George was helping him work through that karma; this went on for years. However, after Master passed away, Jerry never had a dream like that again. The job had been finished.

From Jerry, I learned many gems of wisdom. He was a very advanced soul and is as good of a spiritual teacher as exists these days. One of the things I absorbed from Jerry is that one of the major functions of a Guru and, in particular, one of the major roles of Dr. George, Swami Rama, and Sai Baba, is *to assist us in clearing out the debris and carnage of past lifetimes and assist us to correct the inner and outer flaws which cause these problems.*

When Sai Baba walked among us and stared intently and raised his hand, he is lifting lifetimes of karmic debt off our back. When he writes in the air, he is "re-writing" the Cosmic script of his Drama.

One of the interesting things to ponder in eternity is why we all got rolling in this drama in the first place?

A key insight into the reason is in the amazing sense of humor and amazing kindness and love for mankind that the Masters exhibit. Based on that evidence, I surmise that the answer to Why creation? and Why us? is as simple as this: it is the Joy of God to expand and create and share love.

Regina Rohde Larson

Regina Larson started out life as Regina Rohde, a young German girl born in East Prussia in 1930. At age fourteen the Russian Army was pounding west, defeating the declining Wehrmacht across many fronts, heading inexorably to Berlin.

Her father was a major in the German Army. He had been captured by the British in Crete and as the war winded down, was in a British POW camp in Egypt.

Her mother was terrified of the Russians, in particular, the Siberian troops, who raped, looted, and plundered, at least partially to avenge the atrocities committed against Russian people by the Germans earlier.

The family left their home and headed west. They walked and walked and barely made it ahead of the onrushing Russian Army to relative safety in an area controlled by the British and Americans.

Even though many, many died and many more were consigned to life under the Communist regimes, young Regina continued her life in the American zone of the now dismembered Germany.

She grew up and became interested in metaphysics. One of the first languages the *Autobiography of a Yogi* had been translated into was German. She read it and anything she could get her hands on about yoga and meditation. She was into physical therapy and health massage. She went to work at a health spa on the Baltic in northern Germany. She was praying and meditating daily. Like me, she was distressed to find that Yogananda had passed away. She asked God, fervently, to send her a guru. She wanted one so badly.

One day, at the spa, a tall blonde American named Ray Larson, from Milwaukee, Wisconsin, arrived at the spa. He was an electrician on a Merchant Marine vessel and had suffered some injuries on board. He was recuperating at the spa.

He and Regina fell in love and he asked her to marry him. She assented. They were married and they moved to Milwaukee.

After she arrived, she found Dr. George (and a woman named Mother Perry). She found her guru. She remained in his church ever after.

I have known Regina and her family for over forty years and have always maintained that she is a saint. She raised five wonderful children and still meditates daily.

Dr. George shared with me that it wasn't easy for her. He told me that she had been a monk in many past lives. This life forced her to many outer roles, which were very difficult for her, but her nobility of spirit and her deep love of mankind enabled her to merge with God this lifetime and never have to reincarnate.

Life with Doctor George – Bliss Consciousness

We can have health, wealth, fame, and virtue. We can be known far and wide as a star athlete, movie star, or even as a holy man, saint, or whatever. But, if we cannot sit and mediate and actually experience the joy and bliss of God within, what good is all the above? Not much.

History is replete with people who seemingly have everything, destroy themselves with drugs, alcohol, or violence. I don't need to cite examples — just pick up the newspaper this week and add a few more to the list. I have known many, many people in my life who have huge houses, expensive cars, wives, kids, yachts, mansions, power, connections, etc. However, I have known very few truly happy people. When I grew up, I seemed to have it made. I was a good student, had a wonderful family, and had everything going for me in my culture. However, down deep, I knew that I did not know God and knew that I was not happy.

What surrounded Master George was a force field of bliss. I don't know how else to describe it. When you came into his presence, you automatically felt a whole lot better. If you sat near him in a group harmlessly watching a ballgame on TV, it was difficult to listen to the baseball game because of the uplifting of your consciousness.

This is how you evaluate a real Master. Can s/he help you experience God within your own consciousness and can he assist you in becoming a self-sustaining independent God-Realized being yourself?

Jesus, Yogananda, Sai Baba, and Master George do not want people to worship them. They don't mind if you bow at their feet in respect of the Divinity manifested therein, but they'll only put up with bowing-at-the-feet routine for a couple of times until they see that you are really serious about realizing your own divinity If you are only determined to worship them and avoid responsibility for working out your own Divinity in this body on this earth, now, then I can assure you that they and your soul will prod you with circumstances until you begin to seek the Lord within yourself and realize Divine consciousness with all your heart.

There is a fine line of wisdom here. You must have the humility and devotion to understand that you can't do it without a Guru on the inner plane if not the outer. You must have the awareness that beings like Dr. George, Yogananda, and Sai Baba are our spiritual superiors. From them, we receive the Divine vibrations to help lead us home. From them, we receive Divine Grace to overcome our past karma, to change our deep inner flaws, and to change our hearts to devotion.

However, this is where the fine line of wisdom comes in; we always need to recognize that the same Divinity within Jesus, Yogananda, and others is also within us, yet not quite as much manifested. Jesus said, "Greater things than these shall ye do, because I go to the Father."

What separates us, then, from being the same as Jesus?

Time.

We are in an illusion of time. It has been ordained from the beginning of time that we travel this road. It has been ordained by the Infinite Creator, beyond creation, that we sit at the metaphysical (if not physical) lotus feet of the Guru and tune into the vibrations of increasing fineness — slowly, patiently, lifetime after lifetime, leading us to the Infinite One with our being.

Let me give you some examples of how Master George worked with me. Remember: The goal of these exercises was to allow me to feel and experience the joy of God within myself.

Exercise One

Circumstances would be arranged so that a person that I deemed to be less evolved than me would have power over me and use it cruelly.

First, how dumb could I be that I actually had the temerity to think that anyone is lower in any way than me? Is that dumb or what? Well, I sure had those thoughts.

The first job Master George gave me was working as a laborer on a sewer/water construction crew with a foreman, who was 6' 5" and 250 pounds, and who yelled the first stream of profanity that came to lips. Even though nearly all of his crew had some sort of prison record, they jumped immediately when he yelled.

I was in shock for many months. I pleaded with Master George to release me from this situation. I certainly didn't need the money. I could have gotten many jobs and could have been in college with all my other friends from high school getting PhD's.

However, I got what I wanted — the joy and bliss of God and some surprising revelations.

These circumstances forced me to dig deep within myself to rise above these outer circumstances, inwardly. I found that when I did, I entered a realm of joy, peace, and bliss and could be one with Master George, Christ, and Yogananda. (I didn't know Sai Baba at that time.)

Even in the midst of the clamoring of heavy equipment, foreman yelling, moving here, moving there, cleaning a bulldozer tread, pounding in a truss to hold up the wall of the hole, I learned to reside in the abode of the highest. I became extremely happy.

Interestingly, the foreman after a few months let up on me and actually gave me plum assignments. He took me on long rides to other sites and talked until he was blue in the face about all his personal problems. I got my first unusual revelation from God. I saw what a great soul this man was, despite his obvious outer flaws. I saw his past lifetimes as a heroic soldier. I saw how much God loved him and how rare love and respect are on this planet.

I was feeling amazingly good about the whole thing and then, you guessed it, they sold the company and laid off 35% of the workers. Since I had little seniority, I was one of the 35% and was one of the first workers out of the door.

Ah well — end of Exercise One.

Exercise Two

This was a complicated and long-term one: Forgiveness/non-violence with strength.

Master George said that you should practice non-violence, but you should not be a doormat.

Combined with the fact that I am a very stubborn person and really don't like anyone telling me what to do, this area of my work with Master George was very tough. No one likes someone else to tell them about their faults.

Well, in Dr. George's church, I was surrounded by older people of my parent's generation who all knew what was best for me. For years, these folks, who were my brother and sister disciples, tried their best to "mold" me in their image. I resisted stubbornly, but all the way, I forgave them and sent them love. It was tough. They often complained to Dr. George that I didn't do this or did do that. He would inform me of this and would chuckle often. He was testing me to see if I would fight back. I rarely did, I hit about 95% because I knew that Dr. George and God and my soul demanded that I forgive and send love. I never tried to justify myself either, which, in my mind, was the same as "fighting back."

This prepared me for the terrible defeats and humiliations which happened later in my life by the droves. I must have had some serious karma to work out, because I sure have been doing it all this lifetime.

Cash

Before I start this story, I should mention that Dr. George never asked for nor ever took a collection, ever.

I was in Los Angeles hanging out with Dr. George as he made the rounds of various devotees in that area. Most of these people were members of

Bob Raymer's group (see section on Bob Raymer). I had brought with me a stash of traveler's checks, per usual. (I am so forgetful that if traveler's checks hadn't been invented, I would very likely have already lost more than one fortune.) Dr. George and I were sitting in the back seat of a car being driven around Los Angeles. The driver said, "Dr. George, do you think we should stop at a restaurant for a bite to eat?"

As he said those words, I thought the thought: "Oh, where are my traveler's checks? Pocket? Hotel?"

Just as I concluded that quick thought, Dr. George turned to me, and answering my thoughts, slapped me on the knee and said, "Don't worry Sammy, I'll buy." He grinned and I laughed, knowing he was aware of my basic thoughts and motives.

That, of course, was good because my basic motive was God-Realization.

This was one of many, many times over the years that Dr. George routinely let us know he knew what we were thinking. Often, when he gave a talk, most of what he said seemed irrelevant to me. However, during *every* talk that he gave over the years that I heard, one very striking message would hit me right in the bread basket. Interestingly enough, all the other folks in our church said and experienced the same phenomenon.

Vegetarianism

Master George explained to me that yogis definitely advised meditators to avoid meat for the following reasons:

Vibrations. Master George said that when an animal or bird is killed, it emits fear and anger. Those vibrations go right into our being. Moreover, that same fear and anger precipitates unhealthy chemical reactions in the system of the animal or bird that then goes into our physical system.

Lightness. Meat, he said, take three to four hours to digest; whereas, vegetables take considerably less time. Vegetarianism, therefore, makes your system "lighter" for mediation and metaphysical living because the energies are freed more for raising consciousness to God within instead of digesting that big lump of dead flesh.

Chemicals. Steroids and other chemicals now in meat are unhealthy.

I might add two other reasons, which are that it is just awful to think about killing and slaughtering a beautiful creation of God and eating it; and macrobiotically speaking, it takes far too much energy, land, water, manpower, and nutrients to produce one unit of meat as opposed to a similar unit of vegetables.

Master George's dissertation on vegetarianism immediately opened my mind and I saw how it made a good deal of sense.

Bob Raymer

Bob Raymer was 14 years older than me. He, too, was born and raised in Minnesota. He built his own airplane when he was 16 years old and flew it all over the place. He was the only heir to a significant fortune from his parents. Bob read Yogananda's *Autobiography of a Yogi* when he was 18 and he started meditating. He finally flew his own airplane to Los Angeles, California to find Master Yogananda.

He met him and asked him to be his guru. Master Yogananda told him that, unfortunately, he was leaving the earth soon, and if Bob wanted to "get it," he should go to Milwaukee, Wisconsin and see Dr. George.

Well, the millionaire's son flew his own plane to Milwaukee and showed up at the aforementioned 5000 South 20th St. ramshackle conglomeration of mismatched buildings. He met this older kindly man with old grubby mismatching clothes on. He thought to himself, "Ah, this is a test from Master. I need to help this poor old guy. Well, I can do that." George sat him down and fixed him some tea. He told Bob, "You must be tired. You can go back into that room and lie down." Bob described how he wended his way through a tilting doorway into a room which was not level and lay down on a dusty old couch. He was wondering about this whole thing, when the shakti rose up his spine, his crown chakra opened, he felt the Divine Bliss, and as he was feeling God for the first time, he remembered thinking, "This guy doesn't need *my* help!"

For a number of years, Bob flew once a month to Milwaukee to be with Dr. George. After a number of years, Dr. George told Bob, "You are OK now. You are a teacher and you must now do it on your own and go within. You are ready." So, Bob became a spiritual teacher. He had a large, regular group in Santa Monica in his beautiful condo on Ocean Avenue overlooking the Pacific Ocean. Quite a few celebrities came regularly to his group. He would fly Dr. George out on a regular basis to speak with his students.

I went to Bob's group often when I was in Los Angeles. It was great to meditate with him. The energy brought you right up to the top. You could feel Dr. George, Yogananda, and Sai Baba around Bob like great lights.

Bob also went to India before most Westerners and found Sai Baba. He was the first president of the American Sai Baba Association back in 1967.

Bob thereupon ran Song of the Morning Ranch, a wonderful spiritual community in Michigan for many years.

Dr. George told me that Bob had been Marshal Ney, one of Napoleon's top generals in a past lifetime. For you history buffs, after Napoleon's first exile to Elbe, he came back with a handful of followers. The King sent Marshal Ney with 10,000 troops to arrest Napoleon and send him back. However, Marshal Ney dismounted from his horse, came up to Napoleon, and offered him his sword and vowed his loyalty to his emperor. They thereupon joined forces, raised another army and threw out the king, which eventually led to Waterloo and Napoleon's final defeat.

My Experiences with Sathya Sai Baba (and His Devotees)

Sathya Sai Baba was born on November 23, 1926 to a saintly Hindu family in the small India town called Puttaparthi, in the Province of Andhra Pradesh, about 120 miles north of Bangalore.

The day after his birth, on November 24th, it is reputed that the great holy man, Sri Aurobindo, broke his customary silence and announced that "Lord Krishna has reentered the body."

The town of Puttaparthis was and is very remote; you could not drive to the town by car until 1965. When little Sathya was born, less than 200 people lived in the town. It was excruciatingly poor and primitive. Nothing grew very well there. There were many cobras, scorpions, and other unappealing aspects.

This little boy amazed the villagers with a continuous series of miracles. Even his birth was remarkable. A cobra appeared under the baby and musical instruments played on their own accord. As a very little child, he materialized gifts for his schoolmates, and food for hungry people, including out of season fruits and different fruits from the same tree!

Sathya refused to eat meat or participate in any activity harmful to animals. He invited beggars and poor people home for his mother and sister to feed.

He also had a remarkable talent for music and writing plays. (He continually wrote music for

70 years and could be the most prolific songwriter in history.)

On October 20, 1940, at the age of 14, Sathya announced to his family, "I am no longer yours. I do not belong to you. My devotees are calling and I have work to do." He therefore left his home and began gathering disciples, who came to him, one by one, each having some unique and remarkable miracle having been done for them by Sathya Sai. He taught them devotional songs to God and encouraged them to seek the divinity within themselves.

He healed the sick and materialized matter from nothing all day, every day. He appeared to devotees all over the world, although never leaving his isolated location.

He would pass his hand over containers of food, and the food would multiply to be able to feed all the people who had come.

I have a friend from Vancouver, British Columbia named Bill, who is a medical doctor. In 1995, we were both in India for a few weeks for Swami's birthday. During this birthday, Swami fed 1.1 million peasants free for 10 days! I can attest that I saw them lined up for food 24/7 and sleeping on the ground for what seemed like miles. (Interesting anecdote: A restaurant owner from New York analyzed the truck traffic bringing in supplies and the relative infrastructure. He stated that it was mathematically impossible for Swami to have fed more than 50,000 people.)

Back to Dr. Bill: Bill volunteered in the "medical tent." One day I when stopped by to say hello to him, he said to me, "Where were you yesterday at 7:30 a.m.?"

I thought for a moment and said, "Why, of course, I was in *darshan*." (For 50 years, Swami came out every morning at that time to walk through the masses saying hello and "giving darshan," which means "the sight of the Master.")

Bill continued, "Where was Swami?" I told him that he was just where he normally was at that time, i.e., on the veranda doing a few things before starting the interview with the fortunate folks who he had selected as he walked through the masses. To my total shock, Bill said, "Our group from Vancouver was volunteering at a food distribution point (about a half a mile away) for the peasants. We had some big pots of food and they ran out. Then Swami came and cracked two coconuts over the pots and they filled up and the food kept flowing!" This is a cool Hindu update of the "loaves and the fishes"!

Sathya Sai Baba materialized a grey holy ash called *vibhuti* (sacred ash). It came out of his hands all day long. Nearly everyone with whom he came in close contact would receive a little unit of vibhuti. Customarily, we devotees eat this vibhuti immediately upon receiving it as a talisman, cure, or preventative.

Note: One time a filmmaker filmed many such disbursements of vibhuti. He thereupon showed this film of these manifestations to magicians and illusionists in Hollywood and Las Vegas. These folks were astonished. Analyzing the film with an editing machine frame by frame, they deduced that <u>no magic was involved</u>. They were curious about how this fellow from India could materialize matter from nothing. I myself can attest that I have seen such materializations, many of them close up. Sathya Sai Baba materialized a ring for me in 1992 and has materialized vibhuti for me twice.

One of the more remarkable things that happens in conjunction with Baba is that pictures of him all around the world spontaneously emanate vibhuti! (If the reader would like to know where, please email me and I can send locations you can access to see this phenomena first hand.)

One of the more interesting such occurrences happened with a greatly feared India bandit, the India equivalent of John Dillinger, whose name is Hali Gappa. In the 1960's, Hali was feared throughout South India. Law enforcement could do nothing with him. Hali and his men spotted this remarkable holy man, Sai Baba, and the crowds, of hundreds of thousands coming to see him. They saw an incredible opportunity for theft.

Thus, they did a reconnoitering expedition at the next big event. They were "undercover," scouting around when Sai Baba announced to the crowd that the legendary bandit, Hali Gappa was in attendance. The crowd was shocked. They were even more amazed when Baba called Hali up to the front and "spiritually" changed him literally on the spot. Hali gave up his robbing ways and went back to a small town south of Bangalore to set up an orphanage! He soon had 25 orphans and operates his orphanage to this day.

Swami gave him a big picture of himself to put in the chapel in the orphanage. Soon prodigious amounts of vibhuti were coming out of the picture and Hali gave it out to anyone who came. One day, one of his old outlaw compatriots came for a visit. He saw the vibhuti coming out of the picture and advised Hali that this was a remarkable business opportunity, and that he should definitely not just give it away, but should charge money for it. This sounded reasonable to Hali, who subsequently started charging for the vibhuti. Well, wouldn't you know, the flow of vibhuti immediately stopped!

Hali realized his mistake, and made his weary way back to Sai Baba's ashram. Finally getting an interview, Hali threw himself at Baba's feet and begged forgiveness. Swami scolded him and told him sternly, "No money, no money!" Hali agreed, and then Swami materialized two little ceramic oval discs, about one inch long, one with a picture of Sathya Sai Baba, and the other with a picture of Shirdi Sai Baba. The kicker related to these pictures was that since that time, they continuously have produced and emanated *amrita*, the nectar of the Gods. Amritha is sweet and sticky, like honey, and has a unique perfume-like smell and taste. It defies the physical known universe when you hold those little pictures in your hand and seemingly from nowhere, your entire hand fills up with amrita. Many, many people have come to Hali Gappa's orphanage to see the picture producing vibhuti on the wall and hold the little pictures in their hands slowly filling up with vibhuti. Hali allowed me to put the ceramics into a bottle, which filled up. I took the amritha back to my friends in the U.S.

Sai Baba called his disciples, one by one, over many years. They became a flood. On any given day, many thousands of people have come from nearly every country on earth to receive his darshan and hope for a miracle, an interview, or whatever. Over the years, many holy men and devotees from every country and every religion came to see Baba to have him bless their missions.

I personally have spoken with men and women from every European country, every South American country, and many other countries while spending time in India. Each of these people detailed and reported at least one remarkable, unique personal miracle that Baba had been done for him/her, either in India or by "long distance" in their home country. I have heard some of the most incredible stories known to mankind. If even a small fraction of these stories were true, Sai Baba has to be regarded as a divine incarnation and a legitimate successor to Krishna, Jesus, Buddha, etc.

The following are a few of the stories I have accumulated from folks from all over the world.

Michael, from Germany

I was sitting next to Michael in darshan one day in 1987. Michael was a blond, handsome, and congenial fellow. He spoke good English and let me practice my mediocre German with him. We agreed to meet after darshan for a cup of tea. At tea I asked him where he was from. He said he was from Frieburg, in South Germany, not too far from the

Swiss border. I told him that I lived in St. Paul, Minnesota. He knew where that was.

Then I received a serious shock. I asked him, "How long have you been a Sai Baba devotee?" He said, "About seven years." I asked him how he became interested in Sai Baba. He said, "I was a communist, in the Red Brigades, and sold dope to support the movement." I just about passed out! "You have to be kidding," I said. "What happened?" He replied, "My girlfriend and I were vacationing on the beach in South India. She had heard about this miracle Swami and I agreed to go along with her to see. I was an atheist, so it didn't make any difference to me. We arrived in Bangalore and made our way to Swami's ashram in Whitefield. (Note: In those days, during afternoon darshan, Swami sat outside in the large courtyard on a big throne-like chair). We entered the main gate and saw Swami sitting in a chair, surrounded by thousands of devotees. He looked my direction for a moment and our eyes connected. I was frozen to the ground. I could not move. The *shakti* (kundalini energy at the base of the spine) moved up my spine and opened me spiritual eye. I saw the thousand petal lotus. My crown chakra was opened. I felt and saw God. I was still frozen to the ground. Swami left the people disbanded. I was still frozen. My girlfriend held on to me. I cried and cried. I cried some more. Finally, we moved. I was not the same. I came back in the morning. Swami walked by and smiled at me. I felt total love. We had to go back. I got back to Germany and quit the communist party. I quit the Red Brigades. I found a spiritual teacher in my hometown. She knew about Sai Baba and we started a small Sai Baba group in Frankfurt. I have been a devotee ever since and I come over here at least once a year." (This story reminds me of St. Paul on the road to Damascus.)

Fredrik, from Holland

Fred told me the following remarkable story, which the German fellow and the American (Bill) verified:

"I was sitting in darshan one day. To my left, was a friendly American named Bill. He was an attorney from New York. On his left was a German fellow I knew, named Werner, who was an engineer with Siemens. We were excited because we were in the front row that morning and knew we had a chance of getting an interview. At the very least, we would be close to Swami and something wonderful can always happen under those circumstances. Baba came out of his room and slowly and gracefully walked into the *mandir* (temple). He slowly approached us and stood in front of Bill. Bill reached down and took *padnamaskar* (the act of touching the Master's feet, an ancient Hindu custom). As Bill sat up, Swami to my amazement was speaking in Dutch! He was looking at Bill, but speaking to me in Dutch! It was wonderful. Then he walked on. I started to cry. I told Bill and Werner that Swami had spoken in Dutch. They were shocked, and Bill said that Swami had spoken in English to him and Werner stated unequivocally that Swami had spoken in German! We all went to have tea after darshan and discussed this for a long time. All three of us heard Swami speak in our own languages AT THE SAME TIME!

Graciella, from Italy

Over the years, I have seen Sai Baba materialize many rings, including one for myself. I have seen many different kinds of rings, which Swami has manifested from nothing. It is quite shocking to have a fellow human being materialize a ring for you from nowhere – no magic – materialization of matter from nothing. This is one of my favorite ring stories.

On my 1987 trip, I stayed in Bangalore for a couple of weeks at the Windsor Hotel. It is a nice hotel and has a lot of the old "British Raj" about it. It offered a great buffet and good food in general. Each morning, my friends and I would go down to the lobby to get a taxi to go to Baba's ashram in Whitefield. There were quite a few other devotees in the lobby. One of them was a distinguished older lady from Italy named Graciella, who was there with her family. Her kids would go with her but her husband was not a big devotee and he mainly stayed at the hotel and did other things. He was a very nice man and spoke great English. Graciella and I were talking one morning as she and her kids were waiting with me for a taxi. I had noticed that she had stunning rings on each of her fingers, and bracelets and necklaces. She laughed and told me that she was a jewelry designer; that is what she did back in Italy. She told me about some famous and wealthy people for whom she had designed special jewelry. She showed me each of her rings. One of them on the ring finger of her right hand had a massive diamond mounted on a gold ring. It was the most impressive ring on her hands. I said to her, "That is the most remarkable ring. Did you make that?" She said, "Oh, no, Swami made that one. He told me he would make me the best ring on my hands."

"A" from the United States

"A" told this story at a large Sai Baba convocation:

"Many of my friends had rings Swami made. I loved all those rings and all the stories that went with the rings. I wanted a ring from Swami so badly. Then, it worked out that my husband and I were getting to go to India for the first time. We were so excited. We spoke with Dr. Bill Harvey, one of the major figures in the Sai Baba Organization in the United States. He advised me that if we got an interview with Swami and if Swami asked me what I wanted (which he does in many cases; he asked me that one time) to be sure to say, 'Devotion, Swami, devotion.' Well, I thought about that. Devotion was OK, but what I really wanted was a ring. I was in a quandary whether to ask for devotion or a ring if it so came up. Well, we got an interview, and sure enough, Swami said to me, 'What do you want?' I said, against my better judgement, 'Devotion, Swami, devotion.' 'Very good', he said, and then he materialized a ring FOR MY HUSBAND!"

She brought down the house with that story. Everyone truly laughed and sympathized with her.

Joel Riordan, from the United States

For a short while, Joel was a very good friend of mine. We worked on a film project together. I wish I could have spent more time with him, but I left Los Angeles after I quit the entertainment business, my mom got paralyzed, and I moved back to Minnesota. I talked with Joel on the phone a few times, but I never saw him again in person. He passed away in the early 1980's in Los Angeles.

Joel was a fascinating man. I loved to hear his stories, both about Sai Baba and about the entertainment business, including many wild stories about famous people he had known. He grew up in Vaudeville. His parents had a traveling show. He actually appeared on stage at age two weeks, playing a baby, of course. He was vice-president of Republic Films when he was only 29 years old and had one of the first Volkswagen dealerships in Southern California I the 1950's. He was about 67 when I knew him in the 1970's. He was a Sai Baba devotee, non-smoker, non-drinker, etc. However, in his younger days, he was a veritable wild man. He was an atheist, hard drinker, and party guy, and had lived one of the most interesting lives of anyone I knew.

When Joel was 56, he married a young Italian woman named Diana, who was 24 at the time. She and her mother were Sai Baba devotees. Joel had a case of "buyer's remorse" after a while into the marriage because his male ego was mightily offended when his wife put pictures of Swami up on their walls and was obviously totally enamored by her guru. Joel could only interpret this divine love as a threat to his manhood. He could not conceive of some guy over in India literally stealing his wife's affection from him. Joel complained loudly to his friends and to his wife about "That Character" (i.e., Sai Baba) ruining his marriage. Joel was seriously thinking about a divorce and thought his wife was totally crazy.

Joel told me that one of his friends suggested that he go to India with his wife, see The Character, and maybe get evidence so that he could have his marriage annulled, thereby skirting the California divorce laws giving a ton of his possessions to the ex-wife. Another of his friends suggested that maybe he should be tolerant and let his wife have her religion and be neutral. He went on to say to Joel, "What would it take for you to be neutral? You don't have to be a believer, just be neutral." Joel told me that he said to the guy, "Well, look, I can accept some of the miraculous healings because back in the old days, I saw phony evangelists actually heal people. They got them so high their own minds healed them. There is no limit to the power of the mind and I think the 'materializations' are a real cool type of magic and sleight of hand that 'the Character' has devised. Here's the deal: If That Character can make a rainbow on a dry day in South India, I will be neutral!" Joel told me that he just flippantly threw that line out, as he was wont to do.

Well, Joel and Diana went to India. They were there for a while when they went up one of the little mini-mountains near the ashram, which are now covered with buildings and such. They were standing there, when a rainbow came out of the ground going straight up in the air. When Joel and Diana told me this story at dinner at a friend's house one evening, she said that the rainbow was there for about five minutes, and Joel corrected her and said it was there for about three minutes. Thereupon, it went back into the ground. Joel was obviously astonished. When they were in afternoon darshan, Swami came by, stopped in front of Joel, and said, "How did you like your rainbow, Character?"

True to his word, Joel became neutral. He actually started to become pretty positive toward Sai Baba. Then another unusual thing happened. Sai Baba seemed almost to adopt Joel. He kept him very close for a couple of years. Joel saw the most amazing miracles. Swami had Joel in for interviews, weddings, and other events.

His wife, Diana, now known as Diana Baskin, wrote a remarkable book called *Divine Memories of Sathya Sai Baba* about her view of those days. I recommend this book as one of the two or three best books ever written about Sai Baba. It will move your heart and soul.

I asked Joel, "When did you become a true believer?" He chuckled and told me that even though he saw many, many materializations of matter and many other miracles, still, there was a reservoir of doubt. He told me that one day, he was sitting in a spiritual ceremony for a young boy with his family. Swami materialized a gold chain for the boy. Joel told me that he thought, "Aha. It's the sleeves! Just like a cardsharp, with cards up his sleeves, that's how Swami does these 'materializations.'" Joel told me that immediately upon Joel thinking that thought, Swami stopped, looked at Joel curiously, then rolled up his sleeves, and continued to manifest jewelry and other things for all the folks there. Joel told me that was when he surrendered and went all the way with Sai Baba.

I asked Joel, "Do you believe that Swami is the avatar of the age?" Joel said to me very seriously words that I have never forgotten, "I do not know anything about any of that stuff. All I know is that he is my best friend." I was touched by those simple words as any I have ever heard on the spiritual path.

Robert from Ireland

One day in 1992 in India, I was sitting in darshan early one morning. I am a pretty talkative soul (big mouth, you might say). I especially love to talk with people from all over the earth at Swami's ashram. This particular morning, I was sitting next to an older fellow from Ireland, identified by his emerald green scarf (I had a red, white, and blue American scarf). He told me that his name was Robert. Then he told me that he had congestive heart failure, and was not expected to live much longer, He said that the doctors in Ireland could do nothing for him. He further told me that he was actually born in Calcutta, India back when England still owned India and his dad worked for the British Raj. When finding out his imminent mortality, he decided to come to India and die at the feet of the Great One, Sai Baba.

Thereupon, we both started to meditate in anticipation of Swami's arrival for darshan that morning.

A few days later, I was walking along the main street of the ashram, and here comes Robert with some friends looking very fit and hearty. I said, "Robert, remember me? I am Sam from Minnesota." He happily acknowledged me and told me an amazing story: "Sam, after that darshan, I started to feel better. I went back to my room and rested. I felt Swami's love going through me. Then, that afternoon, in darshan, I went into an altered state, and I saw a very small Swami driving a very small BULLDOZER through my veins and arteries! He was cleaning everything out! After darshan, I have been feeling fantastic and I know Swami has healed me!"

I really enjoyed that story and told it for years to Sai Baba people. Everyone really enjoyed it. In 1995, I was back in India. Who should I see, but Robert! We hugged and talked and I asked him how he was. He said, "Sam, I have been fantastic. The doctors gave me clearance and I have just recently been hiking in the Himalayas with some friends." I was amazed and subsequently added that new bit to the earlier story.

Whenever I met any Sai devotee from Ireland or the UK, I found out that nearly all of them had heard the story about Robert and the small bulldozer through his veins. It is a popular story in certain circles.

In 1999, I was back in India. I saw some folks with emerald green scarfs from Ireland. One day, I sat near a couple of Irish guys and asked them if they knew Robert. They said, "Oh, yeah, the guy with the bulldozer through his veins." I said that's the guy. They said they had heard all about him, but did not know where he was or anything specific. He was from a different part of Ireland. A few days later, I ran into a few other guys from Ireland and asked them the same question. They said, "Oh yeah, the guy with the bulldozer through his veins," but they didn't know much either. One day I was sitting way back, having drawn a high chit, and was just being quiet, when a fellow with an Irish scarf plopped himself down in the middle of the crowd next to me. He smiled and I said hello. We talked for a bit and then I asked him about Robert. He said, "Yes, I knew Robert very well. I am from his town. I was going to sit way over there (he pointed to the opposite side of the mandir) where I normally sit, but something told me to come here. It must be so I can tell you this story: A few months ago, Robert had a dream. Swami came to him in the dream and said, 'Robert, I have given you seven more years. It is now time to go. I have a question for you. In your next embodiment, do you want a wealthy body or a spiritual body?' Robert said in the dream, 'Swami, I want a spiritual body.' Swami said, 'Very good. Now, Robert, you will remember this dream very well when you wake up and I want you to tell everyone in your Sai Center about this dream. And do not fear, for I am here.' Well, Sam, Robert woke up and remembered the dream. He told us all and we cried and prayed and laughed and sang. Then, a few days later, Robert peacefully died in his sleep."

That, dear reader, is one of my favorite Sai Baba stories.

Brian, from Australia

Brian was a young man in his late 20's who I met in India in 1995 at the celebration of Sai Baba's birthday in November. He played the guitar and we got recruited into the same music group to play for the ceremonies. He had a little boy named Joel, who was about five years old at the time. Joel had a pendant with a silver chain and a copper pendant, with Baba's face on it, similar to my ring. I asked about it and Brian told me the following story: "When Joel was two years old, we came to India to see Baba. Joel had been having a lot of mysterious health problems and we were hoping that Baba could help. We obtained an interview, and Swami materialized this chain and pendant for Joel. It was entirely of silver.

We got back to Australia and one night, the pendant turned copper! We showed all our friends and we all agreed that it was one of Swami's "*lilas*" (lila is the Divine play of the cosmos). We all laughed and marveled at how Swami could turn something silver into copper all the way from India. And we wondered why not the chain, too? Then we took Joel to a homeopathic physician. He did tests and said, "Your son has a severe copper shortage." He recommended some supplements. Joel's health problems were solved very quickly and he has been extremely healthy ever since."

John, from Seattle

John was a very large man from Seattle. He told me this remarkable story in 1995 in India (John is speaking):

I was sitting in darshan in India one day. There was a Hindu man on my left and a Hindu man on my right. (They were collectively probably not as big as John.) Each of them had a letter to give to Swami. The man on my left (Number One) said regarding his letter in a very serious manner, "I have financial problems which are so great, I may have to commit suicide unless Swami can help me." Boy, I was concerned for him. Then the guy on my right (Number Two) said, "My personal problems are greater than your financial problems!" Now I was really concerned for both of those guys. Then Swami came out and looked so wondrous. He stopped in front of Number Two, and took his letter. Then, he smiled at me, patted me on the head and blessed me. Then he stopped in front of Number One, and thoughtfully threw Number Two's letter into Number One's lap. Then he went on and finished darshan. After it was over, we stood up. Number Two angrily looked at Number One and said, "You have MY letter!" Number One said, "No, Swami gave it to me!" I was trying to calm them down. We called over the head Seva Dal (ashram security person). Each fellow pled his case. The head Seva Dal said, "I will open the letter. If it is personal stuff from you, Number Two, I will give it to you. If it is anything else, I will give it to you, Number One." They agreed. He opened the letter. To my total shock, in front of my eyes, it was 50,000 Rupees and a blank paper! Number One had his financial problems solved and by the blank paper, I inferred that somehow, Number Two had his personal problems solved!"

The Family from Bombay

In 1992, I met a family from Bombay. The mom and dad were both medical doctors. Many of the peripheral family were professionals. The mom and dad had two twin boys, who were about four years old. They were blind. They had no eyeballs in their sockets. The mom and dad and family had heard about all the amazing miracles that Baba had been doing for years. They came down with the hope that Swami could heal their boys. They told me the following story:

"We got an interview with Sai Baba. We were so thrilled and we were filled with great expectations. We entered the small interview room and sat down. As usual, Baba materialized vibhuti for all of the women in the room. (I have seen that three times when I have been in interviews. One time, as Swami completed materializing vibhuti for all the ladies in our interview, he frisked his hands, looked at me and said, 'Just enough!' which totally cracked me up and I laughed out loud!) Then he sat down and looked at us and said, 'Yes, I know you want me to heal these boys. However, watch.'"

"Swami pointed at the wall and the wall became a motion picture! We were in shock and we saw the two boys in their past incarnation. They were Dacoits (robbers). We saw how they robbed a wealthy man and proceeded to poke his eyes out so he couldn't identify them. Then Swami turned to us and said, 'You see. I could heal them, but by the laws of God, they would soon become blind again. Let me tell you further. Later in that life, they repented from their evil ways and tried to restore money to the people they robbed. They also turned to God and tried their best to practice devotion to God. Because of that, they were accorded a beneficial birth in a good family like yours.' We were stunned and shocked into reality and understood the meaning of their handicap. We asked what we should do. Swami said, 'Teach them to Love All, Serve All, and one day, their sight will be restored.'"

Diane, from Wisconsin

A lady from Madison, Wisconsin told this story in 1986 at the Sai Conference in St. Louis, Mo. I do not know how she got through this story without breaking down. This is essentially what she said:

"My father had cancer. He was beginning to suffer badly and was in the hospital. I went to India to see Baba and was wondering whether I should pray for a healing for my dad or whether I should surrender to the Lord's will. It was on my mind all the time as we traveled to Puttaparthi and all the time I was there.

"Then, one day, we got an interview. I was very expectant. Much to my surprise, Baba motioned me over and materialized a special allotment of vibhuti for me. He said, 'This is very special vibhuti, very good for cancer!' Then he said, 'Do not fear, your father will be with me.' I saved the vibhuti for my dad. I wondered how I would get him to take it, because he didn't really believe in Sai Baba and wasn't that religious, in general.

"Much to my surprise, when I got back home and went to the hospital, he took it very willingly and smiled. Just a few hours later, he quietly passed away. The doctors said that it was a blessing, because that type of cancer could have lasted a long time and was brutally painful in its last stages. I thanked Sai Baba inwardly. He saved my dad much pain.

"Then, some months later, I had a vivid Sai Baba dream. (Note: Sai Baba says that you cannot have a dream of him unless he so wills it. He has also said in answer to a devotee questioning whether it was real when she had a dream of Swami, 'What difference which dream world I come to you in?'). In that dream, Swami came to me with a big smile. He motioned me to follow him. We came into his small room on the ashram. He pointed out the window at a young Hindu couple with a brand new baby. He pointed at the baby and said, 'That's your father!'"

"My dad was with him. He had reincarnated in India."

Pierre, the Frenchman

One of my good buddies on a number of trips to India was a French fellow, appropriately named Pierre. He was from Paris and spent a lot of his vacations in Puttaparthi with Swami. Some years before, Swami had materialized a simple silver ring with an OM sign on it for Pierre. Pierre wore it all the time and it was literally falling apart. He kept it together with tape sometimes. Then one day, he got into an interview with Swami. I saw him not too long after he came out of the interview and he was ecstatic, with a big smile on his face and a brand new gold and emerald ring that Baba had materialized for him! He showed the ring to everybody and I was truly happy for him.

The Magic House in London

There is a wonderful Hindu couple in Kingsbury, a suburb of London, UK, named Hemma and Boskar. They are truly delightful and generous people who have a house about five minutes from the Kingsbury train station. When I was in London in the Fall of 2005, I went to their house a number of times. The reason, beside the fact that they are very special people, is that they have the most incredible miracles going on all the time in their house. They have over 40 pictures and statues of Swami, Shiva, Krishna, et al with vibhuti, *amritha* (divine nectar), *kum* (a red powder used in religious ceremonies in India), red stuff, and many other things flowing out of them! Anyone who goes to London should definitely make their way to this house.

Every night, for the past 12 years, they open their house to any devotee at 7:00 p.m. If they do not happen to be there, friends or relatives handle the house. They do a little prayer and music session each night. Upstairs, is a little chapel with more such pictures and statues, emanating Swami's magic stuff.

On Sai Baba's birthday on November 23rd in 2005, they had a special singing session. They put nine coconuts on the alter. During the chanting, the coconuts all burst open and the red powder came out of all the coconuts! What a miracle!

Non-Believer in Australia

In 1994, I was speaking with a woman from Australia who lived in New York. She was a long-time Sai Baba devotee. I asked her if she had any good Swami miracle stories for me. She told me this remarkable story about her sister, who was not a believer in Sai Baba:

"My sister lived near Melbourne in a patio home around a swimming pool. Her daughter was 10 years old. She was into meditation, namely Vedanta, but was skeptical of Sai Baba. She didn't really understand the miracles but she was kind and loving toward me, and neither of us tried to push the other into any spiritual trip of any kind.

"However, she kept asking me about Swami. She was real curious. I told her that, being a good meditator, she should ask Swami to come to her and prove himself to her in her own way. She said she would do that. So, on a regular basis, as she meditated, she said, 'Swami, show me that you are real.'

"One day, her daughter and friends were cavorting in the swimming pool. The glass patio door was closed. Somehow, because of lighting and youthful exuberance, her daughter came running toward the door and didn't realize that the door was closed. To my sister's shock, her daughter crashed right through the glass and fell onto the shattered glass on the floor. My sister shrieked in horror, went to her daughter's aid and found two remarkable things: 1) Her daughter was totally untouched, the glass notwithstanding, and 2) There was a perfectly formed hole in the glass door of the very shape of Sai Baba, complete with his afro and robe!

"Now she believed that Swami was real. However, she still was hesitant about becoming an actual devotee or student of Sa Baba.

"Then one night, in deep meditation, Baba came to her as Great Beings do to deep meditators, and said to my sister, 'Oh beloved manifestation of God, I do not care whether you believe in this form of divinity or any other form. You follow your heart. I will bless you no matter what path you are on. Love all, serve all. My love is with you always.' Within a few months, her sister went to India to see Sai Baba."

Danny from Tel Aviv

In 1995, while in India, I met a fellow named Danny from Israel. He was very pushy and had an attitude. No one liked him much. I found him interesting and hung out with him a bit. He just didn't seem to fit in with anyone.

One day, he got an interview with Sai Baba. One of his Tel Aviv group told me that when they got into the interview, Swami motioned for Danny to sit by him. Swami never said a word to Danny. He just held his hand lightly while he spoke with all the other folks in the interview. Then, he materialized a beautiful ring for Danny.

I am telling you, you have never seen such a change in one human being in your life! For the rest of the weeks we were in India, Danny and I hung out all the time. He was totally changed. He invited me to come to Israel and stay with him anytime. It was like the character in the Wizard of Oz was suddenly implanted with a heart filled with love, compassion, and humility. I was truly shocked by this event. I send Danny good thoughts and hope he is well.

Richard Bock from Los Angeles

Richard Bock lived in Los Angeles. He was one of the early American Sai Baba devotees. This is a summary of the stories that he told me when I stopped into his little Sai Store in Los Angeles, combined with background information from mutual friends:

Richard was the owner of a company called the Pacific Jazz Record Company. He was, as told to me by some close and loving friends, quite a wild man, doing the hard Hollywood life to a vengeance. One of those friends gave him a book about Sai

Baba in 1967 and told him that he really needed to cool off, chill out, get into meditation, and change some of his potentially harmful habits, or else he wasn't going to live too long.

Richard wasn't paying too much attention, however. Then, he went on a trip to England to sign some jazz acts. He was on a train in a private compartment. Suddenly, he was having a massive heart attack. He stood up, held onto the sink in the compartment, and told me that he was turning blue. Then, he looked down and saw the picture of Sai Baba on the cover of the book in his briefcase which his friend had given him. Richard told me that he spoke out loud to Sai Baba and said, "I do not know who you are, but you better help me right now." Suddenly, he felt calm. The pain and stress went away. He heard calm words say, "Get off the train at the next stop and take a taxi to a hospital." He did just that. He got off the train at the next stop. There was a taxi right there. He told the driver to take him to a hospital. He was checked in and the doctors were amazed. They confirmed that Richard had suffered a major heart attack, which should have been fatal.

While recuperating in the hospital, Richard read the Sai Baba book. He had his staff book him on a flight to India as soon as the doctors would allow him to leave.

He arrived at Swami's ashram. He was sitting in darshan early on in his visit, when Sathya Sai Baba came up to him, tapped him on the chest, and said "Mr. Bock, from Los Angeles, we just barely saved you."

Richard became a lifelong Swami devotee, became a vegetarian, non-smoker, non-drinker, and regular meditator. He did some of the best films on Sai Baba and filmed some quite remarkable miracles.

Ravi Shankar

One of the subjects of Richard Bock's early Sai Baba films was the famous entertainer, Ravi Shankar, originally from India, and whom the Beatles made famous back in the 1960's. In this part of the film, Swami materialized a remarkable piece of jewelry for Ravi and a ring for his sideman.

Lady Sarah Ferguson

In 1997, we were in India, when Lady Sarah Ferguson visited Puttaparthi. Some of the ladies in our group actually saw her. I, myself, never saw her. She was accorded an interview by Swami. In that interview, he materialized a very large gold cross on a gold chain for her. This was duly noted, photographed, and printed in the Bangalore and Bombay newspapers. It actually made the San Jose Mercury News in San Jose, CA, for some reason.

G., from Chicago

I am not allowed to mention her name, for privacy, but his is an interesting Swami miracle. The following is a summary of G.'s talk at a Sai Conference in St. Louis, Mo in 1987:

"I am a nurse. I was coming home from work. I got off the train and was walking to my flat. As I was walking, suddenly, this long-haired, orange-robed 'brother' appeared in front of me. He looked at me and said, 'Why aren't you looking for me?' I was shocked and wondered, 'Who was that crazy brother?' (Needless to say, this comment brought down the whole place in great laughter). I was really puzzled about this. Then, I kind of forgot about it, but a few weeks later, almost in the same place at the same time on my way home, again, this wild fellow with the afro and the orange robe was suddenly in front of me, and this time, he said 'You are not looking hard enough!' Now, I was really thinking about this guy. I truly couldn't figure out what was going on.

"One day, I was in a used bookstore, and saw a copy of Sam Sandweiss' book *The Holy Man and the Psychiatrist*. On the cover was a picture of that wild fellow. He was Sai Baba! I found out everything I could about him. I discovered there was a Sai Center in Chicago, visited it, and found that they were sending a group to India. I signed up and bought my ticket.

On the way to India, the only thought on my mind was to find out somehow if Swami could confirm to me that he actually materialized himself in front of me in Chicago two different times. Fortunately, we got an interview. We entered the small interview room with Swami. He welcomed us and materialized vibhuti for the ladies in the room. Then he sat down and looked at me and said very firmly (addressing my thoughts), 'Yes, yes, I was there!'"

One of My Own Sai Baba Stories

This is my personal story. I still do not understand how this happened, but it did.

I had been to India before, but in 1992, I took five of my close spiritual fiends with me on a trip to see Sai Baba. We flew from Minneapolis to London and then to Bombay on Air India. We landed at the Bombay airport, which was total chaos and bedlam. We had never seen anything like this in our lives. This was major "India shock." It seemed like there were more people of all shapes and kinds at that airport then there were in the rest of the world, all of them pushing, yelling, and trying to get something from you, whether it was to carry your bags, provide transportation, begging, or whatever. Of course, we all considered it a major miracle that our bags got through and that we actually got through customs.

We found out that we had landed at the International Airport and to continue on our journey to Puttaparthi, we first had to make our way to the Domestic Airport. This was a huge challenge in itself. We had landed in the middle of the night after about 20 hours in the air. Finally, after a total chaotic hour, we made it to the Domestic Airport. We sat there all night and got on Jet Airways to Bangalore at about 9 a.m. This trip was pleasant and easy. We arrived in Bangalore, got our bags, and found a hotel in Bangalore. Fortunately, Swami was

106

in his Whitefield ashram (near Bangalore) and not in Puttaprthi (four hours away by taxi). We also noted that it was easy to find out where Sai Baba was. All one had to do was ask any person on the street or in a hotel or taxi or whatever. That was truly remarkable in our eyes.

We took a taxi the next morning to see Swami and had our first darshan. It was truly spiritual uplifting and was everything we had expected and for which we had traveled 34 hours around the world to experience. We had a lot of fun and met many people from many countries, surprised that there were so many people form the following countries: Germany, Italy, Argentina, Brazil and other South American countries, Australia, and Holland, and so few from the United States.

After spending a few days in Whitefield, Swami moved back to Puttaparthi. We followed and got rooms at the ashram. These were spartan rooms, with two beds, a sink, toilet, and cold shower. We had to buy mattresses in the village.

Every morning and every afternoon, we went to darshan. We got up at about 3:30 in the morning and went over to line up to see where we would be sitting in the mandir. With so many people there, we lined up in many lines. The head person of each line pulled a numbered chit from a bag holding them. We discovered that if the head of your line picked chits 1-3, you could get a seat in the first row and have a chance to get an interview or some remarkable interaction with Swami as he walked through darshan. If you got chits 4-6, you were in the second row, which wasn't too bad.

Seva Dals were volunteers from various parts of India who handled security. They certainly needed to have some order there. We discovered that Westerners (except Italians) generally were pretty orderly, and didn't leap up, didn't try to pile over people, etc., as Swami walked by. In contrast, there were many folks from India, God Bless their souls, who did not have much respect for those around them and without the Seva Dals to effect order, could have made a shambles out of a deep spiritual experience for the rest of us.

One day, I was in a line that got a good chit. I staked out a front row position. Swami came by and came right up to me, and said, "How many?" meaning how many in the group. "Six," I said. He said, "Go," meaning go up to the veranda and wait for him to finish and we had a very coveted interview! I stood up, and waved to the rest of our group. They all saw me and they, too, headed up to the front on the veranda. We sat for a while as Swami finished darshan.

We came into the small interview room. There were six of us from St. Paul, Minnesota, a Hindu couple, and six ladies from Chile. We sat down and waited in great expectation.

The first thing Swami did was manifest vibhuti for all the ladies. Jannie, my significant other, was sitting in the back next to me. As he poured the vibhuti from his hand into hers, he wiped his hands together and looked at me and said, "Just enough!" I was caught so much by surprise, having waited to see God in human form, and then having him make a joke about his own miracle, absolutely cracked me up. I was so surprised, and when I am caught with humor by surprise, I always laugh right out loud. I did just that and laughed so loud that Swami looked at me.

Many wonderful things happen in an interview. I have heard marvelous stories about many people's interviews with Swami. Our first one was no exception.

I had a Buddha ring, made of silver, gold, and some stones, with little elephants around the side. It was a very big ring. Dr. George Gaye had given it to me in 1976. He told me "I am giving you this ring for your protection. You will keep it as long as you need it and then it will disappear." Well, Swami motioned at the ring. I took it off my finger and handed it to him. He looked at the ring and said, "Whose face on ring?" I said "Buddha," pronouncing it the customary way with the accent on the first syllable. He said, "No, Budd-ha, Buddh-a," with the accent on the second syllable. He went on to say, "Face not clear, ring too big." I said, "Swami, I would like your face on the ring." He smiled and held the ring between his first and second finger right out in front of all of us, and blew on the old ring, and miraculously, it became the ring I have now, with his likeness on the face of the ring.

He put it on my pinkie finger and it fit. I was ecstatic! I have never tired in 15 years of looking at the ring. I am so grateful for him doing this for me.

Later in the interview, he did some entertainment for us. First, he spoke with the ladies from Chile. There was one older lady, who spoke English and Spanish. The other five younger ladies spoke only Spanish. Then, he materialized a beautiful lingam (see section on lingams) for them and told them, "This is a special lingam for Chile." He handed it to the older lady and gave her instructions on what to do with it, i.e., what ceremonies to use with it. Then, he asked the older lady in English if they had any questions for him. Here is where the fun began. The younger ladies asked him a question in Spanish. The older lady would translate into English. Swami would answer in English. Then, as the older lady was translating into Spanish, each time she tried, Swami would interrupt her and say, "Bad translation, bad translation." She would start again, and he would then say, "Better, better." We really got a kick out of that and the Chilean ladies were really moved that Swami apparently understood their language.

BOAC Pilot Acts Like a Kid

In 1995, we went to India twice. The first time, in January, we stayed on the ashram near a husband, wife, and son from England. The husband, David, was a BOAC pilot and had the normal English upper-class air about him, though a very nice fellow. David and his wife were veterans of the spiritual path and India and Sai Baba. Their son, however, was on his first trip to India. One day, they got an interview in the afternoon. We saw them by their room later. They were so happy because Swami had manifested a ring for their son. It was a silver Krishna ring, having a raised image of Lord

Krishna on the face of the ring. Krishna had his eyes closed. Early the next morning, they knocked on our door. I will never forget the aristocratic and top professional BOAC pilot as happy as a little kid, because overnight, Lord Krishna's eyes on the ring opened!

This is what is called a lila, the sport of the Gods. Always remember, that the Great Ones have great and generous senses of humor!

Wilma Bronkey from Oregon

This is my favorite Sai Baba story of all I have ever heard or seen. Dr. Wilma Bronkey is a longtime Sai devotee. She and her husband, Ivan, live in Grants Pass, Oregon. At the time of this story, Wilma was about 70 years old. She spent her entire life in great unselfish service in many different humanitarian ways. She is a truly great soul. She has had many remarkable miracles from Swami over the years, but this one takes the cake:

Wilma was driving an "older lady" from Oregon down to Arizona. It was early spring, when the weather in the West can do about anything. It was very warm when they left. They drove through Nevada and were coming down the road through Tonapah, Nevada.

It started to snow. It got colder. Neither Wilma nor the woman had any boots or warm clothing. They were, after all, heading for Arizona. The driving was tough, and they made it into Tonapah. It was evening and they tried to find a place to stay for the night. Unfortunately, all the motels were filled. They came to a truck stop/motor lodge. The man at the desk gruffly told them that there were no rooms.

Because of the snow, it was impossible for them to keep driving. Nevada is a very sparsely populated state and there aren't too many services other than the major towns, of which there are few. They tried some other places. They were having trouble driving. Wilma was praying to Sai Baba and asking him to help them.

They tried the original motor lodge one more time. This time, there was a young woman behind the desk. She took pity on them and said reluctantly, "You can stay in the owner's suite, but don't tell anyone that I let you use it." They were so grateful, and were so happy to be warm and dry. There was a wonderful bath, comfortable beds, and in the extreme circumstances, it was like heaven to the travelers. They spent a wonderful night and came down the next morning to sun, warmer weather, and clear roads. When they found their car, they cleared the snow off of it, and then went to get breakfast. When they came back to the lobby of the motor lodge to pay for the room, the man at the front desk was nonplussed when they said they had stayed in the "owner's suite." He maintained that there was no owner's suite. They went outside to show him and he was correct! There was no such suite. Also, the man told them in no uncertain terms that the boss had no suite and also did not hire any women to work there, because of the generally rough trade of truckers, miners, etc.

Wilma realized that Swami had somehow manifested a phantom hotel room in their time of need!

Swami's Sense of Humor

We had an interview in 1995. During that interview, Swami held out his hand and asked softly, "What's in my hand?" Stupidly, we said, "Nothing, Swami." He pulled his hand back and said, "No, everything."

Well, we thought about that, discussed it, and agreed that Swami indeed had the entire creation in his hand, reflecting his status as a full avatar.

Then, two years later, essentially the same group of us got another interview. During this interview, again, Swami held out his hand and said, "What's in my hand?" This time, a little bit smarter, we confidently said, "Everything, Swami." He looked at us in surprise and said, "No, nothing!" We really laughed about that. We realized that Swami had pulled a little joke on us after two years! We accepted it as awareness of his omnipresence and awareness of who we were.

During that trip, there was a young Dutch boy named Johannes, about 14 years old who adopted us. He liked to hang out with us Americans and we liked him. He heard me tell the preceding story. He enjoyed it and all stories about Swami. One day, Johannes and his family got an interview. He and his dad could not wait to tell us this story:

"We got into the interview, and the first thing Swami did was hold out his empty hand and say, 'What's in my hand?' Before anyone could say anything, Johannes here said, 'Both everything and nothing, Swami.' Swami looked at him in mock surprise, and said 'Smart boy.' Then he playfully slapped him across the face and materialized this gold chain and pendant for him!

"The Chain was beautiful and of a special type of 'woven gold.' One of our English chums explained to us the unique difficulties involved in creating such a chain. We really got a lot of laughs about that story."

An Indian Coincidence

One of our friends from Minnesota is named Susan. She and her husband and child were in India seeing Swami some years ago. She was feeling a little blue and was not happy that they did not get an interview with Swami that trip. Then, a funny thing happened, which could probably only happen in India:

Susan was sitting in a hotel lobby in Bangalore. As she was reading a book, waiting for her family to come back, she heard a woman sitting nearby speak in English. She said, "Oh, are you from the United States?" The woman said, "Yes I am." Susan inquired, "Where are you from?" to which the woman replied, "I am from Minnesota." Susan went on to ask, "Where in Minnesota?" and the woman responded, "The Twin Cities." Susan said, "Where in the Twin Cities?" to which the woman replied, "Plymouth." Susan asked, "Where in Plymouth?" The woman explained, and Susan then confirmed to her that she could literally walk a few blocks to the woman's house! The woman turned out to be named Valerie and she and Susan became friends after returning to Plymouth, Minnesota.

One of Joel Riordan's Tales

Please note that I have never been able to verify this story from any other source, but to my knowledge, Joel never fibbed to me about Sai Baba and he had no reason to fib to me about this story. You may take issue with me on it, but I am going to tell you it the way Joel told it to me in May of 1976 in Los Angeles:

"I was sitting with Swami one day in Whitefield. There were a few of us around. Swami announced to us that there were some undercover people from the Treasury Department of India in darshan that afternoon. We sat around while Swami went out and walked around. He made sure that he called these undercover men in for an interview. One of them was the number three man in the department.

"They sat down and Swami told them that he knew who they were and they could ask questions. They said to Swami, 'We apologize, but there have been rumors that you have been materializing money, counterfeiting money, and as you know, the economy of India is fragile and we had to investigate the rumors.' Swami was very sympathetic and said he totally understood their concerns. He put them totally at ease and manifested some vibhuti and jewelry for them.

"Then, Swami explained to them that he did not materialize any money, per se, but that he did 'apport' money from where it had been lost. Apporting is the unique India technique that many fakirs and yogis have used over the centuries to transport objects from one place to another with no visible means of said transportation, i.e., through the unseen. Well, after hearing Swami's words, these undercover guys felt a lot better because apporting was something well within their experience in Indian culture. Swami went on to say that when there were shipwrecks, plane crashes, earthquakes, etc., where money was lost or when folks put money 'down the slot' in Hindu temples all over India, he apported it to the ashram there for his work. Now, the undercover guys were more comfortable. This was something pretty safe and proven (in India, anyway). Then, Swami materialized vibhuti and rings and stuff for each of them.

"Then he summoned me, saying 'Rowdy!' (Note: Swami addressed Joel for many years as 'Rowdy.') I stood at attention, and he handed to a Hindu fellow and me a set of keys and directed us to a small building a little ways away. We led the undercover guys over to the building, used the keys to unlock the door, and entered. I got the shock of my life and so did the other guys because the entire building was filled from floor to roof with orderly stacks of currencies! Rupees, dollars, pounds, francs, marks, etc. We walked in the aisles amidst the stacks of all these currencies in total disbelief. The undercover guys absently took a sample bill here and there and looked at them. We were stunned. We then exited, locked the building, and raced back to Swami. He was smiling at our return. The undercover guys said excitedly, 'Swami, we have to do an audit and check the serial numbers.' Swami totally agreed with them and said, 'Big job, very big job, better start right away.' The undercover guys agreed, and we returned to the building. We unlocked the door, entered, and NOTHING! The building was completely empty! The undercover guys looked helplessly at the sample bills they still clutched in their hands. We exited the building again, locked the door, and went back to Swami. The undercover guys threw themselves on the floor in front of Swami and bowed at his feet! They all became his disciples and never again was Swami investigated by the Treasury Department of India!"

Colonel Rashid, From India

In 1987, I had a good talk with a Colonel Rashid, from the Indian Special Forces. He was in charge of a detail which was providing security for a visit by the Vice-President of India to Swami. (Note: Nearly all major politicians going back to Indira Ghandi in India have been Swami devotees or at least pay lip service to him.) He was a very smart and good man. He told me, "I took my platoon to be blessed by Swami when I was a lieutenant; I took my company to be blessed by

Swami when I made captain; and I took my
regiment to be blessed by Swami when I made
colonel." I thought to myself at the time, "It would
be great if every officer in every army on earth
brought his unit to be blessed by Swami, we
probably would have a lot fewer wars!" He
thereupon told me a story of one of his former
commanding officers when he was a captain and an
aide to this general:

"My commanding general was an atheist
and a Marxist. He was very close to the Russians; it
was a time in the history of India where India was
flirting with Marxism and was very close to the
Russians and at odds with the United States. The
general had worked with the British during World
War II. A British officer had given him a gift of a
beautiful pistol, with a white pearl handle. The
general kept this pistol in his safe at home in New
Delhi, over a thousand miles from Puttaparthi.

"The general did not like 'holy men' and
considered them all fakes and leaches. He did not
like religion in general and thought that India
should implement the Soviet model of operating,
including banning religions.

"He became really furious when he found
out that his wife and daughters had become Sai
Baba devotees right under his nose. He was truly
mad. He told me to organize a detail to go down to
this place called Puttaparthi and we were going to
end this stupidity.

"I organized the trip, and we took a small
detail to Prasanthi Nilayam, The Abode of the

Highest Peace, Swami's Ashram in Puttaparthi, AP, India.

"We barged right in and pushed the pitiful security aside. We were all armed with side arms and pushed our way into Swami's modest private room. He smiled at us benignly. The general pulled out his service revolver, pointed it at Swami, and said, 'You will not steal my wife and daughters. One less holy man here or there will never be noticed. I am going to kill you right now!

"Swami said to him, in the sweetest calm voice, 'Oh, you are going to shoot me? Maybe you should use a better pistol.' Then, to the general's (and my) total shock, Swami handed him the pearl-handled special pistol from the general's safe back in New Delhi. The general held the pistol, visibly melted in front of my eyes, and totally changed, knelt before Swami, kissed his feet and repented of his thoughts and ways. He begged Swami to accept him as a disciple. Swami held his head gently and blessed him. Then, he asked us to leave and spent some time alone with the general.

"The general did not say another word all the way back to New Delhi. For the rest of his life, he and his family were Sai Baba devotees."

The Bangalore Newspaper Editor

Jesus said, "... agree with thine adversary." He also said, "Pray for your enemies." These are little remembered words these days. Here is a Swami story implementing these teachings. We heard this story from an old Hindu fellow who lived at the ashram and gave a speech to foreigners once in a while. I do not remember his name, nor did I ever meet him. However, I heard him tell this story, wrote notes on it, and have told it for years:

The main editor for the Bangalore, India main newspaper, did not like Sai Baba and considered him a total hoax and fraud. He wrote terrible things about Sai Baba, all of them either misleading or false. He slandered and libeled Swami for a long time.

The speaker I refer to above said that one day he was in a meeting with some big shots from the ashram, as well as the governor of the province, the Vice-president of India, and a few other significant figures. The subject of the meeting was this editor and all his libelous comments. They told Swami that they could put economic and political pressure on the man so he would stop making these false comments.

They were in shock and their collective jaws dropped when Swami said the following: "No, you do not have to do anything and you do not have to try to stop him. Please understand that my interest is in HIS happiness and apparently it makes him happy to say bad things about me, so, as long as he is happy, I am happy." These powerful, wealthy, and influential people were speechless at Swami's comment. Swami went on to say, "One day, it won't make him happy anymore, and then he will stop."

The punchline to this story is the following: The offending editor had a son on whom he doted. The son was dying of a fatal illness and the doctors could not help him. The editor's wife, sister, and daughter took the sick son secretly to see Sai Baba. Baba healed the son and saved his life. The doctors confirmed this. The editor, when discovering these details, traveled to see Sai Baba. He threw himself at his feet. He said, "You have given me my son. I will give you my life."

From that time on, the Bangalore newspaper has been a veritable publicity venue for Sai Baba. It regularly has pictures of Swami on it and tells the stories about his miracles and humanitarian deeds.

A Combination Master George and Swami Miracle

When I first heard about Sai Baba in Los Angeles in 1975, I came back to see Dr. George in Wisconsin. I showed him a Sai Baba book with Swami's picture on it and asked him what he thought of Sai. His eyes gleamed, and he said, "Wonderful." Later, Dr. George encouraged some of his students to set up a Sai Baba center in his (Dr. George's) church in Milwaukee. This center still meets at Dr. George's old church forty years later!

Some of the Sai people in Los Angeles considered Dr. George the Great American Yogi. They came out from L.A. to see Dr. George on a regular basis. On one such trip, students Sylvia, Merry Dee, Bill, and his son were with Dr. George in George's car en route from Milwaukee to The Farm (Dr. George's retreat in Northern Wisconsin, a three-hour drive).

They were having troubles with the car. When they reached the town of Wisconsin Dells, they stopped to use the rest rooms. When they got back in the car, they couldn't get the car started. Sylvia said that whenever she had problems with her car at home, she just threw a little Sai Baba vibhuti on the engine and it would run. Dr. George agreed with her, and she got out of the car, threw some vibhuti on the engine, and the car started!

They drove to Friendship, Wisconsin and thereupon stopped to get some lunch. As they got out of the car, Dr. George left it running and told Bill to go over to the gas station across the road, fill it with gas, and have the guy check it out to be sure everything was alright.

Dr. George and the two ladies went into the café and Bill drove the car to the station. He had the guy fill it and asked him to check under the hood. The guy said the oil is fine, but, remarked, "How the heck did you get here?" Bill replied, "What are you talking about?" The guy responded, "Come here and look." (Note: Bill was a graduate mechanical engineer and knew all about cars.) The guy pointed to the ground cable from the battery. There was a three-inch gap and no ground! Bill knew that it was physically impossible for the car to run, but it did! Bill and I laughed for quite a while when he told me this story. We figured that it was a "joint" miracle by Swami and Dr. George. Bill said that when he got to the café, Dr. George said with a twinkle in his eye, "How's the car, Bill?"

Colusa, California

In this little one-horse agricultural town about an hour north of Sacramento, lives a humble Hindu man from Fiji, of all places, who has never been to India. His name is Ammi Chand Magru. He has a wife and some nice kids and a modest house in Colusa. He worked a series of relatively humble jobs most of his life.

One day his house became a Magic Swami Ashram. When I came by to visit the first time in 1994, there was an alter with over twenty pictures and statues emanating vibhuti, kum-kum, and other stuff. There was one picture of Swami's feet which emanated HONEY. When we chanted, the stuff really came out. The kicker was a glass of water, out of which water kept coming with NO DISCERNABLE SOURCE. So much water came out, that Ammi had to put a bowl underneath the glass to handle the overdraft, and then a bigger bowl to cover the overdraft of the smaller bowl, and then a real big bowl handling that overflow! This holy water would really come out when we chanted. Ammi gave this water generously to all the folks who came to the twice-a-week chanting sessions.

On the wall opposite the alter, was a glossy paper picture of Jesus with the red heart (the common picture that we have all seen). I had my guitar along and Ammi asked me if I would lead our group and a few other folks who were there in Western devotional music (since I do not do too well with the Hindu music, although I love to listen to it). I started in leading everyone in English chants, and while we were doing this, THE PICTURE OF JESUS STARTED EMANATING HONEY!, right from the heart of Jesus on the paper picture flat on the wall, with no frame above, below, or behind it, or around it! Just honey coming out of the picture. I have seen some remarkable things in my life and that was sure one of them.

Some years later, in 1998, we came by again, and the honey was still coming out of that picture, and the water kept flowing, and the vibhuti kept flowing out of pictures.

One sad note: For many years, the Sai organization in the U.S. did not allow Ammi's house and group to be an "official" Sai center. This, I guess, is another case where organizations just do not understand saints and miracles.

My Ring, Phase Two

I told you about 1992 when Swami materialized the ring for me. Well, push it forward three years to 1995. Jannie and I were living in White Bear Lake, Minnesota. We were leaving for India in another week. It was early January, 1995.

One morning, I was sitting on our couch in the living room. I was watching Sports Center, getting the basketball scores from the night before in college and the NBA. I went over to the rest room adjacent to the living room. Then, I went to my little office adjacent the other way and sent a fax. Next, I went into the kitchen, adjacent back of the couch, got a cup of coffee, and went back to work on the phone on the couch. I looked at my finger where my Swami Ring was and it was gone. I went into total panic! I dug the whole house up where I had walked. I thought that the ring must have fallen off my finger somehow while I was either in the rest room, the fax send, or the coffee. Wrong, the ring was nowhere. Jannie came home later. She couldn't find it either. She is very clairvoyant and we got quiet. We both realized that the ring had disappeared, dematerialized. I figured that I had done something wrong. I tried to figure out what it was and try to ask God to forgive me and get back in his good graces, to no avail.

We got to India, and the only thing on my mind was trying to get to Swami and ask him about the ring. Day after day went by. I would be in first row in darshan and he would walk by as if I didn't exist. Then, after weeks of stewing and praying and thinking about the ring, one day, between afternoon darshan and afternoon bhajans, I was just sitting doing nothing, relaxing. Then, to my total surprise, out walked Swami. He came right over to me, and stood over me, and said, "What do you want?" Well, dear reader, I had been thinking of nothing other than that ring and why it had gone missing. I had spent weeks sitting there in India waiting and trying to get close to Swami, to no avail, to ask him about the ring, and suddenly there he was right in front of me asking what I wanted, and my mind went totally blank! I looked into his eyes and I couldn't think a thought. He pointed at his feet and said very sternly, "Padnamaskar!" I reached down and hugged and kissed his feet. He WHOPPED me on the top of the head. Then he turned and left. I learned later that by that little ceremony he had promised me to take me across the Seas of Samsara, past the state of delusion to liberation and oneness with God! I was ecstatic. I forgot about the ring and getting access to Swami. I also couldn't figure out why in the heck I didn't ask him about the ring. Oh well, you can't have everything.

Then, a few days later, when I was least expecting it, we got an interview! I had tears of joy streaming down my cheeks as I sat up on the Veranda waiting for Swami to complete the darshan.

We entered the interview room and I moved right up to the front and sat right next to his chair, the closest person to him. I was literally inches away. He materialized vibhuti for the women in the interview. Then he sat down. Before he could do anything, I said quickly to him, "Swami, what happened to the ring you made me?" Whap, whap – he hit me real hard on both cheeks! The shakti went right up my spine and for a moment, I was in the state of Nirbikalpa Samadhi, the dream of my life since I read Yogananda's book at age 16. My true goal. I was there for a short period of time, then, I floated back down into the room. As I regained my normal consciousness, I thought to myself, "Oh well, I don't care if he gave me an entire jewelry store, the bliss of God is what I have sought and reached for my entire life."

Then, after the interview was over, I was the last person out of the small room. He stopped me, put his hand on my shoulder, and looked me in the eye, and said, "Good man, good man. Don't worry, I will get your ring back to you one of these days."

I felt tremendous peace. I literally floated out of that interview and knew that Swami had my ring safe and sound and would give it to me whenever, even if in another lifetime or another dimension. Happy, happy, happy!

The Rest of the Story

Please bear with me with this seemingly uninteresting detail, it is important. I had a little nylon bag in which I kept about 20 golf balls, tees, gloves, etc., specifically to throw in my suitcase when I traveled. In case I had the time and the opportunity to play a little golf when I was on the road, all I had to do was show up at the course, rent a set of clubs, and play. During the six months after we got back from India, I can document nine airplane trips plus one two-week auto trip in which I threw the nylon bag in my suitcase or garment bag.

It was now August, 1995, and I was in Irvine, California at some meetings. It was later in the evening and I called Jannie. She was very quiet and then she said, "I found the ring!" I couldn't believe it. I said "How? Where?" Well, if ever you needed physical proof of Swami's omnipresence, this was it: 1) While cleaning out our big walk-in closet, and preparing to vacuum it, she removed all the stuff on the floor. As she reached the last corner, there was the ring. But, here is the kicker: it was sitting right on top of the nylon bag! The ring itself was right-side up with Swami's face looking directly at her! Jannie later said "It was a heart-stopping moment!" 2) You could say, well, the ring walked way down the hall, past one bedroom, past another bedroom and bathroom, and around two corners into the closet, but there is absolutely no way you can say it could be on top of the nylon bag.

This story was so meaningful to me, because the next ten years were total disaster for me in the outer. Every possible bad thing that could happen did. I made every possible mistake and stupid move that I could. The things that got me through were my lifetime of meditating, my sense of humor, a few good friends who stuck by me through it all, and the ring, symbolizing Swami's omnipresence.

Polio

This story was told by a lady from Indiana at the Sai Conference in St. Louis, Mo in the late 1980's. Unfortunately, I do not remember her name. However, I took these notes at the conference and can summarize her story with the essential details:

The lady was a little girl in Indiana and got polio back in the days when it was prevalent and before they came up with the vaccine. I remember the sad cases of kids my age back then who had the misfortune of being afflicted with that terrible disease. The little girl was in an iron lung. Her prognosis was not good; she was probably going to be paralyzed the rest of her life. However, while in the hospital, she heard a divine voice assuring her that HE was with her, and against all odds, she recovered about 95%. She still had a few small leftovers from the disease, but not much. Many years later, when she heard Swami's voice, she realized that it was Him. She became a devotee and He, indeed, verified to her that it was Him.

Answered Letter

There is an older gentleman in the Midwest named Paul, who could not make it to India to see Swami in person. However, there was a lady from the Sai Center in his community who was going over soon. Paul spoke with her and asked her if she could hand-deliver a letter to Swami in darshan, if he would email it to her. She said, yes, she would print it out and deliver it. However, as we all know, sometimes when you are going on a trip for a month, and have so many details to deal with, you can forget things. The lady forgot to print out the letter and was unable to deliver it to Swami. She apologized to Paul and he understood.

Then, he went onto his computer and opened the file where he had typed the letter. There, on the bottom of the letter, Swami had answered all his questions! Note: I am not saying that the Avatar of the Age is a computer hacker, just a kindly prankster now and then.

No Smoking

We spoke in 1992 with an older Hindu gentleman who was retired from India Civil Service and lived at the ashram. He told us this story about his sheepish brother:

"My brother liked to smoke. We all asked him to stop, because it offended everyone in the family. He was stubborn and kept this bad habit nonetheless. One day he got an interview with Swami. Baba chastised him about his smoking. My brother said, 'Okay, Swami, Okay, I will stop and never smoke again.'

"Well, he did his best, but fell off the wagon periodically. Then one day, Swami summoned me. Swami said that he had suspicions of my brother smoking again, who denied it vociferously. Swami held out his open palm, and had my brother look into the palm. To my brother's shock, he saw a small motion picture with the visual evidence, i.e., a FILM of my brother hiding out behind a building and having a puff!

"Needless to say, my brother has not smoked since."

The Watch that Worked with No Workings

In 1987, some friends of mine from Australia who I had met at the ashram introduced me to an older Hindu gentleman living there. He was a nice fellow and asked politely where I was from. He said he knew someone from India who had worked in Minneapolis. We did some more small talk. I noticed that he had s "Baba wristwatch" with a leather band. It was the Sai Baba equivalent of a "mickey-mouse" watch, i.e., it had Swami's smiling face on it and was made of plastic. There was one small difference: IT HAD NO INTERNAL WORKINGS! Yes, it had no mechanical or electrical movements. It had run continuously for FIFTEEN YEARS. Swami had materialized it for this fellow. Everyone had heard about it and the poor fellow had to show everyone who came by.

Some years later, I heard that Swami had relieved him of the responsibility and de-materialized it and the man did not have to show everyone the watch that worked with no workings.

The Old Swami

Dr. Kasturi wrote in his book, *999* about an Old Swami who came to see our Swami in 1959. At that time, the old Swami was in his eighties.

The Old Swami came to see Baba one day. Baba received him in a kindly manner. Then he surprised the Old Swami by saying, "I see you when you were a young boy, of nine years old, and you did a certain Puja, guided by your father, of saying your mantra one thousand and eight times in one day, with the goal of obtaining a (special) vision of Lord Ganesha." The Old Swami said, "How did you know that?" Baba said simply, "I was there."

Baba went on to ask, "Did you receive the reward for this Puja (i.e., the vision of Lord Ganesha)?" The Old Swami, said "No." Baba thereupon touched him on his heart chakra and the Old Swami had the sustained vision of Lord Ganesha he had sought for so long!

How's Your Smoking?

In an interview with Sai Baba, he looked at me and said, "How's your smoking?" I was shocked. I never smoked in my life. I can't stand it and am a militant non-smoker. I have asked many people to put out their smokes and do not allow smoking in my car or my house or my office. Never have.

Thus, I blurted out in shock, "Swami, I don't smoke. I never smoked in my life!" He looked at me kindly and said, "Oh yes you did. You were about 15. You picked up one of your dad's cigarettes, tried a puff, and said, 'Nah." When the memory suddenly came back to me, I blurted out, "How did you know?" He smiled lovingly and said simply, "I was there."

I can assure you dear reader that I never told anyone that story and had totally forgotten about it myself until that moment.

Dr. Hislops's Crucifix

Dr. Jack Hislop, a retired professor from UCLA, was the head of the United States Sai Baba organization for many years. He was one of the first Americans to visit Sai Baba on a regular basis. In his younger days, he had been involved with other spiritual movements and paths. However, he stated that only Sai Baba could awaken the heart for him, and allow him to feel God in his heart.

Jack wrote a book called *My Baba and I*, which I think is one of the best Sai Baba books and I recommend it heartily. Not wishing to steal Jack's thunder, but wishing to share some remarkable things from the book, and hoping to whet your appetites to read said book, here are a few synopses from the book:

The Crucifix

(The following is from pages 17-21, *My Baba and I*, by Dr. Jack Hislop.)

The crucifix was created by Baba on a most auspicious day, Maha Shivaratri (an annual festival celebrating Shiva). Baba had reached a decision to halt the yearly public viewing of the birth of the lingam, as it flashed from his mouth and comes to rest in his hands, cushioned by a silk handkerchief. Although the public portion of the holy festival of Mahashivatri was now terminated, nevertheless, Baba would create the lingam each year again and again, for it is a principal sign by which we may know the Avatar.

We may also know the Avatar by the sixteen signs that accompany him: creation, preservation, dissolution, knowledge of incarnations, special grace and the power to bestow it; each of these in the past, present and future, thus totaling fifteen with the sixteenth being Paramatma, the Divine, resident in the heart of each being. To these sixteen signs of the divine incarnation of the Avatar, Baba adds another sign, which he terms the most significant of all: Divine Love, universal and impersonal, yet personal.

(Jack goes on to say that he had seen a number of the lingam manifestations up close. He further states that a group of devotees in a few cars went on a trip the day before the big Mahashivaratri celebration):

The cars halted at the side of the road and we started to climb down the bank to the sandy river bottom. I was beside Baba. As we passed a bush, Swami broke off two twigs, placed them together and asked me, "What is this, Hislop?"

"Well, Swami, it is a cross," I answered. Baba then closed his fingers over the twigs and directed three somewhat slow breaths into his fist, between thumb and forefinger. Then he opened his hand to reveal a Christ figure crucified on a cross, and he gave it to me.

He said, "This shows Christ as he really was at the time he left his body, not as artists have imagined him or as historians have told about him. His stomach is pulled in and his ribs are all showing. He had no food for eight days."

I looked at the crucifix, but found no word. Then Baba continued, "The cross is wood from the actual cross on which Christ was crucified. To find some of the wood after 2,000 years took a little time! The image is of Christ after he died. It is a dead face."

(Later, back home in Mexico). The cross is so small that the details on the figure of Christ escapes the eye. Friend, Walter, came down to our home and took some color photographs of the crucifix. The overall length of the Christ figure is only one inch, and Walter was to make some enlargements to bring out the detail. When he mailed us a sample of the prints, my wife and I were astounded. I wrote to him and said that if the pictures were seen around the world, they would create an art sensation. I am sure it the greatest sculpture of Christ ever made. In my estimation, it is the most extraordinary object Sri Sathya Sai Baba has ever created for the joy of his devotees.

A few weeks later, Walter and his wife returned with color enlargements of the cross.

Those, along with the actual cross, were spread out on the dining room table, overlooking the sea. The time was about 5 p.m. The details revealed by the photographic enlargements were so extraordinary that all persons present were concentrating on this amazing vision of Christ, and on the mystery and wonder of Sri Bhagavan. On this afternoon, the sky along the Mexican coast was clear and peaceful. But suddenly, without any warning, there was a loud crash of thunder and as our eyes turned to the windows, lightning flashed from a dark cloud where a moment before there had been only clear sky. A violent wind rushed through the house, causing windows and doors to open and shut with such force that glass was in danger of shattering. My wife said, "It is 5 p.m., the time Christ died on the cross, and what is now happening is described in the Bible." She later brought a Bible and now we looked until we found the pertinent paragraph, which said that at the moment Christ gave up His life, a violent storm arose with lightning and thunder, and winds rent the curtains of the temple. (Later, Baba confirmed that was the case. When someone person asked Swami about the crucifix, he said the following: "Yes, I made it for him. And when I went to look for the wood, every particle of the cross had disintegrated and had returned to the elements. I reached out to the elements and reconstituted sufficient material for a small cross. Very seldom do I interfere with Nature, but occasionally, for a devotee, it will be done.")

The Resurrection of Walter Cowan

In Dr. Jack Hislop's book *My Baba and I* he tells a remarkable story about a friend from Southern California who died and was resurrected by Swami in India. This following is a condensation of the pages 28-31 as Dr. Hislop tells it:

Resurrection, the rising again from the dead, is something which all Christians have heard of and because it is a sacred story, we tend to believe it, if we have not been pounded by doubts from agnostics, atheists, and people who hold to reason and logic more than to faith. And, stories of resurrection in recent times, come from people who are not viewed as "establishment" and people therefore do not give the stories serious attention.

Mostly, what has been said above refers to the western world. The same structure of belief and disbelief about resurrection is not the norm in India, and this story is about events which occurred in India, although Walter Cowan and myself were born in the West.

Walter died in his room at the Connemara Hotel in Madras. He and his wife, Elsie, had arrived there on Dec. 23, 1971, to see Baba, who himself was in Madras to preside at an All-India Conference of the Sai Organizations.

Early in the morning of December 25th, a rumor quickly spread that an elderly American had died of a heart attack. My wife, Victoria and I immediately thought of Walter. We went to the hotel and found Elsie there. Walter had fallen to the floor in the very early morning hours. Elsie had called Mrs. Ratanlal, whose room was just down the corridor. The two women managed to lift Walter to the bed, and he passed away in Elsie's arms a few minutes later. An ambulance was called, the body was taken to a hospital, pronounced dead upon arrival, and the body was placed an empty storage room, and covered with a sheet to await daylight and decisions about the funeral.

Elsie and Mrs. Ratanlal had already been to see Baba when we arrived. He had told them he would visit the hospital at 10 a.m. The two ladies were ready and waiting to join Baba at the appointed hour. They did go to the hospital, but Baba had arrived earlier and had already departed. To the joy of the ladies, but also to their total amazement, they found Walter alive and being attended to. Nobody saw Baba with Walter, nor has Baba chosen to say how or why Walter was resurrected, but on returning to the devotee family who were his hosts, Baba told the people there that he had brought Walter back to life.

Walter's own story throws some light on what happened, and later on, I was party to a fascinating episode, for Walter's life continued to be in danger, and, in fact, Baba told me that Walter died three times and had to be returned to life three times!

Walter described his experience. He said he realized that he had died and that he remained with the body in the ambulance, looking at it with interest. Then, Baba came and together they went to a place, which seemed to be at a great height. There they entered a conference room where people were seated around a table. There was a presiding chairman who had a kind face and who spoke in a kindly way. He called for Walter's records and those were read aloud. The records were in different languages and Walter did not understand what was said until after some time when Baba started to translate. Walter was surprised to hear that he had occupied a lofty status in various times and cultures and had always been dedicated to the welfare of the people. At length, Baba addressed the person presiding and asked that Walter be given over to Baba's care, for Baba had work for Walter to do. Then, when Baba and he departed the room, Walter felt himself descending towards a place where his body was, but felt great reluctance. In terms of direct experience, he had realized that he was NOT the body, and he had no wish to be subject again to bodily anxieties and miseries.

After hearing Walter, I asked Baba if Walter were just imagining the incidents. Baba replied that it was not imagination. The events were real. I then asked if everyone had similar experiences at death. Baba answered that the corpse was common to all, but beyond that there was no common denominator." (SS66)

One of the very significant early devotees from the West to spend serious time in India was Howard Murphet, a distinguished retired military man from Australia. Howard had unique access to Baba and to many of the old Hindu devotees from Baba's early days, i.e., the 1940's and 1950's, before the world found out about Him. The following are some stories which could only be told from Mr. Murphet.

This one is from his book *Man of Miracles*, which has been distributed around the world. I summarize Chapter 13, pages 131-137 here:

Mr. Murphet referred to this miracle by Baba as the equivalent to Jesus raising Lazarus from the dead. It occurred in 1953. Mr. Murphet interviewed both the "Lazarus" of the story, namely Mr. V. Radhakrishna, as well as his daughter, Vijaya, who was 18 years old at the time and witnessed the entire event with all the relevant details.

Mr. Radhakrishna was seriously ill with gastric ulcers and complications thereof, age 60 at the time, a factory-owner, and a well-known member of his community. A devotee for some time, he took his family to Swami's ashram hoping that Swami could heal him.

At the ashram, Mr. R. was given a room not far from Swami's room. However, he did not go out for many of the functions going on at that time, and mainly lay in bed suffering. Swami came to his room to visit him. Mr. R. said to Swami that he would prefer to die rather than continue to suffer in that way. Swami simply laughed at that and made no commitments one way or another.

One evening Mr. R. went into a coma and his breathing was that of a dying man. The family informed Swami, who came to the room, looked at the patient, and said, "Don't worry, everything will be all right," and left.

More time passed and a male nurse was summoned. He stated that there was no pulse and that Mr. R. was either dead or very near death. Then, the patient became very cold. The wife, daughter and her husband thought they heard what is called the "death rattle." Mr. R. started to turn blue and stiff. The wife ran up to Swami and said that Mr. R. had died. Swami laughed and walked away. Later he came down and looked at the body, but left and didn't say anything.

On the morning of the third day after Mr. R. went unconscious, the body was dark, cold, stiff, and starting to smell like a corpse. Other people came and said that the wife and daughter should have the corpse removed from the ashram and cremated. However, Mrs. R. and the daughter had total faith in Swami, and they stated that Swami had said that everything would be alright. They refused to do anything unless Swami ordered it. These people went to Swami and reported the corpse and demanded that the corpse be moved and cremated. Baba said, "We'll see."

Mrs. R. and Vijaya went to Swami and told him what people were saying and what they were insisting she must do. Swami said, "Do not listen to them, and have no fear; I am here!" He said he would be back to see her husband again soon.

Mrs. R. and Vijaya went back down to maintain their vigil with the corpse. They waited and waited for Swami. An hour passed. When they were just about ready to despair entirely, the door opened and there stood Baba in his red robe and shining smile. The two ladies began to cry just like

Martha and Mary, the sisters of Lazarus, weeping before their lord, who they thought had come too late.

Gently, Baba asked the tearful women to leave the room. As they left, he closed the door behind them. They do not know — no man knows – what happened in that room, where there were only Swami and the "dead" man. However, after a few minutes, Swami opened the door and beckoned the waiting ones in. There on the bed, Mr. R. was looking up at them and smiling! The stiffness of death had vanished and his color was returning. Swami turned to the wife and said, "I have given your husband back to you. Now get him a hot drink." When she brought it, Swami himself fed it to Mr. R. slowly with a spoon. For another half-hour he remained there, strengthening the man he had "raised" from the dead.

The next day, the man was strong enough to participate in the ashram happenings. When they left a few days later, the gastric ulcers and complications were gone. He never had them again.

When I spoke with Mr. R., he told me that he knew nothing about what had happened.   (SS71)

Miracle for My Mother

My mom became paralyzed in 1974 when she was 56 years old. The cause was an inflammation of the spinal cord and it became progressively worse over the years. She had a lot of pain and her paralysis got worse and worse as the years went on. She was able to remain home and not go into a nursing home thanks to a support group of all of us plus a remarkable invention by my uncle which enabled her to bathe herself, getting from her walker or wheelchair by a hydraulic device.

We were going to India in January, 1992. I was thinking that while there, I would ask Swami to do a small miracle for my mother, as in maybe healing her, or at the least, having one of the pictures in her home manifest vibhuti as many Swami pictures do for devotees all over the world.

On a separate track, I had been diagnosed as a diabetic. My blood sugar was off the map. Normal was 60 to120 and mine was over 400. My vision was blurred. I went to an eye specialist, Dr. Rice, in St. Paul, Minnesota, who informed me that I had irretrievable eye damage from blood sugar and gave me a prescription for glasses. I could see well at distances, but had to wear the glasses to read a newspaper or a book. My mother was really concerned about my diabetes. I was concerned about her.

We got to India, and I wrote a letter to Swami. It is the customary practice in India to give Swami letters, if you can. (Much of the time, even if you are in the front row in darshan, he will somehow manage to escape your letter handing tactics!). It is always a good thing to be able to get your letter to Swami. I had this letter in my pocket for weeks and could not seem to get it to Swami. Even when we got an interview, I was so blown away that I forgot to ask him verbally or give him the letter, which said "Dear Swami, please do a small miracle for my mother!"

Finally, the last day we were there, I got front row in darshan. I was sitting next to some young soldier boys from an Indian Army unit who had come to receive blessing from Swami. They were nice young guys and very eager. Swami came out and stopped in front of the boys. They took padnamaskar and he materialized them all a bit of vibhuti for each of them. Then he stopped in front of me. I handed him the envelope, FINALLY. He held it, smiled, looked at me and held up his hand and said, "Wait," and then walked on. I was ecstatic. I KNEW that he would do a miracle for my Mom!

We headed back to Minnesota. My friend Bob and my partner, Jannie were on the plane with me as we were leaving Bombay. I leaned back in the seat, and started to read a Louis L'Amour small print paperback. Bob and Jannie both said simultaneously, "Where are your glasses?" To my shock, I was reading that small print paperback with no glasses! I continued all the way back.

I tested my blood sugar. It was normal! I went to see Dr. Rice. He checked my eyes and said there was no damage or flaws whatsoever! I was really happy. I went to see my mom and told her that apparently Sai Baba had cured me of diabetes! She started to cry tears of happiness then she said to my shock, as she pointed to the picture of Sai Baba on her dresser, "I told him every day, "You heal my son!" So, Swami DID do a small miracle for my mother; he cured me!

For the reader, it has been 25 years since Swami healed me. I am now 73 years old. I still am a diabetic, but I keep it under control by diet and exercise. My vision is still good. I can read normal print like a newspaper with good light. In poor light, or very small print, I use 1.25 magnifying reading glasses I get from the Dollar Store for one dollar. I am truly thankful to my mom and Sai Baba. There aren't many 73 year-old people on this earth who can read anything without glasses. My long-range vision is very good.

Replacement Ring

This story comes from our interview in 1995. We had a number of different people in this interview. There were five of us from Minnesota, some ladies from Canada, and some ladies from Poland.

I was sitting right next to Swami, within inches. He looked at one of the Canadian women and motioned her to hand her ring to him, which she did. It was a very ornate gold, diamond, and ruby ring, exquisitely designed. Swami held it out to show me and said sweetly, "I made this one for her." I looked at her and she nodded assent. Swami looked at her and said gently, "I will make you a new ring. Nine Jewels!" She looked suspicious; she really liked the ring she had. Swami held the ruby ring inches from my face between his right thumb and right forefinger. With his left hand, he counted as he did nine blows of his breath on the ruby ring. There, right before my eyes, the ring transformed into a completely different ring, namely a nine-jewel ring! He showed it to me and said, "Nine Jewels." Then, he handed it to her. He said to her,

"You like?" She said, "Swami, I liked the other ring better." He said, "Oh," very kindly, and retrieved the nine-jewel ring, holding it with his right forefinger and thumb in front of my face again. He looked at me and counted with his left hand, and made one, two, three blows, the paused and looked at me and said, "Enough," and sure enough, there was the original ring back, with only three blows! Swami showed it to me and then handed it back to her. She was really happy. She liked that ring.

Solace for a Lady from Poland

In the same interview, as I was sitting watching Swami doing his thing, I couldn't help notice the face of a young woman from Poland. She was very sad. I did not know her. I never saw her again. However, I could see that she was hurting badly inwardly about something. I sent a small prayer her way. Then, suddenly, without warning, Swami literally waved his hand and arm right in front of my face, almost hit my face again in that interview, and he manifested from nothing a beautiful Japamala, a 108 prayer beads on a string. The beads were light blue, gold, and white, just like UCLA's school colors, and he reached over to the aforementioned Polish woman and put the Japamala over her head onto her neck! She burst into tears of joy. She cried and cried and said something I didn't understand. She knelt down and hugged and kissed His feet! She stayed down there for a while. Swami paused, looked down at her and said, "You're not falling asleep down there, are you?"

As usual, when Swami catches me by surprise, I burst out laughing Too loud. Swami looked at me.

My Friend Stan's Ring

We were lucky enough to get an interview in 1997. This time, there were ten of us, plus two young Italian men, and some other folks. One of us was my good friend Stan Brainin, from Santa Barbara, California. Stan was the same age as me, born in 1944. He and I also had the same sense of humor, which meant that we spent most of our time laughing and making jokes about the planet Earth in general, and everything else in specific, ourselves included.

In this interview, I saw something I had never seen when Swami materialized something, when Swami made a silver ring for Stan. As Swami moved his hand quickly and the ring came out, I saw what was like a small lightning bolt, in the act of creation. Others in the interview confirmed this, as well. It was (is) a great ring and Stan was very moved.

Shirley MacLaine Story

In 1998, I walked on the beach for three hours in North Carolina telling Sai Baba stories to Shirley MacLaine. She was very curious about Him and wanted to know all about him. She had asked me to come down to Capra's studio in Wilmington, North Carolina, to assist her raise capital for a movie called "Bruno," which was to be her directorial debut. She got a number of famous folks an academy award winners to play in the movie, including Penny Marshal, Cathy Bates, Gary Sinise, and others.

She is a very brilliant person, as well as a very down-to-earth good and kind person. She is far different from other "famous" people I have met and didn't have that "famous" person ego and veneer.

We walked a long ways and I told her story after story. Then she told me one:

She knew a fellow from Los Angeles who was a film nut and went to see Sai Baba. He was able to take many pictures with his camera, but ran out of film. He got an interview. As Swami sat down, after materializing vibhuti for all the women in the room, he looked at Shirley's friend, and said, "You're out of film." The fellow was shocked. He asked Swami how he knew that, and Swami dismissed the question and said, "What kind of film?" The fellow had an empty canister in his pocket. He pulled it out and handed it to Swami. Swami took it, looked at it, and went out of the room for a few minutes. When he returned, he handed the fellow a whole pile of nice new film! The fellow couldn't believe it! He was ecstatic and told everyone about it.

When he got back to Los Angeles, he went to his photography shop and had the film developed. Later, when he came to pick up the photos, the man from the photography shop pointed at the pictures and said, "Say that frizzy-haired, orange-robe buddy of yours was here a few weeks ago buying film for you!" You can think of all the implications of that story!

A New Rainbow Story

Just recently, I was visiting good friends, Ron and Beverly Carman in Los Angeles. They have a Sai Baba center at their house every Saturday. One day, we discussed the original Joel Riordan Rainbow story which I related earlier in this section. A young Indian lady in the meeting at the house told us a remarkable story. She had heard about Joel's Rainbow story and was hiking by herself up in the High Desert outside of L.A. She plaintively asked Swami inwardly to send her a rainbow, too. Sure enough, Swami came through: a rainbow just like Joel's came up in a clear sky, dry day in Southern California, a gift to a sincere devotee.

Swami Saves Folks from the IRS

I knew a couple in Chicago named Tom and Janice. They had a very interesting story, actually quite remarkable in Swami miracle annals. One interesting thing: we met Janice in India, where she and her two kids traveled all over India by themselves. Janice was blonde, and both her kids (age 4 and 7 at the time) were blonde as well. We found it amazing that she and her kids traveled all over the world like that with such courage and no troubles.

Tom was in a high level financial business. It turned out that he owed the IRS over $290,000!

The debt was growing all the time with interest and fees and the IRS was pressuring and hassling them.

They wrote a letter every three days to India to Swami, asking for help. After a year of doing this, Tom accidentally got into a business deal that netted him over $500,000! They paid off the IRS and bought a nice house in Chicago, which I stayed in.

Australian Homecoming

This story has been told all over the world and we heard it many times from Australian devotees:

An Australian group got an interview at Puttaparthi. They entered the interview room and sat down. After the preliminaries of Swami materializing vibhuti for the ladies, he turned to one of the gentlemen there and said, "Your wife needs you to come home to Australia right away!" The man immediately started to think about how to get his ticket changed, which in India is a major undertaking. Swami, sensing this, said, "No, I mean right now." He pointed to the wall and the wall became the man's front door at home in Australia! Swami said, "Go," and the man went. He got there just in time to save his wife's life in a medical emergency.

The Australian folk verified this later, and the kicker was that his PAPERS were STAMPED properly as if he had legally come in!

Another Colusa Story

I told you about Ammi's magic house in Colusa, California. This story is a fun thing that happened some years ago regarding a wedding. I heard the story from the young groom and some folks from his Sai Center in the L.A. area:

A young man from California and his betrothed wanted to get married at the sacred Swami house in Colusa. They set the date for 11:00 a.m. on a Saturday morning.

The groom sent an invitation to Swami in India to attend the wedding. Of course, no one really expected Swami to show up in person, but the groom felt that he should invite his Guru to such an important event in his life.

The wedding was set, but as we all know, life comes along and presents changes. One of the key participants in the wedding had a delay and the wedding was rescheduled for 1:00 p.m. the same day.

However, the video guy had already set up the video and had it aimed and ready to go. It was running and he forgot to turn it off when he found out about the delay. He went out to have a bit of lunch and came back to find video evidence that Sai Baba actually did appear at the wedding. The camera was aimed at one of the pictures I told you about on the wall at Ammi's temple which emanated normally grey vibhuti all the time. At precisely 11:00 a.m., the original time of the wedding, this normally grey vibhuti on the picture turned purple. I, myself, saw the purple vibhuti, and I had also seen the grey vibhuti earlier.

Miraculous Tuning

In 1996, I was invited to play music at a conference in Edmonton, Alberta. One of the other performers was a man from England named David Bailey. He was a pudgy round fellow who played piano. He taught also piano and had played music for some important people such as the Royal Family and others back in England.

He and I stayed in the same house in Edmonton for about a week. He had a good sense of humor and we both told a lot of Sai stories. He told me one of the most interesting ones I ever heard, and as a musician, it was special to me. This is the story as David told it to me. Also, he had a video of the event, and I saw it on video as well:

Swami had a big music festival at the stadium in Puttaparthi where each country could send a musician who was a Sai devotee. David was England's representative. The U.S. Sai Organization sent a piano player as well.

Now, for those of you who never have been to India, there is a lot of comedy for westerners, as in some very quixotic and strange things that seem to happen there.

For David and the American keyboard players, they were in shock when they came to play music for 250,000 people who had assembled for this event, and found that the "piano" they were supposed to play was an old beat-up 60 key (i.e., too short) electric keyboard!

Such world-class musicians normally had a grand piano. The word went out and the staff searched frantically for a real piano. Finally, with time running out, they found an old moth-eaten stand-up piano, which was at a Christian mission not too far away and had to be trucked to the stadium. That was the good news. The bad news was that the piano was woefully out of tune.

It came time for the American to play. He took one look at the piano and refused to play. Swami was sitting on stage as the Master of Ceremonies. He motioned for David to come up and play. David told me that he gulped and went and sat at the piano. I saw him on the video and he and I had a major laugh as he tested the keys: horrible! We went ahead anyway and played "Claire De Lune" technically perfect, in front of 250,000 people, but it sounded like three cats fighting in the back yard because the piano was totally out of tune.

After the first piece, Swami smiled benignly and waved his hand in blessing at David and the piano, and the piano miraculously went into perfect tuning! David's second piece was absolutely wonderful.

After hearing that story, I was hoping that maybe Swami would help me keep my voice in tune for the rest of my life.

A Good Birth

We were going to India in January, 1997. My partner, Jannie was concerned because her daughter, Sarah, was in her second pregnancy and not doing well. Her first pregnancy had a lot of troubles and the doctors were not all that enthused about her having another child, but she and her husband really wanted another one. Jannie is very clairvoyant, and she could feel that this new problem was possibly life-threatening. She was thinking that maybe she, Jannie, should not go to India, but I convinced her that it would be better to be with Sai Baba and maybe he could help Sarah. She agreed and we departed in early January. There was a little complication, because Sarah and her husband were fundamentalist Christians and did not accept anything about Sai Baba or metaphysics, meditation, etc. The husband was exceptionally narrow-minded and totally scared of anything out of his religious frame of reference, especially Sai Baba.

We were there for a few weeks and one day we got an interview.

Swami asked Jannie in the interview, "And how are you?" Jannie answered, "Very concerned about my daughter, Swami." Now, remember that there are thousands and thousands of people from every country on Earth there and Swami had no outer means of knowing the data he came up with. Swami responded: "Yes, stomach (and he rubbed his stomach). How many months?" (He knew she was pregnant.) Jannie said, "Two, Swami," and he said very firmly, "No, three!" He looked over at me and said, "I know!" Then he said thoughtfully, "She doesn't think like you do," and then, he wrote in the air (quite often, we would see Swami "writing" with his hand in the air; it is our thought that somehow he is re-writing the script of God's great drama to help a devotee, which certainly happened in this case of Jannie's daughter). As he was writing in the air, he said softly, "I bless, I bless," and as he said that and wrote in the air, I knew for sure that he would take care of Sarah and everything would be okay. Jannie felt that too and smiled and said, "Boy or girl, Swami?"

Swami looked up at the sky so to speak and said, "Daughter says, 'If boy, this will be our last child and if girl, this will still be our last child.' Husband says, 'If boy, this will be our last child and if girl, we will have a third child.'" (Note: I didn't hear the exact words because I was so happy when I knew inwardly that Swami was going to heal Sarah that I missed the exact words, however, it didn't matter, because Jannie remembered.)

This interview was on January 28, 1997. We were back sitting in our kitchen on Feb. 5, 1997, about a week later. I was sipping coffee and Jannie was on the phone with Sarah, letting her know that we were back. Here are the fun things:

- Sarah was in mint condition! She told Jannie that she had no pain for the past week and that the doc had said that she was in great shape with no problems.

- Sarah told her mom that she was almost a month ahead of where she thought, like Swami had said.

Jannie turned white as a ghost and her jaw dropped at least two feet when she heard Sarah say, "Yesterday I said to Jonathan, 'If boy then this will be our last child and if girl, it will still be our last child, and Jonathan said, 'If boy, this will be our last child, but if girl, we will have a third child.'" They said the exact words on February 4th that Swami said in India on January 28th!

The other sweet thing about this story is that Swami blessed and healed Sarah even though she had no idea he was doing it and she did not believe in him in the slightest. That was cool.

The Resurrection of Bharosa A.

Bharosa A. is a middle aged bright and cheerful lady with a wonderful family. She is from Katmandu, Nepal. She and her family have been long-time Sai devotees and the family has a Sai temple in their house in Nepal. Vibhuti comes out of pictures regularly there.

Bharosa suffered a debilitating disease and came to the Super Specialty Hospital in Puttaparthi. Unfortunately, she died on the operating table. Her body was on a gurney and death was certified. Because she was from another country, she was placed in the morgue for three days while they were waiting for her husband and children to arrive. They arrived, and Swami greeted them with a big smile. They were disconcerted. He assured them that all was well, and against all odds, against medical verification of death, and against known physical laws, he resurrected her and she lives on to this day, with one little interesting fact: She travels all over the world speaking about Sai Baba and wherever she stays, the Sai pictures emit Vibhuti after she leaves!

In the late 1960's, Americans started to come to India, first in small numbers and then by the hundreds and then by the thousands. Europeans, Asians, Africans, Australians, and South Americans just poured into South India to see Baba.

One such Westerner was Isaac Tigrett, an American who was the founder of the Hard Rock Café. Swami did some serious miracles for Isaac, including saving his life at a distance twice. Isaac later sold out his interest in the Hard Rock Cafés in the late 1980's. Much to his surprise, Swami ordered him to "build the hospital." Isaac thereupon funded, endowed, and built a magnificent 320,000 square foot, totally modern hospital, out in the frontier of Puttaparthi, and treatment was free to everyone. Swami stated that this should be the model of health care for all countries. (Wouldn't it be great if that did transpire some time in history.)

Sai Baba only left India once. In 1968, he summarily went to Uganda, of all places, then headed by the cruel dictator, Idi Amin. The reason: there were many people of Indian descent living in Uganda and Swami knew that they did not have long to live under Amin's crazy regime.

When he came to Uganda, he did his normal marvelous presentations, healings, and miracles. Meanwhile, he advised all Indian folk to sell out and leave immediately. Basically, those who followed his advice lived and those who did not, died.

Starting in the 1950's, most holy men, saints, yogis, etc., in India have made their way to Sai Baba's ashram to get his blessing. Swami chastised one well-known spiritual teacher, telling him bluntly that he should stay home in India, meditate, and purify his consciousness instead of chasing money and fame in the West.

Swami has been gracious to people of all social and economic levels. He also has ignored people of all such levels. One humorous example is when John Lennon came to the ashram. A man named Howard, from San Francisco, who is now a CPA, but was then a young hippie in India, told us this story. John Lennon came to Sai Baba's ashram one day. Howard's friend, a young woman appropriately named *India* (who now owns and runs a conference center in Montana) raced over to Sai Baba, and excitedly informed him that John Lennon was here. Swami looked at her and said in his sweet voice, "John Lemon, John Lemon? Who is John Lemon?" She said, "No, John Lennon. He's a Beatle!" Swami looked quizzically down at the ground, as if looking for the insect named "beetle", and said, "A beetle? Coming to see me?" Well, poor John Lennon spent a day or two at the ashram, and Sai Baba completely ignored him. He never so much gazed in his direction and John left. We can only surmise as to all the meanings of this.

Early on in his mission, Sai Baba started his educational system. He developed grade schools, high schools, trade schools, and a university, all of the very highest quality, and all free to those lucky enough to gain admittance. These schools have the highest standards and discipline. The performance of the graduates in later life is remarkably good. The Prime Minister of India once stated that these schools are a model for what should be the educational system of India and the world.

Sai Baba and music are inseparable. In the middle of a discourse, he will start to sing. His songs are all devotional songs to God, in one form or another. Yogananda once stated that in America, songs are dedicated to romance, but in India, songs are to God. Well, Swami has elevated this mode to a new level. Most likely, he is the most prolific songwriter of all times. He has written many, many songs and taught his devotees to sing them. All over the world, on a weekly basis, little Sai Baba Centers meet and sing devotional songs. In the Sai Baba world, these songs are called "bhajans." It is a custom that everyone in the center leads a bhajan. The leader sings a line and the rest of the group repeats. I personally, because of my American folk music background, and being a guitar and banjo player, have always found it difficult to play or sing bhajans in Telegu, Sanskrit, or Hindi, with the expanded tonal system of Indian music. I find it difficult to sing in a language which I do not understand and I cannot fit the chords to the songs into my parameters. However, there always has occurred a miracle for me, the previous statements notwithstanding: *I have never sat in on a bhajan session even if I could not really relate to the words and music without receiving a major inner spiritual blessing*!

Swami Rama

Swami Rama is one of the more unique figures in spiritual history. He was raised in the Himalayas by a monastery of spiritual adepts and made contact with many of the advanced beings who live in the secret ranges of those mystical mountains. Swami Rama was specifically sent by the Great Beings to the West, to the scientists and doctors to help them lift their vistas from the binding materialistic ways that circumscribe everything they do.

Swami Rama demonstrated "supernatural" powers to the scientists and medical people at Harvard University Medical Center, the Menninger Institute in Kansas, and many other places. In St. Paul, Minnesota, in front of over 20 physicians, he drank a glass of strychnine poison, pursed his lips a bit and said it was "a little bitter." Two of the physicians passed out on the spot. He had told them that he would do it if three physicians would independently of each other verify that, in fact, it was strychnine. Never had a master or a metaphysician ever submitted himself to such scrutiny. They tested him until he was blue in the face. He went into the breathless state so they could see it. Many of his exploits were denoted in Time Magazine and other publications.

Unfortunately, he was the victim of treachery by one of his top disciples who transferred huge assets in questionable ways. Swami Rama was the victim of religious narrow-mindedness: the folks who ran the Menninger Institute were and are fundamentalist Christians who have sealed all the records and will not let this treasure trove of scientific/spiritual data out to the public; and other places felt the subject was too controversial and that they would suffer embarrassment from their scientific colleagues.

However, he trained many great disciples and left a train of miracles and divine love all around the world. Whenever you go into a center run by one of his disciples, you can feel his energy and vibration very strongly and it is a blessing to this day. He is alive and well and still working from the Other Side, and once in a while he sneaks through just to let folks know who he is.

The following is a short biography of Swami Rama. I will be relying on two books, namely *Living With the Himalayan Masters* by Swami Rama himself, and *Walking With a Himalayan Master* by his close, long-term disciple, Dr. Justin O'Brien, also now known as Swami Jaidev. Dr. O'Brien has given me permission to summarize and simplify his writings as needed, and I have agreed to faithfully keep the same meaning. I have submitted this section to Dr. O'Brien for editing. I will be referring to Dr. O'Brien herein as Justin.

Note: I truly recommend to the readers here that they acquire and read the aforementioned two books. Along with *The Autobiography of a Yogi*, *The Path*, *My Baba and I*, *Sai Baba, Man of Miracles*, and *Jesus Lived in India*, these are the most significant works for Westerners interested in metaphysics and meditation. Also, if you want to learn to meditate, you cannot find better places than the systems of Swami Rama and Paramahansa Yogananda. At the back of the book are contacts for these centers of spirituality in America.

Swami Rama was born in Garhwal, Himalayas, north of Kotdwara. Swami often returned to those hills surrounding the valley of his birthplace. Swami told Justin that he was a totally unexpected child. He said, "When my Master confronted my parents with the challenge of having a child, they were hesitant and laughed at the idea, but were full of joy. My father could not doubt the master's words in spite of their ages. My father knew the power of the Himalayan sages. He grew up to be an accomplished astrologer, scholar, and writer. Although married, he always wanted to live the life of a sadhu, a solitary spiritual seeker, and one time he tried it. He left his family for many months attempting to carry it out. After these months of practice, powerful yogi, Bengali Baba visited him. He blessed him and initiated him into the tradition. The master sent my father home, reminding him that renunciation is not required for spiritual perfection.

"So, when my master told my parents that they would have another child, although already older, they were pleased and promised that their forthcoming child would be his. They knew something remarkable would happen around this baby. Shortly after my birth, my master showed up and demanded his claim. My mother cried, but was reminded of their promise. My master then entrusted them with the care of their child until he would return three years later. My father died a few years later and at his death, I was given into the care of my master and taken to live in his cave."

Justin then told Swami Rama that this circumstance reminded him of the Christian Church in the Middle Ages where with a similar contractual arrangement, certain wealthy families gave one of their sons to the local monastery to be raised by the monks in dedication to God and the work of the Church. Justin said that Swami Rama told him: "My master was known as Bengali Baba, or simply Babaji. In the United States, the Self-Realization organization speaks of their lineage as coming from the famous Babaji, but actually, the name is quite common for many elder yogis. In this instance, these two Babajis are related. Both of them were brother disciples of the same teacher, my grandmaster whom my master sent me to stay with in Tibet many years ago. Each of them completed the training with my grandmaster and went their own directions."

These kindly monks raised Swami Rama until he was eleven years old. Thereupon, he was sent to a tougher monastery for seven years. In this monastery, they taught kung fu and Indian karate. One of the best teachers in the monastery was completely blind. Swami said, "He always knew where the opponents were. I used to try to sneak up on him, but he could feel as soon as someone moved towards him He taught us how to strike using our body's electricity."

Besides his varied spiritual training, from both his master and many other yogis and sages to whom his master directed him, Swami Rama also studied in formal schooling under the famous Rabrindranath Tagore (also a student of Bengali Baba). Further, Swami studied at Oxford University in England, as well as doing research at universities in Utecht, Moscow, and Frankfurt. He had a medical degree from Darbhanga Medical College.

Swami told Justin: "You see, my master took me everywhere in these mountains (Himalayas), meeting his associates. We traveled from Nepal, across the Himalayas, and back into India., staying at all the famous shrines. Once, an avalanche started coming down the mountains above us and would have buried us, but my master lifted his arm, and the falling rocks and mud stopped in mid air until we passed on the path. When he lowered his arm again, the avalanche continued."

Justin said to his master that it seemed if most human beings knew nothing. For all our bragging about technology, we have been using only a small amount of brain power, neglecting most of the possibilities of which we are capable. Swami then said: "Justin, everything that technology is bringing forth now is not being done for the first time. Whatever an engineer can produce, the mind can do on its own, without matter."

For many years, Swami Rama was sent all around the Himalayas to see and study with over 100 "tutors" of various specialties. This was the result of a divine plan to train one student, i.e., Swami Rama into *all* paths of yoga, all the scriptures of each tradition, and the powers and techniques thereof. They agreed to train him in all the esoteric sciences born in the Himalayas, the truths of the ancient rishis, handed down from time immemorial from Guru to disciple. Through them he would grasp the energies of this planet, as well as the foundational forces beyond the Milky Way that form all universes and galaxies, present, past, or yet to come. He would learn the astrological lore of India, Egypt, and Persia, experiment with alchemy, and understand the processes of evolution, know his sonship with the Divine Mother and all her manifestations. He would know the secrets of the energies and the chakras in human form and the secular ways of the West.

Before he began this exhaustive training, he would be required to know and master all the *siddhis* (miracle powers) of the yoga sutras, i.e., going into the breathless state, miraculous healing, bi-location, omniscience, etc.

When he started on this journey, his master gave him specific instructions: 1) never lose your temper, maintain calmness; 2) never reply to insults but try to understand why they came; 3) never get emotionally upset at remarks about you but sit down and examine your capacity; and 4) never take material gifts.

This journey took decades and was excruciating in every way to Swami Rama. He was nearly wiped out, physically, mentally, and emotionally. His strong ego was crushed beyond measure. He felt that he had failed over and over. However, his master stuck by him and encouraged him and he finally made it through. He expanded the yoga sciences to new levels and did things that no human had ever done in the history of yoga in the Himalayas.

The following are a few of his remarkable experiences as spoken in his own words:

Once when I was teaching about life and death, a swami came in and sat with my students. I thought that he was a beginner, so I treated him as I treated the others. I was annoyed because he only smiled, constantly smiled, while the others were conscientiously taking notes. I finally asked, "Are you listening to me? He said to me, "You are only talking. But I can demonstrate mastery over life and death. Bring me an ant." A large ant was brought. He cut into three pieces and separated them. Then he closed his eyes and sat motionless. After a moment, the three parts moved toward each other. They joined together, and the revived ant scurried away. I knew it was not hypnosis or anything like that. I felt very small before that Swami and embarrassed before my students because I only knew the scriptures without a firsthand understanding and mastery of life and death. I asked, "Where did you learn that?" He said, "Your master taught me."

At that, I became angry with my master and immediately went to him. Seeing me, he asked, "What happened? Why are once again allowing anger to control you? Are you still a slave to your violent emotions?" I said, "You teach others things which you don't teach me. Why?" He looked at me and said, "I have taught you many things, but you do not practice. That is not my fault! All these achievements depend on practice, not just on verbal knowledge of them. If you know all about the piano but don't practice, you will never create music. Knowing is useless without practice. Knowing is mere information. Practice gives direct experience, which alone is valid knowledge."

Nearly all children are quite selfish by nature. They do not want to give anything to others. I was trained to reverse this tendency. In the mountains, I used to take only one meal a day. I would have one chapatti, some vegetables, and a glass of milk. One day, when it was almost 1:00 p.m., I washed my hands, sat down, and the food was given to me. I said grace and was about to start eating when my Master came in and said, "Wait!" I asked, "What's the matter?" He answered, "An old swami has come. He's hungry and you must give him your food." "No", I answered. "I'm not going to even if he is a swami. I am also hungry and I won't get any more food until tomorrow." He said, "You won't die. Give it to him. But do not give it just because I am ordering you. Give it as an offering of love." I said, "I am hungry. How can I feel love toward someone who is eating my food?" When he could not convince me to offer my food to the swami, he finally said, "I order you to offer your food!"

The swami came in. He was an old man with a white beard. With only a blanket, a walking stick, and wooden sandals, he traveled all alone in the mountains. My Master said to him, "I am glad that

you have come. Will you bless this child for me?"
But I said, "I do not need your blessing. I need food.
I am hungry." My Master said, "If you lose control
in this weak moment, you will lose the battle of life.
Please offer your food to the swami. First give him
water and then wash his feet."

I did as I was told, but I did not like it, nor
did I understand the meaning of it. I helped him
wash his feet and then I asked him to sit down and I
gave him my food. Later, I found out that he had
not eaten for four days. He took the food and said,
"God bless you! You will never feel hunger unless
food comes before you. This is my blessing to you."

His voice still echoes in my ears. From that
very day, I have been free from any urge which had
so often led me to childish cravings.

There is a narrow barrier between
selfishness and selflessness, love, and hatred. After
crossing it, one enjoys doing things for others,
without seeking anything in return. This is the
highest of all joys, and an essential step in the path
of enlightenment. A selfish man can never imagine
this state of realization, for he remains within the
limited boundaries built by his ego. A selfless man
trains his ego and uses it for higher purposes.
Selflessness is one common characteristic that we
find among all great men and women of the world.
Nothing could be achieved without selfless service.
All the rituals and knowledge of the scriptures are
in vain if actions are performed without
selflessness.

Crossing a Flooded River

Students are many, disciples are few. Many students came to my master and requested, "Please accept me as your disciple." They showed their faithfulness by serving him, by chanting, by learning, and by practicing disciplines. He did not respond. One day, he called everyone to him. There were twenty students. He said, 'Let's go." Everyone followed him to the bank of the Tungbhadra River in South India. It was in full flood, very wide and dangerous. He said, "He who can cross this river is my disciple."

One student said, "Sir, you know I can do it, but I have to go back and finish my work." Another student said, "Sir, I do not know how to swim." I did not say anything. As soon as he said it, I jumped. He sat down quietly as I crossed the river. It was very wide. There were many crocodiles and huge logs were rolling with the currents of water, but I was not concerned. My mind was one-pointed on completing the challenge I was given. I loved to be challenged, and I always accepted a challenge joyfully. It was a source of inspiration for me to examine my own strength. Whenever I was tired I would float, and in this way, I succeeded in crossing the river. My master said to the other students, "He didn't say that he was my disciple, but he jumped."

I was close enough to him to know his powers. I thought, "He wants his disciples to cross the river. Here I am. I can do it. It's nothing, because he is here. Why can't I do it?" So firm were my faith and determination.

Faith and determination, these two are the essential rungs on the ladder of enlightenment. Without them, the word "enlightenment" can be written and spoken, but never realized. Without faith, we can attain some degree of intellectual knowledge, but only with faith can we see into the most subtle chambers of our being. Determination is the power that sees us through all frustration and obstacles. It helps in building willpower, which is the very basis of success within and without. It is said in the scriptures that with the help of the *sankalpa shakt* (the power of determination) nothing is impossible. Behind all the great works done by the great leaders of this world stands this *shakti*. With this power behind him, such a leader says, "I will do it. I have to do it. I have the means to do it." When this power of determination is not interrupted, one inevitably attains the desired goal.

One day, Swami Rama was having the inner challenges that all devotees have on the path. He reminded his Master that he had promised to show him God, but nothing yet. His Master fold him, "I will show you God tomorrow morning."

In the morning, Swami Rama took his seat and was ready. His Master said, "Okay, now let me know what type of God you are prepared to see." Swami Rama asked, "Are there many types?" His Master said, "What's your concept and definition of God? I will show you God exactly according to your conviction and definition. So, you tell me the way you think about God and I will produce that God for you."

Swami Rama said, "Wait a minute. Let me think." His master said, "God is not within the range of your thinking. Go back to your meditation seat and when you are ready, let me know. Come to see me anytime you want after you have decided what type of God you want to see. I do not lie. I will show you God."

Swami Rama goes on to say, "I tried my best to imagine what God would be like, but my imagination could not go beyond the human form. My mind ranged over the kingdom of plants, then the kingdom of animals, and then human beings. So I imagined a wise and handsome man, who was very strong and powerful. And I thought, "God must look like this." Then I realized that I was making a foolish demand. What could I experience when I did not have clarity of mind? Finally I went to my Master and said, 'Sir, show me that God who can free us of miseries and who can give us happiness."

He said, "That is the state of equilibrium and tranquility which you must cultivate by yourself." Then I realized that God cannot be seen through human eyes. God can only be realized by experiencing the real Self and then the Self of others. No one can show God to anyone else. One has to independently realize his real self and thereby he realizes the self of all, which is called God.

Blessings and a Curse

Whenever I became egotistical, I fell down. This is my experience. My master said, "Try your best, but whenever you feed your ego, whenever you try to do something selfish, you will not succeed. This is my curse on you." I looked at him in surprise. What was he saying? He said, "This is also my blessing to you, that whenever you want to become selfless, loving, and without ego, you will find a great force behind you, and you will never fail to achieve some good."

A selfish man always thinks and talks about himself. His selfishness makes himself centered and miserable. The shortest cut to self-enlightenment is to cut through the ego, surrender before the Highest One. Unpurified ego is an evil which obstructs one's own progress. But the purified ego is a means in discriminating real self from not-self, real Self from mere self. No one can expand his consciousness if he remains egotistical. Those who are selfless, humble, and loving are true benefactors of humanity.

Teaching in America

Swami Rama set up centers at various parts of the United States. He trained many students in his meditation system. Note: I recommend that readers contact Dr. Justin O'Brien at the coordinates listed below this section if you want good meditation instruction. You will not only get first class technical instruction, with all the help and systems possible, but you will also get the blessing of Swami Rama and his line of Gurus. If you have another Guru and want to maintain that path, Dr. O'Brien and Swami Rama will bless you anyway, no problem. Swami Rama, Justin, Yogananda, Sai Baba, Dr. George, et al, never ever maintained exclusivity. Whatever works for you and helps *you* attain realization of *your* divinity within is cool with all of the Great Spiritual Teachers.

All great yogis have emphasized the breath as the basic connection between the body, mind, and spirit. Thus, they have developed various breath related systems for meditation. Here is a dialogue on this topic by Swami Rama as described by Dr. O'Brien:

"Only through meditation can the human personality fully unfold, for then one meets his or her real self. It is a journey without movement. Along the way you cast aside all the opinions and appraisals with which others have labeled you. Your journey inward must travel past everything that moves in the thought realm. Meditation means you are becoming independent of this world.

"People get stuck with their various images. Does anyone really know what Christ or Buddha looked like? What difference would that make? You cannot be enlightened by an image. You have to travel beyond the borders of the imagination and the discursive unknown. The territory of the unconscious looms as a frightening question mark. For the meditator, there is no escaping. You have to deal with your unconscious. Through meditation, you will meet your unfilled desires. They will flare up in your mind as you struggle to sit still. Old memories with emotion will arise to haunt you. The Buddha and St. Anthony of the desert had the same alluring encounters in their early attempts at meditation. No sage ever made it to the other shore without getting shipwrecked. You are no different.

"If you refuse to cross the ocean, then you have to put up with the limits you have imposed on yourself. What good is it to have faith in God if you evade knowing yourself? You may say you love others and seek the truth, but the question is deeper. Are you fearless? Unless you have conquered fear, even your love is tainted and truth gets compromised. People take all sorts of precautions just so they do not have to face the unknown.

"The principle endeavor in meditation is to arrive at stillness. Entering into the silence of your soul is the only passageway to all its treasures. If your body is not relaxed, then its stress holds you back. That is why one should practice in a systematic way, bringing the external limbs, the lungs, and the nervous system under a rhythmic control. First, take care of the body so that it doesn't demand attention later.

"With meditation, your hunger grows for more than just the world. A new awareness emerges for what is beyond the world. It needs daily nourishment. Mediation supplies the diet.

"When you bring the fruits of your meditation, the concentration and tranquility, to your workaday world, then you have something to measure. Your thoughts, speech and behavior are what count in the outer world. How is meditation influencing those forces? That is what is important.

"Everyone has trouble meditating. I know all the excuses. I used them all myself with my Master. The mind is slippery and tries to fool us into believing that we are a flawless spiritual person that even the angels envy. Let meditation clean house. It's not what you think that prevents your growth, it is the ego's attitude toward your thoughts. And remember, detachment does not mean indifference or laziness; you are here to perform your duties, to love life, and to allow the things of this world to become a means to your ultimate goal." (WWHM, p.118-122)

Remarkable Miracle

Justin and his wife, Therese, had a rental house in the 1970's near Swami Rama's new ashram in Illinois. They had some grapes on the vines outside. They were perfectly ripe and plump. Therese gathered a bucket of them to bring to Swami Rama. She had cheesecloth and a sieve. Her intention was to make some real good juice for her guru, who loved fresh juices.

They went to see Swami Rama. Justin and Swami sat in the living room, sitting in the silence. Therese went into the kitchen and squeezed grapes to make the optimum juice. She poured the juice into a tall glass. Unfortunately, a seemingly large amount of grapes didn't make much juice. Justin heard her sad sigh in the kitchen and she came out with a half-glass of juice and apologized to Swami that she couldn't deliver any more than that.

Swami put his finger over his lips and said "Shhh," and then put his right hand on top of the glass and raised his left hand up the glass, and the glass filled right up with grape juice!

He went on to say, "Because you made it with such love, you should have your desire."

Thereupon, the three shared in the glass of grape juice.

Hilarious Miracle

This one is told in Swami Rama's own words on p. 168-69 of WWHM: "Many years ago I needed a quiet, undisturbed place to do a certain meditation practice that required leaving my body for a few days. A physician friend of mine gave me an empty room in his hospital to use. 'Make sure no one enters this room,' the doctor told the floor nurse. So I folded my legs and sat in my meditation posture on the bed, closed my eyes, and began my practice. After about a week, the doctor was called away on an emergency and left the hospital. He forgot about me in his rush to leave. Meanwhile, the head nurse was looking for an empty room for a new patient, and hearing that no one had come in or out of my room in a week, unlocked the door. She was surprised to see me sitting there on the bed without a heartbeat or any sign of breath. So, she decided that I was dead.

"Orderlies took me down to the hospital morgue. They could not get my legs unfolded, so they simply covered me with a sheet and left me there. It was cold in the morgue. I began to come back into my body because of the temperature change.

"Into the morgue that evening came a simple sweeper, cleaning the floor. He swept his broom close by the table where I was placed just as I pulled the sheet off my face and asked, 'Where am I?' The poor man was so frightened that he screamed, threw down his broom and ran out of the hospital. He was never heard from again."

Swami went on to say, "There is nothing complicated about attaining comprehensive control of the breath. All one has to do is observe the moving capacity of the lungs. Internalize your awareness and you can feel it. By focusing your attention on the motion of the lungs, its control becomes a conscious ability. Your awareness alone brings control."

On Fire

Justin's wife, Therese, got up early one morning when her husband and Swami were away on ashram business. She set up her alter and was lighting a candle. She dropped the candle in her lap and set herself on fire. She was in shock. Her clothes burned quickly, sending flames up and down her arms and legs. She stood up, looked in the mirror and watched the flames. She wasn't afraid, and realized that it was apparently her time to die and accepted it. Then she remembered the other people in the apartment building and did not want them to be hurt. With that thought, fear came. She peered through the flames around her face to Swami's picture and asked for his help. She beat at the flames with her hands, attempting to smother the flames, when suddenly they all went out. Her clothes were a pile of black shreds at her feet on the burned circle of carpet; her hair, eyebrows, and eyelashes were singed, but the skin of her whole body, even her hands, was untouched. She then sat down in the smoke-filled room to do her meditation practice.

When she called Justin several hours later, she also asked to talk to Swamiji. Swami Rama took the phone and said, "Hi, Tessa. You did not die today. I have too much work for you to do yet." (WWHM, P. 326)

Miracle in Minneapolis

Justin tells this story on P. 431 of WWHM:

One afternoon in the 1970's, an enthusiastic physician met his long-awaited appointment with Swami Rama at the Minneapolis Holiday Inn. As Swami helped him off with his winter coat, the visitor suddenly stopped his motion and a frustrated look appeared on his face. "Is there a difficulty?" Swami looked puzzled. The physician said, "I have forgotten the microphone for my recorder and now I will have to drive back home to retrieve it."

Concerned for the man's time while admiring his willingness to drive across the city on a snowy afternoon, Swami asked him to wait a moment. "Where did you leave the speaker, exactly?" Swami asked. "In my bedroom," said the doctor. "Where is your bedroom located?" asked Swami. "On the second floor, next to the stairs," answered the doctor, wondering about the questions. "Exactly where is the microphone in your bedroom?" Swami asked again. The physician paused to remember and then replied, "It's on the top of the dresser next to the south window."

He was just about to ask about his host's interest when Swamiji smoothly moved his right hand from behind his back and asked with a slight triumphal voice, "Is this it?" The doctor stared at the small microphone held out to him, looked at Swami, then back down at his speaker! With a sigh, he slowly put his coat back on, while weakly uttering, "I can't take this, I can't," and departed.

German Psychiatrist

This is an interesting story in Swami Rama's own words (LWHM, P.435-37):

There was a psychiatrist from s small town in Germany. People often called him a crazy doctor because he did not believe much in modern medicine; he was more inclined to search for esoteric knowledge. In 1955, he had recurring visions of my Master (Bengali Baba). He felt that the man in the visions was calling him to India. He made an aborted effort to fly there, but fell asleep at the airport and missed the flight.

Shortly before that, my Master asked me to go to Germany and learn about western psychology and philosophy. I had several letters of introduction. When I landed, the above psychiatrist was at the airport. He came up to me and asked if I was a swami from India. He showed me drawings of the holy man who kept coming to him in his visions. He asked me if I knew someone who looked like that. He said to me," Please help. The man in this drawing has appeared to me in a vision again and

178

again. I have tried to draw the picture of my vision as well as I could. I am sure it is not a hallucination. This vision has created such deep grooves in my mind that I cannot do my work. All that I can think of is this image. You are a swami from India. Perhaps you can help."

When I saw the drawings, I said, "He is my Master." He insisted that I go back to India with him and take him to my Master, but my Master did not want me back right away. He wanted me to remain physically away from him for some time and to become aware of the more subtle bond which exists between us. That is why he sent me to different teachers in different parts of the Himalayas.

I gave the doctor a long letter to show to Dr. Chandradhar and Dr. Mitra of Kanpur, India. In the letter, I asked them to lead him to Jageshwar, where my Master was camping next to the temple and teaching Professor Nixon and Dr. Alexander.

With the help of the doctors of Kanpur, the German doctor met my Master, stayed with him for three days, and then returned to Germany. He then arranged for me to visit different institutes and universities throughout Europe. I met with a great many Western doctors and psychologists.

Sometime later, I returned to India and so did the doctor. He became a *sannyasi* (renunciate). He now devotes his time to meditation in a small thatched hut in the northeastern Himalayas.

A prophecy vision is the rarest of visions. It flashed from the source of intuition and is therefore beyond the concept of time, space, and causation.

Such a vision is received accidently by laymen. However, those who meditate and have attained the fourth state of mind receive such visions consciously. This unalloyed vision always comes true.

Meeting his Grand Master

After a long and hard journey from India to Tibet in 1939, Swami Rama finally made it to a remote site at 7,000 feet with great views of the Himalayas where his Grand Master resided. He stayed there quite a while and received much teaching from his Grand Master (i.e., his guru's guru). This is one story in his own words (LWHM P.395):

One day, one of the lama students came and my Grand Master told us that he would leave his body and enter someone else's body, and then come back to his own body again. He told us to come closer and hold a wooden plate which was like a round tea tray. When we held the tray, he said, "Do you see me?" We said, "Yes." His body stared getting hazy and that haziness was a human form like a cloud. That hazy cloud form started moving toward us. In a few seconds, the cloud disappeared. We found that the plate we were holding becoming very heavy. Then, after a few minutes, it became very light again. We sat down and waited. After about ten minutes, we heard my Grand Master's voice, which instructed us to pick up the plate again. It was heavy. Then the cloud reappeared, and then my Grand Master manifested from that cloud.

I feel that the world should know that such sages exist, and that such powers are possible for human beings.

Summary of Swami Rama

Justin said the following about Swami Rama: "The man from the world's highest mountains was an ambassador of the human spirit, a delegate from realms of awareness that angels envied, a timeless troubadour who wrote poetry to the universe and chanted the name of the divine until he forgot his surroundings. He was a visionary with a message to mend the wounds of humankind. A traveler and explorer of these times, he overcame all the struggles on his path of life and vindicated for each of us the universal quest for the ultimate meaning of life."

Swami Vishwananda

Swami Vishwananda is a spiritual teacher who was born on June 13, 1978 into a Hindu family on the island of Mauritius. From earliest childhood, his sole interest was in spirituality and religious practices. He would visit churches, temples, and mosques because he was drawn to the presence of the Divine and the Sacred. At an early age, he realized his true Self and understood the reason for his incarnation. Since that time, many people have come to him for his advice on spiritual and everyday matters. (Website, Vishwananda.org)

I have met with Swami Vishwananda in Colorado twice, once in April of 2006 and again in

November of 2006. He told us in a talk at Boulder, Colorado that the great sage Babaji visited him in person when he was five years old. Young Vishwananda had suffered a health problem and Babaji visited him in the hospital. Over the years, he stated, Babaji has manifested himself for "Vishwa" many times. He went on to say that he received all the yogi *siddhis* (miraculous powers) automatically at age 14.

I have personally verified that he has materialized rings, prayer beads, and vibhuti for his devotees. I have spoken with a number of his close devotees who have verified this. I have seen a number of rings thus produced. Further, the vibhuti often comes onto his robes. It is a white color, as opposed to Sai baba's predominately grey vibhuti.

More from the authorized website (Note: There are no books on Swami Vishwananda yet):

Once Swami completed his education, he began to be invited to travel to Africa, Europe, and other parts of the world. He has been blessed with the ability and vision to see into the hearts of all and has already helped and touched the lives of many. By giving Darshan (blessing) he helps people open their hearts to the Divine.

In 2005, Swami founded the Bhakta marga (path of devotion). The monks and nuns (called *Brahamacharis)* strive to live a life of devotion to God and services to their fellow human beings. The Bhasti Marga order is a spiritual monastic order that is influenced largely by Hindu and Christian traditions. A first Ashram has been established in

Germany. Under Swami's guidance and inspiration, other projects, including those involving service, are currently underway.

From all the great sages and saints, it is known that man has an immortal and divine Soul. Swami V. is one of those persons who has realized this and is able to connect with his Inner Self at will. It is Swami's main wish to support others in finding the way to their own inner spark of divinity. He is someone who loves God with all his heart and has a very 'natural' relationship to the Divine. He says, "Through the ages, many teachers, saints, and sages have lived. Their message was in its essence always the same, yet wrapped in different words, languages and traditions. What we lack is the will for people to really go within and put the teachings into practice. Especially in today's world, there exist a lot of distractions that lead to 'outer attachments' that are finite and cause suffering again and again when lost. People should become aware of the 'inner attachments' that are eternal and cause no suffering."

I found out that he was born Hindu, but studied Christianity in depth and actually was a stigmatic, i.e., bled from the wounds of Christ every Friday, ending on Sunday; this happened for over a year.

He also loves music. His voice is gentle and firm, and I have been so moved when he sang that I could not help weeping. He is very easy and gentle and kind. He seems like a brother and friend, as well as an avatar, quite remarkable.

Related to Love, Patience and Unity, he has said the following: "Truly realized Saints love everyone the same way. They see that everybody is part of God and his creation. For them the question about race, culture, or religion doesn't arise. We should take their example. Mankind needs to remember that all people come from the same source and all will go back to the same source, just as all humans, who beneath their skin that gives them their outer appearance and differences, have the same color of blood. Our planet and all its creatures were created through love, are sustained by love and will go back to love. We all live through that very same essence.

"One of the most important qualities on the spiritual path is patience. Great Yogis have been, and still are, meditating and contemplating for years and lifetimes in the Himalayas to advance spiritually. The spiritual path is only suitable for someone who is patient. We must not force anything, be it in meditation or in any other thing. When we are ready, everything will come naturally by God's grace. But what is indispensable is introspection and consistency in regular spiritual practice in order to create a solid basis for the divine grace.

"God lives in your heart right now, but to realize that YOU have to make the first move, and you really have to want Him with all your heart and soul and put Him first in line in your desires."

I have personally been with Swami Vishwananda. He is kind, gentle, soft-spoken and radiates goodness all the time.

In November of 2006, I was walking with him in downtown Boulder, Colorado. He noticed that I had a severe limp. He gently asked me why was I limping. I explained to him that I had played way too much basketball and literally ground the cartilage out of my left knee. I had bone on bone arthritis. I told him that an orthopedic surgeon had told me many years ago that I should have a knee replacement. I told him that I had resisted and was trying to cure it by spiritual means. He nodded understandingly. Later I thought about that and approached him and said, "Swami, let me ask you a question: Is this something you can miraculously cure or am I stuck with this as my karma?" He looked off into space and said, "No. I can help. I will get you some oil." Then, two months later, one of his close disciples brought me back some special healing oil from Swami Vishwananda. I applied it for a month or so, and it has cut my pain in the knee by 95%! In addition, I have no pain at night at all. Further, I am starting to gradually increase the seriousness of my workouts. I might even lose some weight, now that I can walk and even jog a little bit with NO PAIN! Thanks, Swami Vishwananda.

A Comparison of the Teachings of Sai Baba, Dr. George, Jesus, Yogananda, Swami Rama, and Other Major Spiritual Teachers

Relationship to God

All of the teachers taught that God is both within and without. They taught that humans must seek God within themselves. For example, one of the most famous of the statements of Jesus was "The Kingdom of Heaven is within you." Yogananda said. "We all have divinity within us and it is our foremost purpose in life to realize that." (Dr. George quoted Yogananda in a talk at The Farm in October, 1966). They taught that God is within every being. They taught that it was of paramount importance that humans SEEK God within and effect spiritual practices which can assist this process.

There are, of course, many differences in the practices of these paths, depending on the time and place. Moslem practices are different than Buddhist practices, but the goal of the practices is the same, i.e., to seek and experience God within.

Jesus probably said it the simplest and the best: "Thou shalt love the Lord thy God with all thy heart, all thy mind, and all thy soul" and "Seek ye first the Kingdom of God and all these things shall be added unto you."

Abraham Lincoln is reputed to have said that he would prefer a church which would put the two commandments of Jesus above the door and make a reasonable effort to follow them. (Normally, he did not go to church.)

Sri Yukteswar, the great guru of Yogananda, stated that ".... God is ever new, ever increasing joy and bliss."

All the teachers state that the experience of God within is accompanied by joy, love, bliss, and peace.

Dr. George said that mankind was destined to evolve into God Consciousness. He stated that life had moved upward from rock to plant to animal to human, and the next stage was divinity within. He said that it took 2,000 human lifetimes to achieve divinity, if one did not take "shortcuts" with disciplined spiritual practices, such as meditation and humanitarian service.

Yogananda also stated in his *Autobiography of a Yogi* it took 2,000 normal human incarnations to attain divinity. Yogananda further went on to state that the centerpiece of his teachings, namely the meditation system called Kriya yoga, was given by the merciful masters of the Himalayas to humanity as a method of hastening human evolution. According to Yogananda, humans have *chakras* in their spines, which animals do not, and the subtle currents going up and down the spinal cord through these chakras determine the rate of evolution of the human. Using the technique of Kriya yoga, a human can significantly increase the speed of evolution and advance spiritually a great deal in one incarnation. This is appealing to those of us who deeply desire liberation from never-ending reincarnation. By practicing Kriya yoga, many people have found it much easier to experience God within. Many people, including myself, have had wondrous inner experiences of God within using this technique.

Yogananda went on to say the following in a lecture in Los Angeles in February, 1939:

"Now is the time for you to make the effort to KNOW God. In meditation, again and again throw the bombs of your deepest yearning against the bulwark of silence, until its walls are broken down and God is revealed. FEEL the love of God; then, in every person you will see the face of the Father, the light of Love which is in all. You will find a magic, living relationship uniting the trees, the sky, the stars, all people and all living things. You will feel a oneness with them. This is Divine Love." And:

"The season of life is very short, and within this span we must try to reap the richest harvest of God realization. All that is necessary is we make the effort to meditate every day and practice the presence of God. The Gita says, 'He who perceives Me everywhere and beholds everything in Me, never loses sight of Me, nor do I ever lose sight of him.'"

Yogananda gave a talk in Los Angeles in November of 1934 at the SRF world headquarters as follows:

"In the Vedas [Hindu scriptures] of India, we find the earliest true concept of God. In her scriptures, India has given the world immortal truths that have stood the test of time. Every material inventor is actuated by material need 'necessity is the mother of invention.' Similarly motivated by necessity, the early *rishis* (i.e., unknown sages of very ancient times to whom the Vedas were revealed and are the basis of all religions) had become ardent spiritual seekers. They had found that without inner satisfaction, no amount of external good fortune can bring lasting happiness. How then, can one make him/herself really happy? That is the problem the wise men of India undertook to solve. Perceiving that every human being is a compound of matter and mind, the earliest Western thinkers believed that two independent forces existed: nature and mind. Later they began asking themselves, 'Why is everything in nature arranged in a particular way? Why isn't one of man's arms longer than the other? Why do not stars and planets collide? Everywhere we see evidence of order and harmony in the universe.' They concluded that mind and matter could not be both separate and sovereign, a single Intelligence must govern all. This conclusion naturally led to the idea that there is just one God, who is both the Cause of matter and the Intelligence within and behind it. One who attains the ultimate wisdom realizes that everything is Spirit in essence, though hidden in manifestation. If you had the perception, you would see God in everything. Then the question is, how did seekers first find him?"

"As the beginning step, they closed their eyes to shut out immediate contact with the world and matter, so they could concentrate more fully on discovering the Intelligence behind it. They reasoned that they could not behold God's presence in nature through the ordinary perceptions of the five senses. So they began to try to feel Him within themselves by deeper and deeper concentration. They eventually discovered how to shut off all five senses, thus temporarily doing away entirely with the consciousness of matter. The inner world of the Spirit began to open up. To those great ones of ancient India who undeviatingly persisted in these inner investigations, God finally revealed Himself. Thus, these saints gradually began to convert their *conceptions* of God into *perceptions* of God. That is what you must do also, if you would know Him. Right now, you do not stay long enough in your meditations. You must meditate and pray until you actually feel Him. If you persist, the Lord will come to you. He will come to you in whatever form you hold dear. With me, He comes as the Divine Mother, or Christ, or my Guru, or the Infinite, or Great Joy. The Lord is the searcher for hearts and He wants only your sincere love."

Many saints and masters over the centuries have experienced God as the Divine Mother. There are many aspects of the Divine Mother. Just hearing the song "Ave Maria" has brought the divine into the hearts of countless people over the years. Just thinking of the Virgin Mary opens the heart of devotion to God. The entire word may be better if folks thought of "God" as the Mother instead of a Father. A mother is much kinder.

Swami Vishwananda told me this about the Divine Mother while I was walking with him in downtown Boulder, Colorado:

"Divine Mother will come to you if you really, really call on her and desire nothing but Her. I see her all the time. She is everywhere, in every atom of creation."

Many great woman Saints and Masters over the ages have exemplified and personified the Divine Mother for their devotees, including Mother Therese, St. Theresa of Avila, Mother Meera, Ammachi, Mother Mary, and Quon Yin. (I, myself, received a "hug" from Ammachi and was greatly blessed.)

Charismatic Christians sing from the bottom of their hearts to God and attain great joy in doing so. Many miracles have happened due to this devotion to God and expression thereto. How often have you walked into a Christian church and heard the power of the organ and the harmony of the vocalists singing inspirational songs which lift your spirit. When I was a kid, I loved the records of the Mormon Tabernacle Choir. They were so beautiful and so uplifting. Likewise, the gospel album of Elvis Presley is so sweet and good you can feel God within very easily listening to him.

One time, I was traveling and in a strange town by myself. I looked in the yellow pages in the motel to find a church nearby. I went to the nearest church. At that time, I had long hair, wore jeans and cowboy boots, and was a traveling musician. I sat in the back of the church. The music was great. Likewise, the preacher was an "upper" instead of a "downer" (i.e., hell and negativity). I actually could see Christ with the preacher and felt beautiful. After the service, I was so inspired, as I was exiting and shaking the preacher's hand, I made the dumb move of saying "Reverend, I could see and feel Master Jesus right with you today!" Well, that was true, but he looked at me like I was whacko. The good news was that Jesus didn't mind, despite my customary big mouth (which I have spent a lifetime trying to curb). I made a mental note to avoid telling others of my own inner experiences except in certain circumstances.

Buddhists both do deep meditation and do powerful divine chants to raise their consciousness so they can expand their higher consciousness within. I love to meditate in Buddhist temples. The deep devotion and dedication of the long history of monks and holy men dedicated to spiritual understanding bless and sanctify even me, who am not a Buddhist. Though Buddhists do not actually believe in "God" per se, they have developed deep and powerful mantras for specific purposes and expansion of "God" Consciousness within. The Buddhists go on the premise that *we* are divine, we are God. They assert the divinity of all beings. Interestingly, there is a Hindu chant, which translated means "You are That" or "I am He" or something similar. Likewise, Jesus said, "Do not your scriptures say that Ye are Gods?" I knew a Christian faith healer who received his gift while in a coma on his deathbed in St. John's Hospital in downtown St. Paul, Minnesota. He told me, that while he was still in the coma, "I was suddenly looking down on my body and a divine voice said

'Ed, you are not the body; you are spirit!" Then, he told me that he woke up, he was miraculously healed and walked out of the hospital. The doctors called it a misdiagnosis.

Kabir was an interesting holy man. As stated earlier, he lived a normal outer life. He said that there was no need for religion or spiritual practices to realize God. Rather, in his inimitable manner, he said, "What is essential is to wake up to the living presence of God IN and AS life itself and as the love and power constantly reinventing all creation, and to live in that sacred knowledge and bliss, radiating the power of that truth through all one's actions and choices." Now, that, my friends is a mouthful. Boy, I wish I could wake up like that. Kabir's consciousness is what we are all seeking by whatever method.

Lahiri Mahasaya was the guru of Yogananda's great guru, Sri Yukteswar. Lahiri used to sit in his little house in Benares, the holy city of India after work in the evenings. Later, after he retired, he was there most of the time. Disciples came from everywhere in India to see him. For hours, he would sit in the lotus posture in the breathless state. He did spoke little, but his vibration expanded and blessed all who came. He actually imbued the folks who came to meditate with him with their own inner divine consciousness. He had devotees from every path and every caste. He recommended practicing the Kriya yoga, but further stressed the necessity of totally emptying the mind of desires, fears, attachments, etc., while meditating so as to fully effect the divine experience. It reminds me of when Dr. George told me, "In the silence of your soul, there you will find all things."

I am not a Catholic, but I love to meditate in Catholic churches. The long-practiced devotion of millions of devout simple souls to their religion can be felt in Catholic cathedrals everywhere. I am always blessed by sitting in the silence in such a church. I enjoy the mass, as well. I truly feel God's presence while the priest is doing his thing.

Sri Ramakrishna Paramahansa attained divinity the classic Hindu way at a young age. Thereafter, as a service and example to all persons everywhere, he proceeded to take a number of paths to divinity, including the Jain path, the Christian path, etc., and announced that he had come to the same goal, i.e., oneness with God, with all the paths. Ramakrishna said to devotees over 140 years ago:

"God appears in every human form and manifesting Himself alike through the sage and the sinner, the virtuous and the vicious. Therefore, when I meet different people, I have now come to a stage of realization in which I see that God is walking by me and I say to myself, 'God in the form of the saint, God in the form of the sinner, God in the form of the righteous, God in the form of the unrighteous.'" One of his most powerful statements was "Unalloyed love of God is the essential thing. All else is unreal" and "What are you going to do when you are placed in the world? Give up everything to Him, resign yourself to Him, and there will be no more trouble for you. Then, you will come to know that everything is done by His will" and "Do you know what I see? I see Him as all. Men and other creatures appear to me only as hollow forms, moving their heads and hands and feet, but within is the Lord Himself."

The Hare Krishna folk use great devotion and singing from the heart to attain divine realization. It is wonderful to be with these souls as they do their devotions. They sing like children, from the bottom of their heart, to God. I love to attend Hare Krishna meetings and temples wherever I go. I especially like the temple in Santa Monica, California. It is a very special place, which I recommend to everyone.

Most saints, masters, and sages have recommended the devotional path as the easiest path to God. Jesus stated, "Suffer the little children to come to me, for such is the Kingdom of God."

Just think of anyone of any religion you have known in your life who you intuitively feel and know is a true person of God, and two things they have in common are a child-like faith and a child-like kindness to others.

Perhaps no one has exemplified the devotional path better than Paramahansa Yogananda. His words literally lift your heart to God within:

"I believe that if every citizen in the world is taught to *commune* with God and *feel* God within, not just to know about Him intellectually or read scriptures or memorize things about God, when we know Him, then peace can reign and not before. When by persistence in meditation you realize God through communion with Him, your heart is prepared to embrace all humanity." (A class for SRF students in 1926.)

"God alone is sufficient, for in Him lies all love, all life, all happiness, all joy, all peace, everything that even in your wildest dreams you could not imagine. Cultivate a relationship with Him. Practice the presence of God every day and never go to bed at night until you have practiced Kriya and are filled with joy." (SRF Temple, San Diego, June, 1947.)

Sai Baba said the following in talks at the ashram in 1983:

"It is needless to search for God. Verify that you *are* the divine. Strive to realize this truth. There is a simple and easy way. Have the faith that every human being is an embodiment of the Divine. Love everyone. Serve all. The best way to love God is to love all, serve all." Also:

"Millions of people all over the world are in quest of God. But where are they searching for Him? In my view, the very idea of a quest for God is mistaken. There is no need for you to search for God. God is omnipresent. He is everywhere. Devotees imagine they are searching for God. This is not true. It is God who is in search of devotees. Where is the devotee to be found who is pure in thought, word, and deed? God is searching for such a devotee." Further:

"You need not go anywhere for God. Divinity is within you. Just as there are many limbs in the body which are activated by one heart inside, the same God is the Life Force for all beings. The entire Universe is a reflection of the Supreme Being." (all from SS32)

One of the major chants of meditators, is "Aum" or "Om," which in Christianity, is "Amen." As you continue on the inner path, you will actually hear the cosmic sound of Om within. If you focus on this sound, it will lead you to the Kingdom of Heaven within you. This is the "Word of God." Note: the "word" of God is not some scripture written and translated by humans, many of them with agendas having little to do with "God." With concentration and practice, you can hear the "Word of God" within your own soul as you meditate. As you focus on the OM, you will gradually experience more and more happiness, freedom and bliss within, and feel God in your own heart and soul.

Master George emanated divine bliss. He and I would sit together silently watching television. It didn't matter what was on the tube. Basically, he was teaching me to feel and tap into the Om vibration no matter what was going on in the outer. Whenever my concentration wavered and my mind would go to what was happening on the tube, he would snort, chuckle, move abruptly, etc., to let me know I missed my concentration on God within. Over the years, thanks to that training, I am able to focus on the Om within whenever I am not actively engaged in working or doing necessary tasks. One wry note: The exception is when a baseball game was on. He knew that I would pay attention to the baseball game; however, I have found that now, after all these years, I can still have some of my best meditations while a baseball game is on television.

Master George said often in talks and sermons: "You should meditate every day with the expressed intent of feeling and experiencing God within. Never miss a day. Make time for God!"

He told me personally one time in December, 1965, "Learn to meditate until you feel the joy of God and *know* that He is right there with you." He told me another time, "When you convince the Divine Mother that you want her more than her miracles, She will come to you."

One time, I had a real urgent need. It was 1965 and I do not want to discuss the actual matter at hand. It is and was confidential and I do not want to embarrass or talk disparagingly about other people. However, I did have a real need. So, I called my foreman (I was working construction) on Sunday and told him I was sick and would not be into work in the morning. I sat in my chair in my room and told Divine Mother that I really needed Her now and needed an answer and a solution. I told her that I was not going to move from the chair until I got an answer. I started to chant Yogananda's chant, "Door of my Heart" and vowed to keep chanting and meditating until I got an answer. I sat there all night. I fell asleep a couple of times, but woke myself up and kept on going. Finally, about 6:00 a.m., a huge energy hit me like a ton. The energy went up my spine and I felt a great peace and love and knew that I was feeling the Divine Mother. It was beautiful. Then calm reigned and I saw a series of clear pictures of what I needed to do and what I needed to say. I came out of my mystical experience and made notes on what I had experienced. Then, I went out and implemented them and my total problem was resolved to the satisfaction of all the relevant folks! Thank you, Divine Mother.

Relationships with Other Humans

The Biblical Golden Rule: "Do unto others as you would have them do unto you" is the standard of all religions and all the teachers I studied. This is very simple and succinct and says it all.

The second of the two commandments of Jesus summarizes the teachings of these teachers related to our relationships with other humans, namely, "Thou shalt love thy neighbor as thyself."

All spiritual teachers, with the exception of Mohammed, not only recommended not harming other beings, but further, to actually try to help them actively in a positive manner. One of the things I learned in India is the tradition that Jesus was run out of India by the Brahmins who objected to his teaching that there was only one caste, the caste of humanity (see section "Jesus Lived in India"). The Brahmins at that time had control of the money, the political power, and the religious "right."

There has always been a conflict in organized religion of every kind between the dogma/theology and the practice of kindness/forgiveness/tolerance for all beings, even if different. People are so insecure within themselves that they have an urge to get rid of anyone who differs with them regarding religion or theology. This is sad because God and spirit are unlimited things, and religion and theology are limited and circumscribed things. Noting this unfortunate tendency by humans, the Masters of history have spent most of their outer lives trying to set examples of kindness, sacrifice, service, humanitarian works, etc., so that their followers would be cured from this disease of anger, violence, war, cruelty, etc., that afflicts the human race.

Let us discuss a wide variety of such happenings in spiritual history.

Sathya Sai Baba – Hospitals

In the United States these days, we all know about the problems with medical insurance, health care costs, etc. There are approximately 70 million Americans who do not have health insurance. The emergency rooms are filled with the poorest people bringing their kids in because they have no other place to go. Most bankruptcies and many divorces are caused by unpaid medical bills, and the U.S. is better in the medical area than most countries.

Enter Isaac Tigrett, the founder and major shareholder of the Hard Rock Cafes. (The following is taken from a talk given by Isaac at the 1992 Sai Baba conference in Atlanta, Georgia, September, 1992). Isaac went to India on a lark in the early 1970's. He came to Sai Baba's ashram one day and sat in the back, not expecting anything. Isaac was curious, having heard about this amazing miracle-working swami. Much to his surprise, Sai Baba came up to him amongst all the thousands of folks from all over the world who were sitting there viewing the great one. Swami materialized vibhuti into Isaac's hand. Isaac was shocked. He was really impressed as in, how many times in your life have you seen right in front of your eyes a person materializing matter from nothing?

In Los Angeles. Isaac was drunk one night (he had not started real spiritual practices yet), driving his new Porsche at 85 miles per hour on top of one of the canyons in L. A. He passed out. Just as he was going over the cliff, he woke up. There was Sai Baba sitting in the passenger seat smiling with his hand on Isaac's shoulder. The Porsche went over at 85 mph and was totally wiped out 300 feet below. Isaac was UNTOUCHED! As soon as he could after this event, Isaac went to India to see Baba and try to thank him for miraculously saving his life. He sat in darshan day after day and Swami completely ignored him. Isaac was there for weeks but could not come near Sai Baba. Finally, he left and went back to his business. On a regular basis, for two years, he went back, but was ignored again and again.

Then, while in Denver opening the new Hard Rock Café (and still a little wild in the entertainment business), he DIED in a hotel room of a drug overdose! As he was dying, Isaac remembered someone advising him that when one is dying, it is advisable to call on one's Guru. So, realizing he was dying, he called on Sai Baba. Immediately, Swami was there. Swami smiled and escorted Isaac on the Other Side to a tribunal. Swami "pled" Isaac's case in front of the tribunal, mentioning some of Isaac's past lifetimes wherein he did some very good things and deserved another chance. Then, much to his surprise, Isaac was back in his body on the bed in the hotel room in Denver. Sai Baba was massaging his chest. Swami smiled, stood up, and dematerialized, with a blessing to Isaac.

Again, Isaac went to India regularly. For thirteen more years he went to India and Baba completely ignored him. Then, Isaac and his wife sold their stock in The Hard Rock Cafes for a large sum of money, exceeding $100,000,000 and they decided to retire. They took half the money and put it into a humanitarian trust in Switzerland. Their intention was to go to see Sai Baba, hopefully thank him for the past, and offer him the money.

Again, Swami eluded Isaac for quite a while. Then, finally, he called them in for an interview. He teased Isaac about the money and said, "What do I need with your money? I do not want your money." Isaac felt about two inches tall. Then, Swami relented and acknowledged Isaacs good and kind heart and said (much to Isaac's shock), "You build the hospital." Needless to say, Isaac probably thought, "What hospital?" Well, by the time it was done, Isaac had funded, endowed, and was in essence the general contractor for a 328,000 square feet hospital in Puttaparthi, India, free for all patients! This hospital is designed by

Prince Charles' architect and has all the modern state of the art technology for the five basic body groups, including heart, lungs, etc. Big name doctors of Indian descent from all over the world come to volunteer and receive $50 per month plus room and board! It is a wonder of the world.

Sai Baba simply said, "In India, wealthy people can have health care, but poor people cannot. This service is open to anyone." Not only do they treat thousands of patients, but being associated with Sai Baba, many miracles happen in the hospital as well. I personally spoke with a number of doctors at the hospital in Puttaparthi who laughingly told me that they do their best medically, and then Swami comes along and regularly, miraculously heals many people!

Swami Rama set up a comprehensive medical center in Jolly Grant, about 18 miles north of Rishikesh in the Himalayas. It is a medical city on 250 acres with nursing school, medical school, and complete medical services. Many miracles take place at the hospital. Swami Rama's vision was to have an international center which would be free for the poor people or those who could not pay. They do very well for the poor people and train many nurses. Teams go into the remote areas do common sanitation, which has decreased the fatality rate of children by over 80%. They have introduced alternate methods of cooking to save folks from the harmful effects of cooking with dung.

Ammachi the great woman saint, has opened up large medical centers in South India which are free for the poor people. They are on the same mode as Sai Baba's hospitals and are an amazing blessing for those who really need it.

Kindness

Teachings of Sathya Sai Baba related to this topic:

"There are a number of weaknesses that have invaded human beings; as a result, they lose kindness and become cruel. The behave like wild animals dwelling in the jungle. Krishna taught that it is not the true nature of a human being; it is the very opposite of humanness. The very word human or humane is used to denote kindness. Of all the different flowers of devotion, God accepts the flower of human kindness with greatest love." (SS36)

"There is no need to search for God. Why are we searching for God? Because we do not have sacredness in us. As we do not have kindness in us, we are in search of the embodiment of kindness. If only we have kindness in us, the embodiment of kindness would be with us, beside us, behind us, in front of us, below us, above us, inside our homes and outside. Would anyone search for a thing which he has with him? One searches for a thing he does not have." (SS26)

Master George stated on time in a sermon on a Tuesday night in Milwaukee, "The most important things in the universe are forgiveness and kindness. The cosmos would end without them."

Swami Rama stated the following: "Lead your life with this quality, but let no one walk over you. Do not use kindness as a substitute for *standing up for yourself*." (personal dialogue with Dr. Justin O'Brien)

I, personally, have always been an extremely impatient person. I am also sometimes loud and pushy. After I had been meditating for a number of years, I started to actually see the Divine within other people. I found out that I couldn't help being kind to other folks, and when I was not because of my own personal flaws, I had a tough time meditating, and I felt bad. The more I meditated, the more I felt bad when I didn't live up to my teacher's ideals.

Brotherhood

Sai Baba says the following related to this topic:

"Have an open heart. Do not relish the narrow path of restricted love. Love all. Do not develop prejudices against men in power or position. They too are our kith and kin. We all stand together."

"I preach only one religion of love for all, which alone can integrate the human race into a brotherhood of man under fatherhood of God. I know only one language of the heart beyond the mind or intellect which relates man to man and mankind to God, thereby creating mutual understanding, cooperation and community life in peace and harmony. On this basis, I want to build one humanity without any religious, caste, or other barriers in a universal empire of love with could enable my devotees to feel the whole world as their own family." (SS13)

Paramahansa Yogananda stated the following in a lecture in Hollywood, California, in October, 1943:

"Love gives without expecting anything in return. I never think of anyone in terms of what he can do for me. And, I never profess love to someone because he has done something for me. If I didn't actually feel love, I wouldn't pretend to give it, and since I feel it, I give it. I learned that sincerity from my Master. There may be some who do not feel friendly toward me, but I am a friend to all, including my enemies, for in my heart I have no enemies." (10)

Sri Ramakrishna Paramahansa stated, "I would incarnate as a dog, if I could help my brothers and sisters."
Master George told me one time. "You should look for God within all beings, and see yourself in others."

Since I have been a serious meditator, I have also become aware of all the problems greedy people, companies, and governments cause the planet. I have to resist becoming a revolutionary, sometimes. I have tried to do my part related to what is good for society as best I can. I have always tried to speak up about the evils of the big multinational corporations and their influence on all of our lives, and have tried my best to vote for candidates who care about the downtrodden, the environment, minority rights, and are against unnecessary wars. I have tried my best to support efforts helping with the poorest and down and out. One of my biggest frustrations this life is being unable to deal with the problems that face so many people on this Earth. I wish I had billions of dollars so I could do something about the folks who really need it.

Charity

Sai Baba has said the following related to this topic:

"Gifts made with that one in view, to receive the Grace of the Lord are *Sathwic* (i.e., spiritual). However, gifts made expecting something in return is like fame and publicity, esteem and power, or made in a huff or made reluctantly under pressure; these are to be classed as *Rajasic* (i.e., not good). Charity should be given with reverence and faith." (SS65)

"Man has become a puppet in the hands of his own ego. There is no unity at all. There is just a big zero. Even the things you call sacred and pure fall far short of having those ideal virtues. Unity and sacredness can be achieved only through the medium of sacrifice, not through comfort and luxury. Therefore, embark upon the task of sacrifice. Through sacrifice you will come to know that your real nature is charity. Charity does not mean that you have given some money to an individual or an organization. The removal of all the evil thoughts that are within you is true charity. Charity will, in turn, confer purity upon you. Once you have purity, there will be unity. And once you have unity, you can reach divinity." (SS38)

Sai Baba probably holds the Guinness Spiritual Book of Records in just plain basic charity in one lifetime. First, it was very difficult to donate money to him, per se; he only owned the robes on his back and lived in one simple monk's room for his entire life. He provided free quality education for thousands of kids over many years. He built two hospitals which are free to the patients. He constantly gave gifts to everyone he came in contact with. I was in India one year when he fed 1.2 million peasants free for 10 days. I saw them lined up all day and all night. He set up a clean water project for 750 villages, 3,000,000 people who never had clean water before, and expanded it every year. He shamed all of his followers to be like him and has stated for many years, "My life is my message," and it sure was.

Jesus recommended that when someone asked, you should just flat loan them the money and not think about it.

I had some incredible examples of generous spirits in my life, including Dr. George, my mom and dad, and others. I just hope that if I ever got serious money that I would not horde it and would help anyone I could.

Dr. George gave of himself and his assets, selflessly to anyone who needed it. I saw so many instances of that. Likewise, my mom and dad taught me to never refuse anyone who truly needed it.

Forgiveness

Jesus stated in Matthew:

"When you pray, say the following: 'Our Father, which art in heaven, hallowed be thy name. They kingdom come, thy will be done, on earth, as it is in Heaven, and give us this day our daily bread, and forgive us our debts, as we forgive our debtors, and lead us not into temptation, but deliver us from evil, for thine is the kingdom, the power, and the glory forever. Amen.'"

"For if you forgive men their trespasses, your heavenly Father will also forgive you, but if you do not forgive others, neither will God forgive you your trespasses."

Also, in response to Peter's question of how many times we should forgive someone, like seven times? Jesus said, "I say unto you, not seven times, but seventy times seven."

Sathya Sai Baba stated:

"The act of forgiving will bring about a change in the person, and also in the one who forgives." (SS66)

"Only a person who has this *Kshama* (attitude of forgiveness) can be considered to be endowed with sacred love. This cannot be learned from textbooks." (SS58)

"Forgiveness is a quality that every man should possess. That forgiveness is Truth itself, it is Righteousness, it is the Veda. It is the supreme virtue in this world. Hence, all people should develop the quality of forgiveness." (SS44)

Dr. George used to say in his talks all the time that it was "impossible to meditate well if you could not practice unconditional forgiveness." One time, he told me personally, "You were a soldier and warrior in many lives. This life, you must be unarmed, you must learn to take it on the chin and forgive and send love."

I can attest that I have spent my entire life doing just that. The good news is that by forgiving, it really makes me happy and allows me to meditate really well.

Service to Others

Sai Baba said the following:

"Even if you are unable, or unwilling, to serve others, at least if you avoid doing harm, this is a form of good service" (SS4)

"When a devotee seeks with humility and purity to give *seva* [service] and *prema* [unselfish love] to My creatures who are in need of such selfless service and sublime love; when he considers all creatures as My children, as his beloved brothers and sisters, as the blessed manifestations of my Immanence, then in fulfillment of my roles as Sathya Sai, I descend to help, accompany and carry that *yogee* (devotee). I am always near such a yogee to guide him and to shower My love on his life." (SS21)

"What is the purpose of being a man? It is not for leading an animal existence. Man exists for service. Every man has to return to society by way of service what he has received from it. That service should be rendered selflessly in a spirit of sacrifice. Service is thereby converted to spirituality." (SS27)

Master George said, "God works, why shouldn't you?" He further stated, "It is just as important to help others as to meditate." And "It is not right to just sit and meditate and not help others." Another time, he said to me, "Hinduism is wrong when they see a poor man and say, 'Oh well, it's his bad karma' and do not try to help him, and Christianity is wrong when they ignore meditation and the inner experience of God."

I have had a real difficulty in this life with this aspect of the spiritual path. My record of service to others, in my opinion, is pretty dim compared to the great Masters and saints. I have a long way to go to even get within visual distance of Mother Therese and others. This is one area where I have been working on improving myself.

Kindly Deeds by Master George

In Milwaukee back in the 1970's, there was a man named Verlon Grothe. Verlon was a big hefty man who weighed more than 350 pounds. He was in the vending machine business and was successful at it. His mother came from West Bend, Wisconsin, where Dr. George grew up.

Verlon got very ill. He was in a coma and had some inoperable situations. The doctors told his mother that it was pretty much all over for Verlon. He was only 45 years old, but had lived hard.

His mom came to see Dr. George on a Tuesday afternoon. I was there when she came and heard about the situation. She said to Dr. George, "I am Lutheran. I do not understand what path you are on and I do not understand about the meditation and stuff, but I do know that you are a true holy man and that you can heal my son. Please heal my son." Dr. George blessed her, gave her some assurances, and she left.

The next morning, early, Dr. George and I were driving to the Farm. We stopped and had breakfast. Then, we drove to the St. Luke's Hospital near 27th and Oklahoma in Milwaukee. It was about 7 a.m. Dr. George told me to sit in the lobby while he went up to see Verlon. I sat and read the newspaper for about 15 minutes. He came down and we got into the car. He always drove. As we pulled away, I asked him, "Did you pray for him? Are you going to heal him?" He didn't answer my question directly. Instead, he deflected it and said, "Turn on the radio." I turned on the radio and we drove to the Farm. He never said a word about Verlon.

We came back into Milwaukee on Sunday evening. Mrs. Grothe was there waiting for Dr. George. What a remarkable story: We stopped by the hospital on Wednesday. On Thursday, Verlon came out of his coma. He demanded to know why they had him in the hospital. The doctors were amazed. The next day, they did tests. There was nothing wrong with him. They discharged him on Saturday! The interesting thing was that he had absolutely no clue what Dr. George had done, he probably still doesn't and probably would not have listened or believed his mom if she had told him. His mom, however, was eternally grateful. She tried to give Dr. George a significant sum of money. He totally refused and sent her on her grateful way.

My mother was a student of Dr. George, as well. She became paralyzed in 1974. I asked Dr. George if he could heal her. He told me sheepishly, "Divine Mother will not give me permission." I learned very hard that sometimes folks have to go through their lessons or their karma for a higher purpose. It was very difficult to see my mother paralyzed and hurting. She lived for 27 years and got more and more immobile with more pain each year.

For the last four years of his life, Dr. George drove from Friendship, Wisconsin to Grand Rapids, Minnesota (where my mom and dad lived) once per month. The trip was 384 miles one way. He did it, rain, sleet, or snow. My mom would not have made it without those trips.

Jose was a longtime Yogananda and Dr. George student. He had to move back to Texas for economic reasons. When he came back to Wisconsin with all of his kids, he wanted to be near Dr. George. One day, at the Farm, he and I were boarding up a wall on a new section of a building we were adding onto. Around the building, about 40 yards away, with two buildings in between, and in a garage, Dr. George was on the power saw, cutting something. Jose nailed a board up on the wall and realized he needed something to stand on because he had reached the limit of his reach. He set down his hammer, looked around, and said, "Sammy, do you see anything to stand on?" Just as he said those words, around the corner came Dr. George bearing a footstool. He said nonchalantly, "Here Jose, you need this?" He set it down and left back to the garage. Of course, there was no normal human way this could have happened. It proved to Jose that his teacher was in touch with his thoughts and needs in a stark down -to-earth manner. Jose crossed himself repeatedly and said, "Mama Mia, blessed guru." I laughed out loud. It was cool to see that one.

Leslie was a tough cookie. She was a strong person, had great authority, and was extremely bossy. One disagreed with her at one's peril. She bossed everybody else's children in the church, if the parents were not strong enough to stand up to her. She sometimes could push your buttons. She also had a very generous heart and would help anyone in need. Leslie was a very loyal student of Dr. George.

For a number of years, there was an extremely wealthy man from Florida we will call JB. JB flew Dr. George to Florida once a month for teaching. He also came to Milwaukee regularly. In 1958, he put a considerable amount of money into an account for Dr. George to build a new church, i.e., to replace the dirt floor log pew church previously described. JB, however, got into a tussle with Leslie. He was so ticked off that he told Dr. George, "Either she goes or I go, and if I go, my money goes with me." Dr. George said goodbye. End of Story. His loyalty to a true disciple was significant.

Jesus said: "For I was hungered and you gave me food; I was thirsty and you gave me drink; I was a stranger and you took me in. I was naked and you clothed me. I was sick and you visited me. I was in prison, and you came unto me. Then shall the righteous answer him, saying Lord, when saw we thee hungry, and fed you? Or thirsty and gave you drink? Or naked and clothed you? Or saw you sick or in prison and visited you? And then I will tell you: 'Verily I say unto you, as you have done to the least of these my brethren, so you have done it to me.'"

Truth

Jesus said, "You shall know the truth and the truth shall make you free."

Sai Baba said:

"Truth is not merely telling the facts about what you see or hear or know. These are temporal truths. In its full sense, truth can be applied only to what comes out of your heart in its pure and unsullied form as the voice of conscience." (SS99)

"Seek the Truth; you are seeking God. Truth is God. Truth exists. So, too, God exists." (SS99)

"You have been sent into the world, in order that you may use the time and the opportunity to realize the truth that you are not man, but God. The wave dances with the wind, basks in the sun, frisks in the rain, imagining it is playing on the breast of the sea. It does not know that it is the sea itself. Until it realizes the truth, it will be tossed up and down. When it knows it, it can lie calm and collected at peace with itself." (SS45)

"Where there is Truth, there dwells Lakshmi, the Godess of Prosperity. Truth is changeless and eternal. It is vital to man's life. If, in the midst of misery and suffering in the world, there is goodness, it is because of Truth. In ancient times, kings ruled over their kingdoms on the basis of truth. Because of lack of Truth, there is no peace and security in the world. Truth always protects a nation." (SS99)

"The human condition today is full of falsehood. It is sunk in wickedness. So no one can understand the significance of Truth. Truth is generally understood to mean speaking exactly what has been heard by the ears. No, this is not the meaning of Truth. What has been heard undergoes change. Truth is changeless. It is the same in the past, present, and future. Have faith that Truth exists thus and can be experienced." (SS99)

Master George said in a lecture in 1973: "Truth is big. Truth is sometimes contradictory. For example, some lifetimes, a human needs to be humbled. In other lifetimes, he or she is raised to higher levels in the outer. Sometimes a person has power. Other lives, the person has none. Some things are true at different times and different places. However, there is a truth beyond these surface truths. These are the basic principles of life, the basic principles of the spiritual path. These do not change and are not relative."

Another time, he spoke with a few close devotees in 1975 and said the following: "What is truth? If a man is being chased by bad people and runs east, is it truth for you to say he was running west to help the man? Yes, it would be untruth to tell the bad man the objective truth. Is it truth to tell another person about his or her faults as you perceive them? No, it is truth for you to forgive the person and seek to cure those same 'flaws' within yourself."

He told me (with a chuckle) one day in 1975, "Sometimes contradictions are both true." I thought about that for quite a while. My interpretation of that is that "truth" is sometimes determined by relative circumstances and not absolute.

We are in an age where truth is very hard to find in nearly any venue. Disinformation, misinformation, "spin," dissembling communication, distortions, half-truths, partial truths, and downright lies. I think that a synonym for truth today could be, "What is good and kind and best helps folks." Given that definition, most politicians and most wealthy men and women need some serious help.

All the Masters I studied had a real reverence for honesty and "the truth." The question, of course, is just exactly what is "truth"? As a general rule, the masters have tried to keep it really simple. While they could probably have spoken in complex profundities, simplicity seems to be the order of the day for nearly all of them. As a rule, they led simple lives, unselfish, and totally dedicated to help those around them in whatever way they could.

They basically averred that the following were true, and any issue beyond these were subject to the varieties of time, location, and culture.

In that spirit, the following are short simple Summary Statements by Dr. George over the years.

- Seek God with all your energy.
- Put the search for God first.
- Avoid extremes.
- Have a generous and kind heart.
- Be happy.
- Try to make others happy.
- Meditate or pray regularly.
- Do organized service to others.
- Help the ones who are down and out.
- Be kind to animals.

- Do not drink, smoke, or use drugs.
- Many advised to become vegetarians.
- Be good to your family.
- Do not love war or fighting. (You may have to do it, but do it only as your duty to your family or culture.)
- Brighten the corner where you are.
- When possible, obey the laws of the land.
- Surrender to the will of God.
- Your purpose on earth is to develop the divinity within you.
- Respect and see the divinity in all beings.
- Rise to the spirit of religion instead of the literal words.
- Do not judge other people.
- Forgive unconditionally when wronged.
- Release anger, fear, doubt and worry.
- Take pleasure in another person's good fortune.
- Concentrate on the inner as opposed to the outer.
- Respect all life.
- Recite the name of God mentally or verbally whenever you can. (Jesus said, "Pray without ceasing.")
- Do not be arrogant and control your pride.

- Naughty or nice, we are all God's children.

The following are some of Sai Baba's "Maxims," as compiled by Charlene Leslie-Chaden in her phenomenal book, *A Compilation of the Teachings of Sai Baba.*

- All is one. Be alike to everyone. The world is one; be good to everyone.
- Money comes and goes, but morality comes and grows.
- Be good, see good, and do good. That is the way to God.
- Silence is the only language of the realized. It is only in the depth of silence that the voice of God can be heard. Silence stills the waves of one's heart.
- Man is not born to go in the quest of *Anna* (material prosperity). He is born to go in quest of Atma.
- Man without God is not a man. God without man is always God.
- Realize that the Divine is present in every living thing as the indwelling Atma.
- All religions are roads leading to the one and the only goal, that is God. So regard them with equal respect. All religions teach that you should purify your mind, know your own self and develop Prema.

- The truth is only yourself, what you see during the day is a day dream, what you see during sleep is a night dream.
- Since God is the indwelling Atma of all living beings, doing service of good to a person is in reality worshipping God. Similarly, talking ill or doing anything bad to a person is in reality doing bad to God Himself or talking ill of Him.
- Good and Bad, happiness and sorrow, which appear to be different and opposite, are in reality two faces of the same coin.
- Love lives by giving and forgiving. Self lives by getting and forgetting.
- The good life is a journey from the position of "I" to the position of "We."
- Whatever you may do, if you do it with the feeling that you are doing the same thing to yourself, you will never do anything bad.
- Practice before you preach. Do not yourself do the mistake which you find in others.
- A bad act cannot give you good results. A good act cannot give you evil results. You plant the seed. It grows into the tree the seed contains.
- Implicit faith in the divine is the road to spiritual success.
- The Lord loves not the *Bhakta* (devotee), but his *Bhakti* (devotion), remember this.

- Having got this sacred chance of life as a human being (which is very difficult to get), if we conduct ourselves like animals, we will be wasting our lives and not justifying this gift of God.
- God is an ocean of mercy. *Bhakti* [devotion] is the easiest way to win His grace. God's grace is like sunshine, available to all.
- If anyone points out a fault in you, you must thank him, because by yourself you will not be able to find out your own fault. As your eyes are directed outwards, you can find the faults only in others.
- Recognizing one's error is the beginning of wisdom.
- As close as you are to God, so close is God to you. One who realizes that god is omnipresent will recognize that God is closest to him and that he is nothing but God himself.
- Only the repetition of God's name can win Him, and only by sincere Prema and Bhakti can one feel God, not by money or theology.
- Haste makes waste. Waste makes worry. So, do not be in a hurry. Slow and steady wins the race.
- Spiritual pride is the most poisonous of all varieties of pride. It binds and leads the person suffering from it to ruin.

- Ceaseless contemplation of the Lord will give you ceaseless taste of sacred nectar.
- The proof of rain is the wetness of the ground. The proof of devotion is the peace the aspirant has attained.
- Above all, do every act as an offering to the Lord, without being elated by success or dejected by defeat. This gives the poise and equanimity for sailing through the waters of the ocean of life.
- Welcome disappointments, for they toughen you and test your fortitude.

Swami Rama met a Sage in the Himalayas who told him the following about truth:

"There are no contradictions in the teachings of the Upanishads (one of the Hindu scriptures). These teachings are received directly be the great sages in a deep state of contemplation and meditation." He explained, "When the student starts practicing, he realizes that this apparent world is changeable, while truth never changes. Then he knows that the world of forms and names which is full of changes is false, and that behind it there exists an absolute Reality that is unchanging. In the second step, when he has known the truth, he understands that there is only one truth and that truth is omnipresent, so there is really nothing like falsehood. In that stage, he knows that reality which is one and the same in both the finite and infinite worlds. But there is another, higher state in which the aspirant realizes that there is only one absolute

223

Reality without second, and that which is apparently false is in reality a manifestation of the absolute One. These apparent contradictions confuse only that student who has not studied the Upanishads from a competent teacher."

Yogananda said:

"Yoga is a system of scientific methods for reuniting the soul with the Spirit. We have come down from God and we must re-ascend to Him. We have seemingly become separated from our Father, and we must consciously reunite with Him. Yoga teaches us how to rise above the delusion of separation and realize our oneness with God. The poet Milton wrote of the soul of man and how it might regain the lost paradise. That is the purpose and goal of Yoga: to regain the lost paradise of soul consciousness by which man knows that he is, and ever has been, one with Spirit." (9)

"Before creation existed, there was Cosmic Consciousness: Spirit or God, the Absolute, ever-existing, ever conscious, ever-new Bliss beyond form and manifestation. When creation came into being, Cosmic Consciousness 'descended' into the physical universe, where it manifests as Christ Consciousness, the omnipresent pure reflection of God's intelligence and consciousness inherent and hidden within all creation. When the Christ Consciousness descends into the physical body of man, it becomes soul, or super consciousness, the ever-existing, ever-conscious, ever-new bliss of

God into individualized encasement in the body. When the soul becomes identified with the body, it manifests as ego or mortal consciousness. Yoga teaches that the soul must climb back up the ladder of consciousness to Spirit." (Talk in 1944 at the Hollywood SRF Temple.)

I have worked very hard this lifetime to follow these teachings of Truth by Yogananda, Dr. George, and Sai Baba. I can attest to the reader, that if you practice meditation regularly and do your best to expand your love and service to others, that it is a mathematical certainty that you will experience the Truth that you are Spirit. I can attest that I have many flaws and have made many errors and mistakes this lifetime, yet, I have always continued to meditate and seek more and more of God within. Somehow, miraculously, I can feel and experience many of the things that Yogananda wrote and talked about. I am striving for more and more.

On my first trip to India, my friend told me on the airplane, "You should pray and tell Swami (Sai Baba) what you want. I replied that I really couldn't think of anything I wanted from him, then I thought quietly to myself, and I did not say anything to anybody, but, inwardly, I said, "Swami, here is what I want: I want the best meditation I ever had in my life."

We got there and had been there for about a week or so, and one day, about 9 a.m., I went over to the mandir (temple) and put my pad down, and sat down on the pad with my back up against the outer mandir wall. I started meditating. Five hours later, I had not moved a muscle. I went into the best bliss I ever had experienced. My friends came and brought me back to earth. They laughed and told me that people walked by me all day, looking and talking about me. I never noticed any of them. My friends laughingly told me that I sure looked like a real yogi. Boy, I sure felt like one. This experience, more than any of the hundreds and hundreds of miracles I have seen and heard about convinced me of the reality of Sai Baba as a Divine Incarnation.

Peace

Jesus said in Matthew: "Blessed are the Peacemakers, for they shall be called the children of God" and "Ye have heard that it has been said, 'an eye for an eye, a tooth for a tooth. I say to you: you should not resist evil, but whosoever smiteth thee on the right cheek, turn to him the other also, and if a man will take your coat, give unto him your cloak as well, and whoever shall compel you to go a mile, go with him another mile, give to him that asks from you, and from him that would borrow from you, do not turn away from him" also: "You have heard it said that you should love your neighbor and hate your enemy. But, I say unto you: Love your enemies, bless them that curse you, do good to them that hate you, and pray for them which despitefully use you and persecute you."

Swami Rama said the following in a personal dialogue with his student, Dr. Justin O'Brien:

226

"Peace belongs to your essence, but you need to find it. Thus, you need to practice meditation and maintain a balanced lifestyle. This combination will gradually establish serenity" and "Sustain peace under all conditions. This will obviously take a lot of practice."

Simply put, all the Masters recommend, when possible, a peaceable outer *and* inner life. They, of course, advise against hurting any other being. They also strongly recommend forgiveness, tolerance, and kindness.

They all go on to firmly request of their followers something even more difficult than outer peace, namely *inner* peace. Very possibly, one of the toughest challenges to mankind was the following statement of Jesus: "He who is angry with his brother is a murderer." Where do you go with a statement like that?

Dr. George used to say that desires cause many problems. One of these problems that he mentioned was the fact that unfulfilled desires caused frustration and disrupted inner peace. He advised that we reduce our spurious desires for one thing or another and "go with the flow," saying inwardly to God, "thy will be done." He advised to have faith in the ultimate plan of God for the overall good of our souls and our being. He taught us that our plans and desires often worked like a reverse practical joke on us. Many, many times, one or another of us had one idea, desire, or plan in mind, only to be thwarted, frustrated, or stymied, and then later to find out that what actually did happen to us was for the better.

I can remember one fellow (whose name I cannot use), who wanted to marry a particular woman. He asked Dr. George to marry them, but Dr. George refused. The fellow was upset with Dr. George and went ahead and got married using another preacher. Well, it turned out to be very frustrating. The woman, though beautiful outwardly, had a number of very big psychological problems. She was exceedingly mercurial in temperament, i.e., one moment she would be fine, and then the next moment she would lose her temper, blow her stack, and remain angry for hours or days. The poor fellow finally could not handle it, and got a divorce. He later recognized the wisdom of Dr. George and mentioned that he should have followed his caution.

Likewise, at a Sai Baba Retreat in St. Louis, Missouri, many of us heard a similar story. In this case, a young international couple was in India at Sai Baba's Ashram in Puttaparthi, India. The man was from Central America and the woman was from Europe. They were very much in love, and pestered Baba to marry them. He resisted, and resisted. Finally, the influential families put pressure on everybody, and Sa Baba agreed to marry them. At the wedding, he materialized wedding rings for both of them, as he normally does. Then, he said a curious thing: "In six months, very happy, very happy!" No one knew what he meant, but the young groom telling this story to us brought down the house in ironic laughter when he said that soon after the honeymoon, the relationship was a disaster! They fought and disagreed about everything, and he admitted that it was just as much his fault as her fault, and after six months of torture, they both eagerly and happily got an annulment! They were, in fact, very happy after six months.

Sai Baba said the following related to peace:

"Only thoughts of God and intense love for Him bring peace. As worldly thoughts diminish, thoughts of God increase. Normally the mind desires these worldly things all the time. As the desires are cut out one by one, the peace becomes stronger." (SS12)

"Wash your hearts with your tears of joy, so that God might install Himself therein. Engage always in good deeds and beneficial activities....do not inflict pain by word or deed or even by thought. That is the way to gain true peace and that is the highest gain you can earn in this life." (SS45)

"Where there is Love, there is no hatred. Where there is no hatred, there is peace. We should propagate peace all over the world and it can be done only through love. What is love? Oneness of feeling is love. If you foster the feeling that the same Atma resides in all, you will be at peace." (SS99)

"Man strives for peace in many ways. Where is peace to be found? It is not in the external world. Peace must be found within. Outside, you have only pieces. You must seek to manifest the peace within you. There are millions in the world who preach and propagate what is good. But, not one in a hundred *practices* the good teachings. The world will pay no heed to those who do not practice what they preach." (SS99)

Master George had some interesting things to say about peace. One time, he told me in person, privately, right after we had seen a pretty bad program on television about Viet Nam: "I could be sitting in the middle of that battlefield, with the shells and bullets flying all around, and I would be at perfect peace." Another time, he told me, "Only through daily regular meditation will you find peace within." In a sermon in 1965, he said, "There will be no peace on earth as long as people eat meat." In a lecture in 1967, he said, "Only God can give you peace. You will always be restless within until you surrender to God within." One time, while talking with a few of us in 1970 about the Divine Mother, he said, "Be sure to always ask Divine Mother for direct experience of Her. Release all other prayers and desires. Ask only direct inner experience of Divine Mother and She will give you the peace you seek."

I can attest that these words are totally accurate. The only peace I have found is through meditation and helping others. When I meditate until I feel the joy of God, then and only then do I have peace within.

Human Actions

The most significant statement by a Master related to this topic is by Lord Krishna in the Bhagavad Gita: "Whatever actions you do, release the fruits of these actions to the Lord. Be even-minded in praise or blame, victory or defeat."

Sai Baba stated the following:

"God is the only 'Doer' of all acts and He is the only 'enjoyer' of all fruits. All acts are done by Him and all fruits go to Him. He is present everywhere and in everything as Atma." (SS29)

"It is essential to perform every action as an offering to God. The impulse for every action comes from the heart, whether the action is good or bad. The heart is the abode of the Lord. Hence, every thought arising from the heart and every action resulting from it should be regarded as an offering to the Divine." (SS62)

"Atma is the source of all action just as the current is the source of light. You are only instruments in the hands of God. God acts through you. And since He performs the actions, only He is entitled to enjoy the fruits of the actions." (SS71)

"Whatever things we do with this body are leading to a rebirth of this body. Any actions, good or bad, can be compared to seeds. In order not to sow seeds, we should do all actions without desire.

All actions should be done in and only for the pleasure of God." (SS35)

Master George had some unique views on actions:

"It is absolutely indispensable to work. Whoever you are, wherever you are, it is very important on the path to work." (He told us this in many ways over the years.)

In a talk given in 1972, he said, "Thoughts are just as important as outer actions. A person may have the nicest manners, be polite, and say good things, but if his thoughts are full of judgement of others, or if he is angry, or if he thinks himself above others, his good actions mean nothing."

One day, while we were working outside, building a building, he told me, "Whatever you do, dedicate it to God. It doesn't matter what you do (i.e., in the form of work) as long as you dedicate it to God and do it with love and willingness."

Many times he said in different ways, "Whatever you do, do it happily and in a good spirit."

What I have done over many years is try to practice the following: 1) I try my best to release the desire for the "fruits" of my actions. It is almost impossible, but I keep trying; 2) I try to dedicate everything I do to God, whatever job I am assigned. This is a little easier and I have been practicing at it for a long time; and 3) I try to remember that the saints and masters and sages all say that "God is the doer," and, of course, I forget and egotistically think that I am the doer and thereupon fall flat on my face.

Ahimsa (Non-Violence)

As per above, Jesus said the following:

"Ye have heard that it was said by them of old time, 'Thou shalt not kill and whosoever shall kill shall be in danger of the judgement.' But I say unto you, that whosoever is angry with his brother without a cause shall be in danger of the judgement." Also:

"Therefore, if you bring you gift to the alter and there you remember that your brother has a problem with you, then leave your gift before the altar, and go back to be first reconciled with your brother and then come and offer your gift" and "Ye have heard that it has been said, 'an eye for an eye, a tooth for a tooth.' I say to you, you should not resist evil, but whosoever smiteth thee on the right cheek, turn to him the other also and if a man will take your coat, give unto him your cloak as well, and whoever shall compel you to go a mile, go with him another mile, give to him that asks from you, and from him that would borrow from you, do not turn away from him" also "You have heard it said that you should love your neighbor and hate your enemy. But, I say unto you: Love your enemies, bless them that curse you, do good to them that hate you, and pray for them which despitefully use you and persecute you."

Sai Baba said the following related to Ahimsa:

"The meaning of 'ahimsa' is that either in thought, word, or deed, you should not cause harm to anybody." (SS55)

"When you realize that God is in everyone, you will practice non-violence." (SS99)

"Ahimsa really means that you should not cause harm to anyone through your vision, hearing or talking." (SS18)

Master George said to me one time, "You should be non-violent, but do *not* be a doormat."

Another time, he said that the real non-violence was having no anger, fear, judgement, or frustration with any other being. I remember him saying that, and thought about it for a long time. He told me this in the summer of 1970.

It has been a real challenge for me to be non-violent, especially with my thoughts. However, I give myself a good grade overall in this area. I have focused a lot of energy toward being non-violent. My biggest challenge is on the highway. I have been really working on gritting my teeth, and saying to myself, "They, too, are children of God."

Mahatma Gandhi stated the following:

"I have found that life persists in the midst of destruction. Therefore, there must be a higher

234

law than that of destruction. Only under that law would well-ordered society be intelligible and life worth living. It takes a fairly strenuous course of training to attain a mental state of nonviolence. It is a disciplined life, like that of a soldier. The perfect state is reached only when the mind, body, and speech are in proper coordination. Every problem would lend itself to solution if we determined to make the law of truth and nonviolence the law of life. Just as a scientist will work wonders out of various applications of the laws of nature, a man who applies the laws of love with scientific precision can work greater wonders. Nonviolence is infinitely more wonderful and subtle than forces of nature like, for example, electricity. The law of love is a far greater science than any modern science."

Animals

Swami Rama said the following about animals: "Animals are sometimes very perceptive, especially dogs. They imprint on humans for their evolution. However, remember that an animal is not a child!" (personal dialogue with his student, Dr. Justin O'Brien). Justin went on to say that Swami Rama always had a dog or more with him, and he could communicate with birds who "reported" to him. The following is a description by Swami Rama in his own words about an interaction with a tiger in the wilds of the Himalayas:

"Once I was traveling all alone in the Tarai Bhavar toward the mountains in Nepal. I was on my way to Katmandu, which I the capital of Nepal. I walked twenty to thirty miles each day. After sunset, I would build a fire, meditate, and then rest. I would begin walking again at four o'clock the next morning and walk until ten o'clock. Then I would sit near water under a tree through the middle part of the day, and travel again from 3:30 until 7:00 in the evening. I walked in my bare feet carrying a blanket, a tiger skin, and a pot of water.

"At about 6:00 one evening, I became tired and decided to take a short nap in a cave which was about two miles from the nearest road. I spread my blanket on the floor of the small cave because it was a little damp. As soon as I lay down and closed my eyes I was pounced on by three little tiger cubs who made gentle little cries and pawed at my body. They were hungry and thought that I was their mother. They must have been only twelve to fifteen days old. For a few minutes I lay there petting them. When I sat up, there was their mother standing at the entrance to the cave. First I thought she would rush in and attacked me, but then a strong feeling came from within. I thought, 'I have no intention to hurt these cubs. If she leaves the entrance of the cave, I will go out.' I picked up my blanket and pot of water. The mother backed off from the entrance and I went out. When I had gone about fifteen yards from the entrance, the mother tiger calmly went in to join her babies.

"Such experiences help one to control fear and give a glimpse of the unity that lies between animals and human beings. Animals can easily smell violence and fear. Then they become ferociously defensive. But when animals become friendly, they can be very protective and help human beings. One human being may desert another in danger, but animals rarely do so. The sense of self-preservation is of course very strong in all creatures, but animals are more dedicated lovers than human beings. Their friendship can be relied upon. It is unconditional, while relationships between people are full of conditions. We build walls around ourselves and lose touch with our own inner being and then with others. If the instinctive sensitivity for our relations to others is regained, we can become realized without much effort."

Sai Baba said the following about animals:

"Animals did not come for the purpose of supplying food to human beings. They came to work out their own life in the world." (SS19)

"The human form is unique in that divine force is as much as 80 percent present, whereas in the animal, only about 15 percent. Man can raise himself to union with God, whereas the animal can never be free of his natural state. The body of man is necessary because it is able to reveal the unseen God." (SS49)

"Love is present not only in human beings, but also in all creatures, birds or beasts. Nor is that all. It is in fact all-pervasive. Love pervades everything in creation. Man's humanness is vitiated when he fails to recognize this love." (SS99)

The following is one amazing story about Sai Baba and his elephant, Sai Gita. It was witnessed by hundreds of students at Swami's University, as well as many faculty members and local citizens. I will summarize it in my own words, having read about it and heard it verbally from a number of people.

Swami has his main headquarters in Puttaprthi, India at the ashram which is called Prasanthi Nilyam ("Abode of the Highest Peace"). On a semi-regular basis, he leaves for his other main ashram in Whitefield, a suburb of the big city of Bangalore. Whitefield is about 190 km away from Puttaparthi. There is always a lot of discussion on the ashram about when there are hints that Swami is going to be leaving for Whitefield. Especially for foreign devotees, who have come all the way to India to see Baba, it involves changing locations, travel, hotels, taxis, etc. Often, when Swami makes his move, it resembles a remarkable stampede of folks rolling down the road in taxis to Whitefield. I, myself, have done it a number of times. One time, we got advance knowledge, and were prepared with a taxi to follow right along with Swami's car.

This story occurred when Swami attempted to leave without any warning to go to Whitefield. After morning darshan and bhajans, he just got in his car and had his driver take off. They rolled down the main street of Puttaparthi heading for the highway. This route led them past the University on the right and the home of Sai Gita, Swami's

238

elephant on the right. As Swami's car slowly came down the road, many devotees and students raced out to the road to receive "car darshan," which we jokingly call the experience of connecting with Swami as he drives by. As Swami's car got to the stable of Sai Gita, suddenly she breached the wall, crushing it under foot, and came right out onto the road. Swami had his driver stop. Hundreds of students, faculty, and citizens surrounded his car and the elephant, and were amazed as they saw Sai Gita put her trunk right on the hood of the car! She wouldn't move. They all saw Swami get out and gently tell her that he was leaving for Whitefield. That didn't do any good. They saw great tears go down her face and trunk from her sad eyes. Swami patted her and talked to her some more. She just would not move. Finally, he relented, and asked her if she would feel better if he did not go that day. She immediately perked up and allowed Swami's car to turn around. After he returned to the ashram, she obediently and peaceably returned to her stable.

Master George said the following about animals:

In 1965, he told me "Animals take a lot of karma from humans. They can increase their evolution by their sacrifice and service in that manner."

When one of the members of his church wanted to get a dog or a cat for one of his kids, Dr. George advised him, "During the short time I have left to work with you on this earth, it would be better if you didn't have a pet in the house. They sometimes affect the vibrations and make it more difficult for you to meditate. On the other hand, if you want to get her a pet that would live outside the house, it would be beneficial for her to learn caring skills and responsibility." So, the family got a goat, who lived outside. It worked out well.

In 1966, Dr. George told me the following: "Worms are extremely important to the planet. Without them, there would be no soil. One time, I put myself into the consciousness of a worm. Those poor guys really work hard!"

In 1958, a young wolf came to The Farm. A number of devotees saw Dr. George go and talk with the wolf. He spoke with the wolf for a while. Then, the wolf left. Dr. George told the devotees, "He was a young wolf and got lost. I told him which way to go so he could find his pack."

At The Farm, there was a large king snake. King snakes are harmless to people, but are excellent "mousers." Normally, they are nocturnal. Dr. George told the snake to stay out of sight during the day, because he would scare the little kids, of which there were many at that time. One day, Dr. George sadly said that the snake would not listen to him and kept coming out and scaring the kids. The snake was never seen again.

Dr. George further stated that one significant difference between humans and animals is that humans have seven chakras, energy centers in the spine. These are key to spiritual advancement.

When I was a kid, we had an orphan dog, a big collie, named Pal, who adopted us. He actually was the neighborhood dog. He took care of all the kids in the neighborhood and was the local guard dog. He seemed to know exactly who belonged and who didn't. I had buddies ride their bicycles up to our house and Pal greeted them with great friendliness, and the mailman, milkman, etc., who were necessary folks, were respected by him. However, any suspected stranger had better beware. Pal could scare the socks off of him. One time, my uncle, aunt, and family came when we were not home. They laughed because they said Pal came running like he was going to tear them up, but stopped, sniffed a little, and then wagged his tail and waited to be patted. It is interesting the awareness animals have. We could have the same sensitivity if we weren't so engrossed in greed and ego.

Astrology

Sai Baba stated, "People should pray for the blessings of Divine Grace. They need not worry about the prospects in the new year (1995). With God's grace they can overcome any situation caused by planets. People always complain about planets. In fact, people are plagued by only two planets: egotism and possessiveness. To free themselves from those two, they need God's grace." (SS33)

Dr. George never said too much about astrology. One time, he said to me off-handedly after I read my horoscope in the newspaper, "There are very few folks on this planet who truly know

241

and understand astrology. Most of them are in the Himalayas."

Sri Yukteswar, the guru of Yogananda, said the following about astrology:

"Charlatans have brought the stellar science to its present state of disrepute. Astrology is too vast, both mathematically and philosophically, to be rightly grasped except by men of profound understanding. If ignoramuses misread the heavens, and see there a scrawl instead of a script, that is to be expected in this imperfect world. One should not dismiss the wisdom with the wise. All parts of creation are linked together and interchange their influences. The balanced rhythm of the universe is rooted in reciprocity."

"Astrology is the study of man's response to planetary stimuli. The stars have no conscious benevolence or animosity. They merely send forth positive and negative radiations. Of themselves, these do not help or harm humanity, but offer a lawful channel for the outward operation of cause-effect equilibriums which each man has set into motion in the past."

"A child is born on that day and at that hour when the celestial rays are in mathematical harmony with his individual karma. His horoscope is a challenging portrait, revealing his unalterable past and its probable future results. But the natal chart can be rightly interpreted only by men of intuitive wisdom: those are few." (1)

Yogananda said the following about astrology:

"My guru said, 'The deeper the self-realization of a man, the more he influences the whole universe by his subtle vibrations, and the less he himself is affected by the phenomenal flux.' These words of Master's often returned inspiringly to my mind.

"Occasionally, I told astrologers to select my worst periods, according to planetary indications, and I would still accomplish whatever task I set myself. It is true that my success at such times has been accompanied by extraordinary difficulties. But my conviction has always been justified; faith, in the divine protection, and the right use of man's God-given will, are forces formidable beyond any the bad astrology can muster." (1)

I have had my "western" astrology detailed chart done and had my "Vedic" astrology chart done over in India. They had one commonality: My job and interest this lifetime was God, seeking and knowing God. The rest of the stuff had huge differences in it. I have a little more confidence in the Vedic astrology.

The Atma

The great sage, Lahiri Mahasaya, who brought the knowledge of Kriya yoga from his great guru, Babaji in the Himalayas to mankind in the 19th century, demonstrated the meaning of the word *Atma* (also known as the Divine Spirit within all beings) in this unique manner in the words of Paramahansa Yogananda:

"One of my most precious possessions is a small photograph of Lahiri Mahasaya. This picture had a miraculous origin. It appears that the master had an aversion to being photographed. Over his protest, a group picture was once taken of him and a cluster of devotees. It was an amazed photographer who discovered that the plate, which had clear images of all the disciples, revealed nothing more than a blank space in the center where he had reasonably expected to find the outlines of Lahiri Mahasaya. The phenomenon was widely discussed.

"A certain student and expert photographer, Ganga Dhar Babu, boasted that the fugitive figure would not escape him. The next morning, as the guru sat in the lotus posture on a wooden bench with a screen behind him, Ganga Dhar Babu arrived with his equipment. Taking every precaution for success, he greedily exposed twelve plates. On each one, he soon found the imprint of the wooden bench and screen, but once again, the master's form was missing.

"With tears and shattered pride, Ganga sought out his guru. It was many hours before Lahiri Mahasaya broke his silence with a pregnant comment: "I am Spirit. Can your camera reflect the omnipresent Invisible?"

"Ganga replied, 'I see it cannot. but Holy Sir, I lovingly desire a picture of the bodily temple where alone, to my narrow vision, that Spirit appears fully to dwell.' The master kindly replied,

'Come then, tomorrow morning. I will pose for you.' The next day, the master posed as the photographer focused his camera. This time, the sacred figure was sharp on the plate. The master never posed for another picture." (1)

I have heard many stories in India about saints and masters who do not leave a shadow because, they, indeed are Spirit or the Atma. I remember the first time I felt free from the body. I had been meditating for weeks, seeking, asking, seeking, yearning for God. I was working out in the woods and just stood there to rest and I felt the shakti go up my spine, and I actually inwardly experienced that I was not the body, I am Spirit, the Atma.

Sai Baba said the following about our indwelling divinity:

"It is sheer foolishness on the part of man to identify himself with a house while he is only a simple resident in it. It is the same as identifying oneself with a car which one is driving. Similarly for the car of the human body, the Atma is the driver who operates the senses, the organs, etc. It is the Atma which makes the eyes see, the ears hear, and the hands work. It is the driver who forms the life of the car because he is the one who operates the different parts of the car and makes it run. Though the eyes, ears and other senses are very much existent in the body, they do not function once the Atma leaves the body. It only proves that Atma is the true master of the body. An earnest inquiry into the human system reveals that the different organs in the body are only instruments, the Atman is the master. The conglomeration of Minds, Buddhi (intelligence) and Samskara (tendency) is Atma." (SS99)

"You are the Atma, the Supreme Master. You have the potential to realize this through the discriminating power of the intellect. Once you recognize this truth, you will also understand the human nature, which is a combination of values like Truth, Righteousness, Peace, Love, and Non-violence and you will then rid your animal qualities. Then you will realize the cause of diseases and the method of curing them." (SS99)

"Atma is eternal. It cannot die or decay, diminish or disintegrate. Only those who have not realized the Atma principle suffer from the delusion that the body is themselves. Until then, even the most learned are led into that error. Being enamored of the body as if it is you is 'ignorance.' Being aware of the Atma, which you really are is 'wisdom.' Getting the knowledge of the Atma is as precious a piece of good luck as getting a diamond in the dust. The Atma is the gemstone embedded in this mass of flesh." (SSI8)

"The Divine Atma, which dwells in the heart of every human being, is not recognized by man because it is covered by the clouds of desire. The splendor of the sun is revealed when a wind drives away the clouds that hide the sun. Likewise, when the wind of love blows away the clouds of desire in the heart, the ego and possessiveness are driven out and the effulgence of the Atma within is revealed in all its glory." (SS25)

"The Atma is always content and blissful. The attachment to the Atma will not undergo any modifications; even when the senses and the body fail, the Atma will remain and infuse bliss. It is unlimited and indestructible." (SS50)

"Why fear when I am here. 'I am' refers to the Atma, who is always everywhere. The Atma is like the lion, without fear." (SS69)

"The Divine Atma, which dwells in the heart of every human being, is not recognized by man because it is covered by the clouds of desire. The splendor of the sun is revealed when a wind drives away the clouds that hide the sun. Likewise, when the wind of love blows away the clouds of desire in the heart, the ego and possessiveness are driven out and the effulgence of the Atma within is revealed in all its glory." (SS99)

Regarding the Atma, Dr. George usually referred to it as "the spirit within," "God within," "the Kingdom of Heaven," or "The Higher Self." He rarely if ever used the term, "Atma," to my knowledge. However, regarding "God within," et al, he had the following things to say:

"Man needs to ask himself, 'Who am I?' and seek that answer consciously in meditation within himself." (Informal talk in September, 1965 at The Farm.)

"God is within you; He is your own Higher Self. It is your principal duty on Earth as a human to realize this and to experience this divinity within. There is no higher duty." (Sermon, on a Tuesday in October, 1976 at the church.)

"Do not ever forget that YOU are the divinity, not the body, not the ego, not the personality, but the *real you*, clouded by delusion of many lifetimes of mistakes and troubles. Do not forget who you are!" (Sermon, church, 1972.)

In a sermon on Tuesday night in 1968, Dr. George said, "It is essential that man (i.e., humans) realize consciously inwardly that they are *Spirit*, and are not the ego or the body."

He said a number of times, "Yogananda said that if you do not have a guru in the outer, the Atma within will guide you."

In 1972, he told me, "Remember: God is not a gray-bearded old guy out there some place. He/She is Spirit and *you* are spirit! Be and experience your omnipresence."

I remember clearly my first experience in omnipresence and the actual inner consciousness that I was not the body and was spirit. It was in the Fall of 1965 and I was walking to my car after working sewer/water construction one day. Earlier, one of the tough guys on the crew had pulled a nasty on me, and instead of fighting, I inwardly forgave him and sent him love. I ignored him outwardly, and kept sending him love. He calmed down and actually in a clumsy way tried to amend his ways.

As I walked, suddenly, my entire being was filled with light and love. I had to stop walking on that Milwaukee street. I felt like I was light as a feather and I felt Dr. George and Jesus come to me in a huge blue friendly light. The real me was huge, omnipresent, beyond the body and thoughts. As I came down, I experienced great joy, better joy than I ever had. I floated home.

Avatars

Dr. Justin O'Brien (Swami Rama's disciple) said that Swami Rama said the following about avatars: "There are eras when avatars will show up on earth, usually when humanity is in dire straits and needs such incarnations badly."

Yogananda said the following about Avatars:

"The characteristic features of Indian culture have long been a search for ultimate verities and the concomitant disciple-guru relationship. My own path led me to a Christ like sage whose beautiful life was chiseled for the ages. He was one of the great Masters (avatars) who are India's sole remaining wealth. Emerging in every generation, they have bulwarked the fate of Babylon and Egypt." (1))

"The Northern Himalayan crags near Badrinarayan are still blessed by the living presence of Babaji, guru of Lahiri Mahasaya. The secluded master has retained his physical form for centuries, perhaps for millenniums. The deathless Babaji is an *avatar*. This Sanskrit term means *decent*. In the Hindu scriptures, avatar signifies the descent of divinity into flesh." (1)

"The great guru (Lahiri Mahasaya) saw in silence most of the time, locked in the tranquil lotus posture. He seldom left his little parlor, even for a walk or to visit other parts of the house. A quiet stream of *chelas* [devotees] arrived, almost ceaselessly, for a darshan of the guru.
To the awe of all beholders, Lahiri Mahasaya's habitual physiological state exhibited the superhuman features of breathlessness, sleeplessness, cessation of pulse and heartbeat., calm eyes unblinking for hours, and a profound aura of peace. No visitors departed without upliftment of spirit; all knew they had received the silent blessing of a true man of God." (1)

Sai Baba said the following:

"The word Avatar means 'descent.' It is the descent of God on the earth in human form. Its purpose is to establish Dharma, the supreme Law of rightcousness in the world again and again. There are two aspects of the Divine birth. One is the descent that is the birth of God in humanity. Another is the ascent that is the birth of man into the Godhead or rising into the Divine nature or consciousness. The supreme Divinity resides in the heart of everyone and yet concealed from us by the *yogayama* (maya or delusion). The Divine birth is different from ordinary birth. The God-head takes birth through his own maya. The God dwells in and yet stands upon and over Nature as its Lord and Master. That is the special feature of an Avatar." (SS34)

"God is like an airplane flying in the sky. When there is a need in this world for an avatar the plane lands, picks up the passengers, namely those who are spiritually prepared and goes back again. I am an Avatar in human form If I came as *Naryana* (God), people would be afraid of me. You see, God is the seed, the original seed of all creation. God resides in all beings and all things. My job as an avatar is to help all people realize and experience this." (SS8)

Dr. George told me in 1965 that there were four avatars on the earth. He said that when there were 12, the world would change. Sai Baba stated at one time that there are now 12 avatars on earth! Maybe there is some hope.

Dr. George told me that his guru, Paramahansa Yogananda was an avatar. George said that he (Yogananda) was an "Avatar of Love." Dr. George verified that Sai Baba was also an avatar. However, he said that Sai Baba was a "cosmic" avatar and the highest being to come to earth.

Dr. George would not say anything about himself, other than the following mysterious comment: "I knew who I was when I was being born. At first, I resisted, but then I knew I was coming to be with Yogananda, and I agreed."

I have been so lucky this lifetime. I have actually met and known two avatars and two great masters, namely Sai Baba and Swami Vishwananda, and Dr. George and Swami Rama.

Birth as a Human

Sai Baba said the following:

"All at birth are pure and innocent. But as they grow, they develop arrogance, pride and ostentation. But, this is not proper. People should cultivate humility and discipline, which are the hallmark of humanness." (SS33)

"You have been born because you did not pass in certain subjects. There is some balance of experience which you must acquire to complete the course. If you become convinced through Self-realization that your true nature is Supreme Consciousness, then you have finished the course. You have passed." (SS62)

"Whatever is born is destined to die. However, today, human beings want to find a reason for death, but they are not wanting to know the reason for birth. We always ask why and how one has died, but we do not ask why one is born. As we do not know the cause of one's death, we also do not know the cause of one's birth. For superficial purposes, we think that one has died because of an accident of or sickness. This is not so. For death, birth alone is responsible. If we recognize that birth is the reason for death, we will not feel sorry for death. Of all the fears of man, the fear of death is the strongest as well as the most foolish. After all, none can escape death, having committed the error of birth. TO get rid of the wheel of birth and death, awareness of the undying unborn Self which is one's reality is the only method available to man." (SS3)

"A human birth is the most sacred one among the 84 lakhs (840,000) of different living beings in this creation. To attain such a sacred birth is a great fortune, indeed." (SS3)

"Having taken birth thousands and thousands of scores of times (billions), finally, as a result of the accumulated merits, at some time, the being gets the human birth. Having obtained the human birth (which is difficult to get and which is the major step toward liberation), who is more sinful than him who does not uplift himself and seek Divine Realization." (SS29)

Dr. George said the following about human birth:

"Human birth is priceless. Each person should use this birth to realize God within." (lecture)

"Man evolved from the rock, to low-grade plant, to higher grade plant, to living cells, to low grade animals, to higher grade animals, and then to being humans. Our next step in evolution is Christ Consciousness. Jesus, Buddha, Krishna, Sai Baba, and Yogananda set examples of what we are going to be." (personal conversation)

"We are evolving to divinity." (He told me this personally in 1964.)

"They should celebrate when a person dies and mourn when he is born." (He told me that often.)

"When you die, unless you are liberated, you will be born again, under the setting and terms and conditions that are best for your growth." (He told us this at The Farm in personal dialogue.)

Sri Yukteswar, the great guru of Yogananda, said the following on this subject, p. 177, *Autobiography of a Yogi*:

"The Book of Genesis in the Bible is deeply symbolic and cannot be grasped by literal interpretation. Its 'tree of life' is the human body. The spinal cord is like an upturned tree, with man's hair as its roots and afferent and efferent nerves as branches. The tree of the nervous system bears many enjoyable fruits, or sensations of sight, sound, smell, taste, and touch. In these, man may rightfully indulge; but he was forbidden the experience of sex, the 'apple' at the center of the 'bodily garden'.

"The serpent represents the coiled-up spiritual energy which stimulates the sex nerves. 'Adam' is reason and 'Eve' is feeling. When the emotion or Eve-consciousness, in any human being (i.e., man or woman) is overpowered by the sex impulse, his/her reason or Adam also succumbs.

God created the human species by materializing the bodies of man and woman through the force of his will. He endowed the new species with the power to create children in a similar 'immaculate' or divine manner. Because his manifestation in the individualized soul had hitherto been limited to animals, instinct-bound and lacking the potentialities of full reason, God made the first human bodies, symbolically called Adam and Eve. TO these, for advantageous upward evolution, He transferred the souls or divine essence of two animals. In Adam or man, reason predominated. In Eve or woman, feeling was ascendant. Thus was expressed the duality or polarity which underlies the phenomenal worlds. Reason and feeling remain in a heaven of cooperative joy so long as the human mind is not tricked by the serpentine energy of animal propensities.

"The human body was therefore not solely a result of evolution from beasts, but was produced by an act of special creation by God. The animal forms were too crude to express full divinity. The human being was uniquely given a tremendous mental capacity...the 'thousand-petal lotus' of the brain, as well as acutely awakened occult centers (Chakras) in the spine.

"God, or the Divine Consciousness present within the first created pair, counseled them to enjoy all human sensibilities, but not to put their concentration on the touch sensations. These were banned to avoid the development of the sex organs which would enmesh humanity in the inferior animal method of propagation. The warning not to revive subconsciously-present bestial memories was not heeded. Resuming the way of brute procreation, Adam and Eve fell from the state of heavenly joy natural to the original perfect human.

"Knowledge of good and evil' refers to the cosmic dualistic compulsion. Falling under the swam of Maya through misuse of feeling and reason, humans relinquish their right to enter the heavenly garden of divine self-sufficiency. The personal responsibility of every human being is to restore their 'parents' or dual nature to a unified harmony or 'Eden.'" (1)

The preceding was extremely interesting to me. Yukteswar is indeed a deep philosopher. I recommend that everyone gets Yukteswar's book, *The Holy Science*. It is a fascinating short book.

Chakras

Sai Baba said the following things about Chakras:

"The Chakras are situated in the brain and the spinal cord which are within the skull and vertebral column. If there is a damage to a particular region in the brain or the spinal cord, the sensory and motor nerves concerned with this region are affected and weakness and sensory loss occur at the corresponding peripheral areas of the body. Therefore by imagining the chakras at these peripheral areas, one is actually thinking of the chakras in the spinal column." (SS48)

"The stage of desire operates in the first two chakras, the stage of endeavor in the nest two and the stage of awareness is most evident in the last two. The awareness is there, latent in everyone, ready to surface when the veils of ignorance are removed. The individual life-force resides like a lightning flash in the womb of a blue cloud between the ninth and twelfth rings of the spinal column. It will be alert and awake only when sadhana (spiritual practices) of any type is done after the cleansing of character and habits." (SS7)

Master George said the following related to Chakras:

"Man has seven centers in his spine and two more in his astral body above his head." (personal talk)

"It is very important to concentrate on your heart chakra when you chant and sing to God." (He told me this in 1964.)

"When you meditate, lift your energies to your crown chakra." (He told us this in 1970 at The Farm.)

"The significant difference between humans and animals is the seven chakras in the human spine." (a regular statement of his)

I truly recommend the Science of Kriya Yoga, and get training from either SRF or Ananda Village (both listed in the back of this book).

Compassion

Sai Baba had plenty to say about compassion:

"The one whose heart is full of compassion, whose words are steeped in love and whose body is used in the service of fellow men is neither affected by evil powers, nor by the adverse influence of the age of Kali." (SS26)

"People start crying when they watch someone suffering in a cinema. But when they come across a person suffering in real life, they make fun of such people. IS this a human quality? No! Kindness must be extended in all places. Today, lack of compassion has become the fashion of the day. Man belongs to mankind, but he does not have kindness. A man without kindness is no man at all! We have to develop such kindness and compassion." (Speech given at the Ashram, Feb. 17, 1996.)

"Compassion is when love is mobile and flows. Personal love is when love is not mobile, but remains fixed on husband, wife, child, etc." (SS9)

Master George talked about compassion nearly every time he spoke. He lived and showed his compassion to all beings all the time. Looking into his eyes, you knew he cared and knew he would do anything to help you to become free from this earth of pain and misery. He helped us work out our past karma all the time. He told me many times, related to working out karma, "You do some, the guru does some, and God does the rest."

Undoubtedly, the greatest visible example we have ever seen right in front of us on television was the life and work of Mother Therese, the great Catholic saint from Albania who lived and worked in the worst horrific parts of India to give simple compassion to the lowest of the low.

Another remarkable example of compassion (and wisdom) was the former U.S. Secretary of State, George C. Marshall. In the history of warfare, there was only one case of the victor rebuilding the defeated. This was called The Marshall Plan, which rebuilt Germany and Japan after World War II.

One of the greatest public gifts to mankind came during the worst of the fighting in World War I. At Christmas, spontaneously, troops of the British and the German armies came out of their trenches, exchanged gifts, sang hymns, and prayed together. They knew they were brothers. Of course, once the commanding generals of both armies heard about this, they shut it up in a hurry and made sure that they demonized the enemy so their troops would forget about this brotherhood stuff and get back to killing.

Sai Baba and Yogananda, as children, would give away the family larders to feed homeless beggars, often to the chagrin of their fathers. Jesus' entire life was a manifestation of compassion. Sai Baba extolled the life of Mother Therese many, many times. He told many Indian people that he wished they could be like her.

My mother taught me by example. She had one very unique quality: She had a sincere happiness in someone else's good fortune. Even when she was paralyzed for 27 years and in great pain, she exhibited this noble quality. I have met few people who did this. Thus, I try every day to emulate and follow that teaching. One thing: It makes you happy.

Consciousness

Sai Baba also has spoken a lot about consciousness:

"Stillness and Silence mean the nature of Pure Consciousness. He who has reached it will be in the highest peace and highest bliss. Pure Consciousness is Truth, Wisdom, and Bliss." (SS26)

"Supreme Consciousness is the ocean, nature is just a wave of that vast ageless and boundless ocean…and the individualized soul is just a drop of that wave. You cannot give up the wave or the sea. You can only merge, leaving the name and form to drop off. Once you enter the depths of the sea, it is all calm, it is all peace; agitation, noise, confusion all are only on the outer layers." (SS4)

"When you have achieved the consciousness that God is in you, with you, for you, that awareness must reshape every thought, word and deed, and make you wish good, speak good, and do good." (SS46)

Paramahansa Yogananda stated the following about consciousness:

"If you keep your brain, your mind, your body filled with happy memories, the greatest good of all, GOD, will come and remain with you. Remembering only the good experiences of the past, you shall eventually remember your oneness with Spirit. You will remember that you have come down from Spirit into this flesh, into this little cage of bones which is a prison of disease and trouble. Get away from the mortal consciousness. Remember in meditation that you are one with the vast spirit." (Talk at the Hollywood Temple, September, 1943.)

"We are in a dream state. The only way to wake up is to refuse to recognize anything as reality except God. Otherwise, you will again and again sink to your knees in a mud of suffering that is of your own making, until you realize that neither good fortune nor evil fortune is real, that He alone is real. Only he is wise who lives in constant remembrance of God. To think of Him always is to find freedom from this earthly dream of birth and death." (Talk at SRF Headquarters, December, 1939.)

Master George said the following:

"Everything is consciousness. There is consciousness in everything."

"Be conscious of God within you. Be conscious of spirit. Be conscious of Love and Joy." (Also a regular statement of his.)

"Even rocks have Consciousness." (He told me this one time when we were digging a well and had to move a large rock.)

"Many animals are aware of a lot of things which humans are not aware of. Trees, also, have great consciousness. There is even competition among trees." (He told me this in 1967.)

"Raise your consciousness as often as you can to God. Repeat God's name in your subconscious all the time. Be aware of God within. Look for miracles and manifestations." (He spoke these words in a sermon in 1972.)

I saw Dr. Cleve Baxter in Toronto in 1974. He wrote about awareness in plants and had developed sophisticated lie detector equipment for the FBI, CIA, and the Defense Department. He attached the electrodes to plants and did amazing experiments. Here are some of them that I remember from his talk:

Six scientists were in a room with a big plant and electrodes attached to it. One of the scientists came over and snipped a leaf from the plant in half with a pair of scissors. The plant, as manifested through the aforementioned lie detector equipment went ballistic. The scientists were shocked. The next morning, as they entered the lab, one by one, no reaction, until the scientist who had actually done the cutting came in, and the plant went off again!

In another experiment, they tried different types of music. The plants thrived with the classics, soft jazz, and simple folk music. They were OK with many 50's and some 60's rock and roll. However, they really suffered with what we would call acid rock, metallic rock, or hard rock. One of the scientists who conducted the experiment said it had to do with the underlying chords as well as the medium of performance. He said that some chords are consonant with the universe. The results of this experiment were that Mozart, Handel, and Bach were the most beneficial to plants. Also, simple folk songs with a guitar and singer were good, as well. (I can imagine what a plant would do with Rap and Hip Hop!)

Dr. Baxter told about their experiments with thoughts and kindly words to plants. Plants, without exception, responded positively to loving thoughts, kind words, and encouragement.

Dr. George told me that trees work exceptionally hard. He also explained to me how trees were sometimes in competition with each other. He said over and over that trees were mankind's best friend. It makes me spitting mad to see how the big corporations rape and plunder the forests of the world to increase their bottom lines. If it wasn't for the courageous efforts of some environmentalists, America would be denuded of trees like India and other places.

Death
Sai Baba has had much to say about death:

"Death is but a passage from this life to the next; it is the change from old clothes to new, as the Gita says. But some cynics laugh at this comparison and ask, what about the death of new-born infants, children, youths, and middle-aged persons? Their bodies cannot by any stretch of meaning be classified as worn out! Well, the clothes might not be old, but the cloth out of which they were made must have been from very old stock, so that though new clothes were prepared out of it, they had to be discarded soon." (SS10)

"Our body is transient like a water-bubble, but life is a long journey. In this long journey, we change our bodies many a time, as we change our dress. In fact, death is nothing but a change of dress"! (SS63)

"Life is eternally stalked by death, but man does not like to hear this. It is considered bad luck to even hear the word, even though every living thing is every moment, proceeding nearer and nearer to that event." (SS50)

"If you are asked, what happens to man after death, you can point to yourselves and declare: 'This is what happens, they are born again" (SS43)

"It does not matter how long each one lives. Everyone must leave his body sometime or other. It is very necessary that so long as we live in this body, we use the available time for understanding God." (SS8)

Master George spoke about death quite a bit:
"Yeah, some people think that Gabriel is going to Toot-toot on his horn and all the corpses are going to rise up out of the graves and start dancing." Then he laughed uproariously. (He told my mother and me that in 1970.)

"There is absolutely no reason to fear death. All of you have died many, many times. When you die, just be sure to call on your guru. Also, try to leave the body consciously, try to be thinking of God when you die. That is why all the masters and saints have always recommended constant repetition of the name of God, because you never know when you will die." (Sermon, 1966.)

"Dying is easy. Living is hard." (Both Dr. George and Clint Eastwood said these words. Clint said them as Josey Wales in his great western, *The Outlaw Josie Wales*.)

"When you die, you go to where your consciousness is. If you do not have heaven in your heart and mind and soul right now, you won't have it after you die." (He told me this in 1977.)

"Everyone thinks that Jesus will save them from their sins. He never said that. He said that if you forgive and serve others, then you will be forgiven. However, most people have a whole lot more karma from many past lives and it will take more than a few lifetimes to work out all that karma." (He told me this in 1965.)

"When you pass away, most of the time you will be met by loved ones with whom you are familiar. You will go to a level which you have earned and which is consonant with your spiritual development." (He said these words, or similar, many times.)

"Laugh at death. Death often is your best friend. Be happy for those who pass away from this plane of tears. They have a time of happiness and peace until they have to come back here." (He said these words to a group of us at The Farm after a devotee passed away in 1971.)

Those words were most exemplified by Dr. George's great guru, Paramahansa Yogananda, when, after his passing in 1952, his body remained uncorrupted after his death and he physically manifested to a number of devotees after his death. Here is the story as told by Yogananda's disciple and great spiritual teacher, Swami Kriyananda (Donald Walters) in his book, *The Path*:

"One of the first proofs we received of our guru's victory over death came from Forest Lawn Memorial-Park, in Glendale, CA, where the casket that contained his body was kept unsealed for twenty days pending the arrival of two disciples from India. On May 15th of that year, Mr. Harry T. Rowe sent Self-Realization Fellowship a notarized letter: 'The absence of any visual signs of decay in the dead body of Paramahansa Yogananda offers the most extraordinary case in our experience...No physical disintegration was visible...This state of perfect preservation of a body is, so far as we know from mortuary annals, an unparalleled one....The appearance of Yogananda on March 27th, just before the bronze cover of the casket was put into position, was the same as it had been on March 7th. He looked on March 27th as fresh and as unravaged by decay as he had looked on the night of his death.'"

"The casket was closed after twenty days when word came that the two Indian disciples would be unable to make the journey. Later one of them reported that Master (Yogananda), after his *mahasamdhi* (a yogi's conscious exit from the body), had appeared to him *in his physical form* and embraced him lovingly.

"Norman (another disciple) had a similar experience. 'I was lying in bed one night,', he told me, 'when the door suddenly flew open. Master walked in, just as plain and as solid as I see you now. He gave me a few strong words of advice, then left. The door, which he never touched, closing behind him.

"Daya Mata (the long-time head of Yogananda's organization) tells of how Master appeared to her in his physical form, years, I believe, after his *mahasamadhi,* when she faced a serious decision in the work. 'I touched his feet,' she says. 'They were as solid as my own. Though he said nothing, I understood his meaning as clearly as though he had spoken.'"

"I have told earlier the story of Master's appearance also, and warning to Professor Novicky in Prague, Czechoslovakia, when a communist informer tried to get him to betray his interest in yoga.

"Most of us were, for a time, grief-stricken at Master's passing. But Mrs. Royston told me of going one day with a few of the nuns to his crypt at Forest Lawn. 'The others were standing in front of the crypt,' she said, 'weeping, but I didn't at all feel we'd lost him. I called to him silently. Suddenly, I knew he was standing beside me. I felt rather than saw him, but I heard him quite distinctly, "I'm not in there! he exclaimed.' It seemed to surprise him that disciples, schooled in his teachings, should be devoting so much attention to his mere body!"

"One disciple, disconsolate for weeks after Master's passing, received a telephone call from Rajasi Janakananda (James Lynn, Yogananda's foremost disciple, who was a self-realized being, himself) in Encinitas. 'I didn't realize you were suffering,' he told her, gently. 'Master appeared to me last night and asked me to comfort you. He said to tell you that you *must* be happy...he is always with you."

I can attest that Master also appeared to Dr. George in his astral form after his death, and for many years thereafter. Dr. George explained to me that he saw Yogananda very clearly and heard him, but it was not his solid physical body, it was more ephemeral.

I think the reason he said that is because many times since his passing he has appeared to me the same way. Unfortunately, I have a difficult time hearing his words; I am not so developed. I feel his love and joy and presence, so that's pretty good.

Yogananda said the following: "Laugh at maya...earthly life as a delusion...Watch life as a cosmic motion picture, then I cannot work its delusive on you anymore. Be in God-bliss. When you can stand unshaken amidst the crash of breaking worlds, you shall know that God is real. He doesn't mean to hurt you. He has made you in His image. He has made you already what He is...That is what you do not realize, because you acknowledge only that you are a human being...you do not know that this thought is a delusion." (Talk in Los Angeles in June of 1949.)

Dr. George told me that Yogananda told him personally: "Right now, you are playing a part in God's great drama. One of these days, you will go backstage for a 'costume change' and come back for a different role. You may play a hero or villain, you may play in a tragedy or a comedy or an epic. The important point is to play your role as well as you can, while not being attached to it."

As I have written about, I have had two experiences with death or near-death. Also, when I meditate, I feel liberated from this body and have had many, many experiences over the years related to the unreality of death. My mom, my dad, my sister, Dr. George, Yogananda, and others have come to me many times, very real, and very loving. I can feel as clear as a bell the connection. For those of you who have loved ones who passed on, you should get quiet and receptive and ask for them to come. They certainly will. It is true that they are standing right by your side.

Also, there are many qualified and good clairvoyants in human form now who are gifted and can "bring in" your loved ones and get messages for you from them. Let me tell you a few stories:

My dad passed on in 2000. He was a real character in life and had a gregarious spirit, and was also a professional gambler in his younger days.

One day, some people were threatening me in a business transaction. It was very stressful. I prayed and meditated, but was still unsettled. I called a good friend of mine, Judy Boss, in St. Paul, Minnesota, who is a remarkable clairvoyant. I told her about my situation and she "tuned in." She said, "I see your dad here. He is smoking his pipe and chuckling. He says, 'They're bluffing!' I laughed out loud. I could actually feel my dad's presence, but couldn't hear his words like Judy. I thanked her and immediately called my attorney and we called their bluff and they folded quickly. "Nice try," I thought after we rectified things, and thanks Judy and thanks to my dad.

One time, I was on the road playing music at a fair in the early 1970's. For a period of weeks, I had been thinking steadily of Yogananda. I reminded him that he had passed away when I was only eight years old and never had a chance to meet him in the physical. Every day when I meditated, I called on him and asked to be able to see him just as he was in the body. Some weeks passed and I was on stage, picking my banjo, and suddenly, there in front of my spiritual vision, were Dr. George and Yogananda, clear as a bell! I studied him as I saw him. He was smiling, silent and smiling. Somehow, my subconscious kept me picking the banjo in the key of "G." Then, my concentration wavered, and I was back there on stage, picking in the key of "G." I had forgotten what song I was singing, so I quickly thought of one in the key of "G" and finished it up and got off stage. Thanks, Yogananda and Dr. George.

When I first met my long-time partner, Jannie Williams, I was significantly impressed by her remarkable and unique psychic abilities. Both Judy (Jannie's sister) and Jannie have at their core a total dedication to God and lack of ego related to their gifts, as well as a sincere desire to serve and help others, with no thought for themselves. Both of them should receive heavenly "medals" for sharing their gift so graciously with those of us who are not so gifted. One day, Jannie and I were sitting, meditating and praying. Suddenly, Jannie said, "Your friend Jerry is here from the other side." I thought, "Jerry? Jerry who?" She answered my thoughts: "He says his name is Jerry Smith and you went to high school with him. He says he was killed in Viet Nam." Well, that was all true, and I was totally flabbergasted and shocked. There was no human way Jannie could have known that. I asked him how he was, and he told us that he was working with a group on the Other Side who helped soldiers killed in battle find their way on the Other Side. As we have learned since, many young men, who are killed in battle or in an accident, are sometimes totally disoriented and cannot find their way on the Other Side. They are often angry about being dead, once they realize they are dead, and they are so shocked to go from the fullness of youth into an after-life state. I asked Jerry how we could help and he said, "I can see a lot of your past lives. You were a solider and warrior many times and you have a great sympathy for soldiers. I can also see that you and your partner are very connected to various Great Ones. We need yours and their help. If you so volunteer, I will come to you and bring you souls who need a lot of help." So, for a while thereafter, Jerry would bring us souls in the spirit world to bless and help. We asked Dr. George, Yogananda, and Sai Baba to help them. In specific, we asked that they learn how to forgive so they could go on. We found out that if you have not forgiven your enemies on Earth, you have not escaped anything at death. You are still stuck with them and the lack of forgiveness in your heart, which greatly restricts you on the Other Side.

My sister Gail has come to me regularly over the years, especially when I am having difficulties. Her presence is always very comforting and very friendly. She is such a great being and good friend.

In my early days of meditation, I always felt a very friendly Indian chief next to me in the Spirit. I did not find out until many years later, with the help of a number of clairvoyants, that said Chief was Sitting Bull. I have a strong connection with him from the past and he is always there for me on the inner plane. It is good to have friends in high places!

Lahiri Mahasaya said the following: "Always remember that you belong to no none, and no one belongs to you. Reflect that someday you will suddenly have to leave everything in this world-so make the acquaintanceship of God now. Prepare yourself for the coming astral journey of death by daily riding in the balloon of God-perception. Through delusion, you are perceiving yourself as a bundle of flesh and bones, which at best is a nest of troubles. Meditate unceasingly, that you may quickly behold yourself as the Infinite Essence, free from every from of misery. Cease being a prisoner of the body, using the secret key of Kriya (i.e., Kriya Yoga), learn to escape into the Spirit." (1)

The Resurrection of Sri Yukteswar

Yogananda's guru, Sri Yukteswar, passed away on March 9, 1936 while Yogananda was in India. Sometime later, Yogananda goes on to describe the resurrection of Yukteswar:

"Sitting on my bed in a Bombay hotel at 3:00 P.M. on June 19, 1936. I was roused from my meditation by a beatific light. Before my open and astonished eyes, the whole room was transformed into a strange world, the sunlight transmuted into supernal splendor. Waves of rapture engulfed me as I beheld the flesh and blood form of Sri Yukteswar!

"My son!" Master spoke tenderly, on his face an angelic bewitching smile.

For the first time in my life I did not kneel at his feet in greeting but instantly advanced to gather him hungrily in my arms. Moment of moments! The anguish of past moths was toll I

274

counted weightless against the torrential bless now descending.

"Is it *you,* Master, the same Lion of God? Are you wearing a body like the one I buried beneath the cruel Puri sands?"

"Yes, my child, I am the same. This is a flesh and blood body. Though I see it as ethereal, to your sight it is physical. From the cosmic atoms, I created an entirely new body, exactly like that cosmic-dream physical body which you laid beneath the dream-sands at Puri in your dream-world. I am in truth resurrected-not on earth, but on an astral planet. Its inhabitants are better able than earthly humanity to meet my lofty standards. There, you and your exalted loved ones shall someday come to be with me."

"Deathless Guru, tell me more," I said.

"As prophets are sent on earth to help men work out their physical karma, so I have been directed by God to serve on an astral planet as a savior," Yukteswar explained. "It is called Hiranyloka, or 'Illumined Astral Planet.' There I am aiding advanced beings to rid themselves of astral karma and thus attain liberation from astral rebirths. The dwellers on Hiranyloka are highly developed spiritually; all of them had acquired, in their last earth-incarnation, the meditation-given power of consciously leaving their physical bodies at death. No one can enter Hiranyloka unless he has passed on earth beyond the state of *sabikalpa Samadhi* into the higher state of *nirbikalpa Samadhi*.

"You have read in the scriptures that God encased the human soul successively in three bodies-the idea, or causal body, the subtle astral body, seat of man's mental and emotional natures; and the gross physical body. On earth, a person is equipped with his physical senses. An astral being works with his consciousness and feelings and a body made of 'lifetrons' (i.e., conscious prana or life energy). A causal-bodied being remains in the blissful ream of ideas. My work is with those astral beings who are preparing to enter the causal world."

"Great Master," I said, "please tell me more about the astral cosmos."

He said, "There are many astral planets, teeming with astral beings. The inhabitants use astral planes, or masses of light to travel from one planet to another, faster than electricity and radioactive energies. The astral universe, made of various subtle vibrations of light and color, is hundreds of times larger than the material cosmos. The entire physical creation hangs like a little solid basket under the huge luminous balloon of the astral sphere. Just as many physical suns and stars roam in space, so there are also countless astral solar and stellar systems. Their planets have astral suns and moons, more beautiful than the physical ones. The astral luminaries resemble the aurora borealis – the sunny astral aurora being more dazzling than the mild-rayed moon aura. The astral day and night are longer than those of earth.

"The astral world is infinitely beautiful, clean, pure, and orderly. There are no dead planets or barren lands. The terrestrial blemishes-weeds, bacteria, insects, snakes-are absent. Unlike the variable climates and seasons of the earth, the astral

276

planets maintain the even temperature of an eternal spring with occasional luminous white snow and rain of many-colored lights. Astral planets abound in opal lakes and bright seas and rainbow rivers.

"The astral universe, not the subtler astral heaven, Hiranyloka, is peopled with millions of astral beings who have come from human life on earth, as well as countless other beings. They all reside in different astral planets in accordance with karmic qualifications. Various spheric mansions or vibratory regions are provided for good and evil spirits. Good ones can travel freely, but the evil spirits are confined to limited zones. In the same way that human beings live on the surface of the earth, worms inside the soil, fish in water, and birds in air, so astral beings of different grades are assigned to suitable vibratory quarters.

"In the vast realms above the dark astral prison for evil-doers, all is shining and beautiful. The astral cosmos is more naturally attuned than the earth to the divine will and plan of perfection. Every astral object is manifested primarily by the will of God, and partially by the will-call of astral beings. They possess the power of modifying or enhancing the grace and form of anything already created by the Lord. He has given His astral children the freedom and privilege of changing or improving at will the astral cosmos. On earth, a solid must be transformed into liquid or other forms through natural or chemical processes, but astral solids are changed into astral liquids, gases, or energy solely and instantly by the will of the inhabitants.

"The earth is dark with warfare and murder in the sea, land and air. But the astral realms know a happy harmony and equality.

"The astral body is an exact counter part of the last physical form. Astral beings retain the same appearance which they possessed in youth in their previous earthly sojourn.

"In order to please his beloved devotees, the Lord takes on any desired form. If the devotee worshipped through devotion, he sees God as Divine Mother. To Jesus, the Father aspect of the Infinite One was appealing beyond other conceptions. The individuality with which the creator had endowed each of his creatures makes every conceivable and inconceivable demand on the Lord's versatility." My Guru and I laughed happily together.

"Communication among the astral inhabitants is held entirely by astral telepathy and television. There is none of the confusion and misunderstanding of the written and spoken word which earth-dwellers must endure.

"The earth-liberated astral being meets a multitude of relatives, fathers, mothers, wives, husbands, and friends, acquired during different incarnations on earth, as they appear from time to time in various parts of the astral realms. The person is therefore at a loss to understand whom to love especially; he learns in this way to give a divine and equal love to all, as children and individualized expressions of God. Though the outward appearance of loved ones may have changed, more or less according to the development of new qualities in the latest life of any particular soul, the astral being employs his intuition to recognize all those once dear to him in other planes of existence." (1)

Yukteswar goes on to explain that physical desires rooted in egoism and sense pleasure entrap earth beings. Likewise, on a higher level, astral desires include the music of the spheres, light, changing lights, and the power to precipitate all objects and experiences as forms of light. Once free from the astral worlds, the causal beings are infinitely more subtle. However, they too seek liberation into the Infinite Ocean of Bliss, which is our final destination, for all of us!

Desires

Jesus said the following in Matthew:

"Blessed are the poor in spirit, for theirs is the Kingdom of Heaven."

"Lay up yourself not treasures upon this earth, where moths and rust doth corrupt, and where thieves break through and steal. But lay up for yourselves treasures in heaven, where neither moth nor rust doth corrupt and where thieves do not break through and steal" and "No man can serve two masters; you cannot serve God and worldly desires."

"Therefore, I say unto you, take no thought for your life, what you shall eat, nor yet for your body, what you shall put on. Is not the life more than meat and the body more than raiment? Behold the fowls of the air, for they sow not neither do they reap, nor gather into barns, yet your heavenly Father feedeth them. Are you not much better than them?"

"If any man will follow me, let him deny himself and take up his cross and follow me. For whoever will save his life shall lose it. and whoever will lose his life for my sake shall find it. For what does a man profit if he shall gain the whole world, and lose his own soul?"

"If you want to be perfect, go and sell what you have and give it to the poor, and you shall have treasure in heaven and then come and follow me."

"Verily I say unto you, that a rich man shall hardly enter the Kingdom of Heaven, and again I say unto you, it is easier for a camel to go through the eye of a needle than for a rich man to enter into the Kingdom of Heaven."

Sai Baba considered "desires" a very important subject:

"The man with the most desires is the most poor. Until we realize the desireless state of pure bliss, we are in poverty." (SS50)

"Desires for worldly objects produces pleasure and pain, whereas desire for God confers bless and does not produce pain." (SS2)

"Let all desire and attachment be for God. He alone is eternal and He alone is the source of all joy." (SS8)

"One is very fortunate to get a human birth, but because we are filling such a human life with various material desires, we are filling our life with sorrow. If we cannot get sorrow at all and there can be no one more happy than one who has no desires." (SS41)

"By chanting the Lord's name, desires can be reduced, while legitimate wishes get fulfilled." (SS23)

"These are not real troubles at all. The real cause of sorrow is attachment to the body and identifying one's self with the body. All sorrows arise from the feelings of 'I' and 'Mine.' It is essential to reduce attachment to the body." (SS41)

Dr. George stated the following about desires:

"Desires are what keeps man coming back to this earth. Sam, you must reduce and control your desires. Say to Divine Mother, 'I want only what you want'; you will be much happier." (He told me this in 1972 working at The Farm.)

"Say to God: 'I will use my will, but guide thou my will.'" (He said that in many talks over the years.)

I have had a lot of problems with desires this lifetime, among them are 1) trying to make it "big-time" in the entertainment business; 2) trying to change the planet in a big way, instead of focusing on changing myself; and 3) wanting to be well-known and popular. Sometimes, I get tired of my stupidity and wonder when I will ever become a Master of myself. The only antidote I know for my flaws is concentrating harder and harder on God, chanting the name of God all the time in my mind and heart, forgiving, releasing fears, desires, etc., and surrendering to God's will. Man, that surrendering to God's will is really tough for me. Dr. George told me that I was a "hard case."

Devotion

All saints, sage, masters, and avatars have stressed the need for devotion in the heart to love and worship God. Swami Rama said the following on this topic in a personal dialogue with his student, Dr. O'Brien: "Some devotees are inclined in this direction toward an external ideal. Thus, they need a concrete symbol. In our tradition, we internalize the devotion." Justin went on to say that Swami Rama would advise some students to do devotion to an outer manifestation, depending on the student's temperament and state of evolution.

Sai Baba said the following on devotion:

"All education, all wealth, all ritualistic worship or penances are of no value without genuine devotion to God. Devotion can elevate the lowly to the highest level. Without faith in God, even an eminent person gets degraded." (SS51)

"God can be worshipped in many ways. His name can be repeated. His glories chanted, his true nature contemplated in meditation. In every instance of the worship of the personal form of God, the main essential is the Divine name." (SS19)

"Merely going to the temple and offering worship, offering a coconut expecting some reward – all these are a wrong way of understanding devotion. In order to fulfill the desires, quite a few people resort to this sort of method. They are converting devotion into a business proposition. They do business with God: I give you this, and you give me that! This is not devotion. You should attain the Atmic Bliss. You should earn God's love. Even if you have an atom of God's love, you can conquer many things in the world. Once you have earned God's love, you can attain the Atmic Bliss at all times." (SS45)

"Whatever scholarship one may attain, whatever power and position one may enjoy, one cannot be happy without the peace of mind that is got by pure devotion." (SS44)

"Devotion to Rama or Krishna (or Christ, presumably) becomes meaningless if you do not practice their teachings. The worship of the Lord should be accompanied by leading a Godly life. Only then can bliss be experienced." (SS22)

Dr. George talked a lot about devotion. It was one of his more significant topics:

"God can only be experienced in the Heart. The Lord responds to deep devotion and longing from the heart and will come to the devotee whose devotion to Him is greater than other desires." (Talk at The Farm, July, 1973.)

"Devotion is the highest path. In this age of Kali, it is also the easiest. It is very difficult to do the path of wisdom or be an ascetic. God is love and responds to love." (Talk at The Farm, July, 1973.)

"For most people, it is easier to think of God as Divine Mother. It is easier to feel and experience God as Divine Mother, or beloved Guru. That is why God gives us saints, master, gurus, and avatars to identify with, to make it easier for us to experience Him." (Sermon, February, 1968, The Farm.)

"You can make any mistake on earth, but if you have devotion, somehow, some way, it will work out." (He told me this personally in December, 1967.)

Everyone has some good features and some strengths to go along with their flaws. I am lucky because devotion is my strong suit. I truly love God and love to meditate and love to sing to God. That is my greatest joy and I keep focusing on it all the time.

Ego

Sai Baba said the following interesting things about the ego:

"There is one thing that comes into man from the outside. That is the ego, which is formed by attachment to outside objects. With desire for the world cut, ego automatically vanishes." (SS61)

"Egoism causes a lack of inner peace. Man creates and magnifies within himself a great variety of selfish habits and attitudes. This causes him great discontent with himself. The effulgence of man's divine nature is obscured by egoism. Therefore, when egoism is destroyed, all troubles end, all discontent vanishes and true bliss is attained." (SS46)

"The ego is most easily destroyed by devotion to God, by dwelling on the magnificence of the Lord and by humility and service to others as the children of the Lord." (SS51)

"Criticizing others and finding fault with them comes out of egoism." (SS1)

"If there is ego and you think Swami is yours, then Swami gets imprisoned by your ego and cannot come to your help. But, if you think, 'I belong to Swami', then Swami becomes free to look after you and bring you spiritual progress. It is all a matter of humility of God will knock out your ego since it stands in the way of surrender." (SS47)

Jesus said the following on this topic:

"Blessed are the poor in spirit, for theirs is the Kingdom of Heaven" and "For whoever shall exalt himself shall be abased and whoever humbleth himself shall be exalted" and "Blessed are the meek for they shall inherit the earth."

Dr. George said this about the ego:

"Most of the spiritual path is the destruction of the ego." (Sermon, church, January, 1965.)

"One of the most important things the Guru does for you is help you become detached from the ego and laugh at it." (Sermon, church, August, 1977.)

"Your egos can get you into a lot of trouble. God can get you out of trouble." (The Farm, informal talk, May, 1973.)

Like nearly everyone else on this planet, I have been victimized by the sometimes remarkable ignorance and blunderings of my ego. It seems it is absolutely impossible to control, like the Great Ones say. I have looked into the eyes of Dr. George, Sai Baba, Swami Vishwananda, and Swami Rama. The unique thing about them, is that *there is no ego.* I know that sounds strange and unlikely, but you can actually feel it. I am not the only one who has made that observation about these Great Beings. Judy, Jannie, and other psychics can verify that in the unseen, these type of beings come across with a totally different aura and consciousness. We all get glimmers of this state when we meditate and when we do something totally unselfish for others without thought of reward. They are there all the time.

I have found the only cure for a runaway ego is to meditate, love God, chant the name of God, chant to God with all your heart, and serve others.

Food and Diet

Sai Baba has had many words on diet and food. Here are a few of them:

"Devotees have learned to offer whatever they eat to Swami first before eating. Has not Swami himself said that all the bad effects found in the food are nullified by offering them first to God?" (SS50)

"It is not enough if you eat good quality food alone. An excess of a good thing also becomes bad. Likewise, insufficiency too is bad. The main problem and defect of all mankind is that people eat too much food." (SS11)

"Today ...all people should give up meat eating. Why? Meat eating promotes only animal qualities. It has been well said that the food one consumes determines one's thoughts. By eating the flesh of various animals, the qualities of these animals are imbibed. How sinful is it to feed on animals, which are sustained by the same five elements as human beings! This leads to demonic tendencies, besides committing the sin of inflicting cruelty on animals. Hence, those who genuinely seek to become devotees of God have to give up non-vegetarian food." (SS15)

Dr. George said the following about food and diet:

"Yogananda said it was best to be a vegetarian if you want to learn how to meditate. Meat takes too long to digest and weighs you down when you're trying to raise your energies." (Dr. George told me this the first day I met him in 1964.)

"Because of your blood type and your system, you should eat some fish a few times per week. Fish have a different nervous system than animals and will not give off the negative vibrations you get from eating meat." (Dr. George told me this the second day I knew him.)

"When an animal is killed for food, the animal gives out strong vibrations of anger and fear. The person who eats the meat picks up those vibrations." (He told me this personally in June, 1964.)

Swami Rama said the following on diet/food: "Ultimately, the vegetarian diet is the best diet. For a devotee to be practical, he/she should cut down on animal fats as he/she gets older, past 45 years of age. If you must eat meat, eat lighter meats, such as chicken or fish. Tibetans have to eat meat in that barren country." (Spoken to Dr. O'Brien)

Yogananda said in a talk in 1926 the following:

"Make it a point to drink plenty of liquids, and I do not mean soda-water beverages. It is necessary to wash away toxins in the body. However, avoid drinking liquids with meals, and this can be injurious to digestion. One tends to wash down the food without chewing it properly. If starches are not partially digested in the mouth, then they do not digest fully in the stomach. To chew food well is important; the stomach has no teeth. Hasty eating is harmful, particularly if large amounts of liquid are taken with the meal, thus diluting the gastric juices. Also, drinking liquids with meals gives a tendency to obesity. It is important to keep the bloodstream healthy. Beef and pork may release into the bloodstream toxic poisons and microbes. The white corpuscles try to destroy the microbes, but if the latter are strong and if the white corpuscles are insufficient to resist them, toxic reactions set in." (10)

I became a vegetarian in 1964. Before then, all the time I was growing up, I constantly got a horrible rash on my arms and legs called eczema. It would really strike me in the winter when it was dry and cold. I was so embarrassed to be in the locker room with the guys seeing the awful-looking stuff on my arms and legs. It itched like crazy. There was no cure. I tried various creams and lotions, to no avail. From the day I became a vegetarian, I have *never had eczema again.*

Also, being a vegetarian truly helped me meditate a lot easier.

It was tough being a vegetarian in this country back in the 1960's and 70's. Few restaurants served anything other than fat fried meat. Folks were chagrined when they offered you a meal and you did not eat meat. I remember that I thought to myself, "Well, I will not eat meat unless someone graciously serves it to me and not wishing to offend them, I will eat it anyway." I tried that twice and got sicker than a dog, so, after that my tact left as my veggies arrived. I am a "loose" vegetarian, in that I eat eggs, dairy products, and some fish.

Energy

Sai Baba stated the following about this topic:

"To sit straight is important. Between the 9th and 12th vertebrae is the life force. If the body is in a straight position, the life force may rise up through the straight body and give the quality of intense concentration to the mind. In like fashion, the divine power, which is always present, may flow into you, if the meditation is correct and the body straight." (SS41)

"Where is the Cosmic Energy? The Cosmic Energy is all pervasive. It is in you, above you, below you and around you. You, yourself are the Cosmic Energy, but you are not able to realize it." (SS11)

"The magnetic power (or the power of attraction) is present in all objects in the world. All the thoughts in a man's mind have this magnetic power. The power of this energy was recognized from ancient times. India is the nation that recognized the divine source of this energy, experienced its power and propagated the truth about it to the whole world." (SS4)

Dr. George talked often about Divine Energies
"Everything is vibration and energy. God is the highest energy." (Dr. George said those simple words to me in July, 1965 when we were very tired at the end of a hard day working at The Farm.)

"When you do the Kriya yoga, raise your energies up your spine as you inhale and exhale." (Dr. George said this every December in the church when he did the Kriya yoga Initiation.)

"Recognize energies and be aware of them. Raise yourself above low energies. Stay out of places of low energy. Associate with people of high energy and if someone is down, try to cheer them up and raise their energies with love, kindness, and understanding. Even a little bit of love and kindness will help someone a lot." (Sermon, The Farm, June, 1965.)

I may not be much of a clairvoyant, but I am totally aware of energies. I can feel good and bad energies. Many times, I have noticed a very important or wealthy individual who is "great" on the outer but has real bad energies. Likewise, I have seen many unknown bottom-of-the-rung folks who have great energies and are a silent blessing on the earth. I have often come into a hotel or restaurant and walked right back out again because of the energies.

When I traveled and played music or traveled for business and had time to spend, I always sought out the public library in town. Libraries always have good energies. Oceans, lakes, rivers, streams, and mountains are big-time for me, in the energy field. Sitting by water is so healing. Likewise, there is nothing better in the energy area than hiking in the mountains. I know everyone is different, but for me, a healing energy is watching a baseball game, whether on television or in person, it makes my day.

However, being around a being such as Sai Baba, Swami Vishwananda, or Dr. George is the highest energy. If you get quiet in Baba's or Vishwananda's darshans and you do not feel the incredible beautiful energy, then you are unfortunate; you need to seriously wake up and change yourself.

Enlightenment (Self Realization)
Sai Baba said the following on this topic:

"There is no need to retire into a forest or cave to know your inner Reality and to conquer your lower nature. Win the battle of life by being in the world but free from attachments. That is a victory for which can be congratulated." (SS27)

"Realization, which is not possible through logic, which is not possible through offering of sacrifices, and which is not possible through discussion and other disciplines, can only be achieved through love." (SS9)

"Search for Bliss, the bliss that emanates from love, love with no blemish of attachment. Be like bees hovering on the flower of the glory of the Lord, sucking the sweet nectar of Grace, silently and joyfully." (SS20)

Dr. George said the following about this subject:

"The whole purpose of your life is to attain Self-Realization." (He told me this many, many times over the years and said it in most of his lectures and sermons.)

"If there are enough people of Self-Realization in America, it will be spared much of its karma. The work of the Masters and spiritual people is to make sure the prophesies do *not* come true!" (He told me this in December, 1968 at The Farm.)

"Out of a hundred people, one seeks enlightenment, and out of a hundred of them, one finds it this lifetime." (Dr. George used to say this often in his sermons and lectures.)

Swami Rama said these pithy words to Dr. O' Brien: "Self-realization – that's it! There is no happiness without it. Use the world as an instrument to assist your Journey."

Sometimes it comes as a surprise to you when you feel your own divinity. Knowing my faults like I do, I am always pleasantly surprised when I feel God within. Dr. George told us over and over, "Realize who you are!" and "You are not sinners; you are learners and evolvers."

Evolution of the Soul

Sai Baba has said the following words on this topic:

"There is a category of devotees who can feel Swami's presence through strong vibrations and inflow of energy as and when they still their thoughts and concentrate on the Name and Form of the Lord. Tears of bliss roll down the cheeks of such devotees when they set up communication with Swami. Higher than this is another category of devotees who have vision of the Lord in the form of brilliant Light. They can, at will, watch every movement of the Gods and goddesses. They develop the faculties of clairvoyance and clairaudience. Even though they may not be actively involved in the activities of the Sai Organization, they always live in a state of bliss and enjoy Sai's presence in subtle ways."

"A still higher level in the evolution of the soul is reached when a human surrenders his will to

294

the Will of God and makes the choice to let his whole life, everything he does, every thought, be of His will. He does everything for and with God."

"The next higher stage is reached when a devotee experiences the truth, that all is God and there is only God. It is a revelation that touches him deeply. To him is opened the door to the inflowing of the God-force so that it reaches the innermost part of his being. It is there within, it is there without, and when he surrenders, he allows the two to join in perfect unison, and lives and works only as the instrument of God for the welfare of humanity." (SS59).

Dr. George said the following on this subject:

"We have had millions of incarnations and have evolved from the lowest form up to human. Our next step is Christ Consciousness." (He told a few of us this at the Farm one summer day in 1965.)

"Everything is always growing, changing, and evolving. You cannot stand still. You must move forward, willingly or unwillingly." (Dr. George said this in a sermon in the church on Tuesday night in April, 1970.)

"When Jesus said, 'You must be born again, both of the water and the spirit,' he meant reincarnation. He was talking about the water of the womb and the spirit reentering the human form for another lifetime." (Dr. George said that often in talks and conversations.)

Sri Yukteswar, the guru of Yogananda, said the following on this topic:

"*Kriya yoga* [the scientific meditation method taught by Yogananda] is an instrument through which human evolution can be quickened. The ancient yogis discovered that the secret of cosmic consciousness is intimately lined with breath mastery. This is India's unique and deathless contribution to the world's treasury of knowledge. The life force, which is ordinarily absorbed in maintaining the heart-pump, must be freed for higher activities by a method of calming and stilling the ceaseless demands of the breath.

"The Kriya yogi mentally directs his life energy to revolve, upward and downward, around the six spinal centers. One-half minute of revolution of energy around the sensitive spinal cord of man effects subtle progress in his evolution. That half-minute of Kriya equals one year of natural spiritual unfoldment. One thousand Kriya practiced in eight hours gives the yogi in one day, the equivalent of one thousand years of natural evolution. ... The scriptures state that man requires a million years of normal evolution to perfect his human brain to experience Cosmic Consciousness." (1)

I have personally seen how much Kriya yoga has helped me. I can look at myself now, as compared to twenty and thirty years ago and see a whole lot of improvement, both in inner experience and in outer manifestation. I also have had many memories of past lives. I was a wild one and did some rough things, especially in the way of warfare. I have grown a whole lot in consciousness and spirit since those lives. That is another reason why it is wise to forgive others; we have no idea where they are in evolution.

Happiness

Sri Yukteswar, the Guru of Yogananda said:

"I see that you are imagining that the possession of miraculous powers is knowledge of God. One might have the whole universe, and find the Lord elusive still. Spiritual advancement is not measured by one's outward powers, but only by the depth of his bliss in meditation. Ever-new joy is God. He is inexhaustible; as you continue your meditations during the years, He will beguile you with infinite ingenuity. ...How quickly we weary of earthly pleasures. Desire for material things is endless. Man is never satisfied completely, and pursues one goal after another. The 'something else' he seeks is the Lord, who alone can grant lasting joy." (1)

Swami Rama told this story about a sage in the Himalayas and happiness, the following being Swami Rama's words:

There was a Swami who lived quietly deep in the Himalayas between Utterkashi and Harsil. I went to see him, and when I arrived he asked, "What is the purpose of your coming?" I told him, "I want to receive a mantra." He said, "You will have to wait." When Westerners go to someone for a mantra, they are prepared to spend a lot of money, but they do not want to wait. I tried the same thing. I said, "Swamiji, I am in a hurry."

"Then come back next year," he said. I asked, "If I stay now, how many days will I have to wait."

"You will have to wait as long as I want you to wait," he replied. So, I waited patiently one day, two days, three days. Still the Swami wouldn't give me a mantra. On the fourth day, he said, "I want to give you a mantra, but promise that you will remember it all the time." I promised. He said, "Let us go to the Ganges."

Countless sages have done spiritual practices on the banks of the sacred Ganges and have been initiated there. I stood by the river and said, "I promise that I will not forget this mantra." I repeated this promise several times, but he still delayed. At last he said, "No matter where you live, *live cheerfully.* That is the mantra. Be cheerful at all times, even if you are behind bars. Anywhere you live, even if you have to go to a hellish place, create heaven there. Remember my boy, cheerfulness is of your own making. It only requires human effort. You have to create cheerfulness for yourself. Remember this mantra of mine."

I was both very happy and very sad, because I had expected him to give me some unusual sound to repeat. But he was more practical. I apply this "mantra" to my life and find it successful everywhere. His spiritual prescription seems to be the best of physicians, a real key for healing oneself.

Sai Baba has said the following on this topic:
"Happiness is essential for God-realization. It is one of the major gates to divinity. It is not just a fault if a person is not happy; it is one of the most serious of all faults. It is a barrier to realization. Mostly, people are unhappy because of worldly pursuits, attachments, and enjoyments, too much interest in the world. To get free of this fault, the person has to realize that desire is never-ending, like the waves of the sea." (SS6)

"Everyone must learn the secret of happiness, which consists in refusing to shed tears for anything less than God." (SS28)

"People today are treating the body as the source of all happiness. Such happiness is not true and permanent. It is momentary. Educated persons are not striving to earn spiritual, permanent, and real happiness." (SS99)

"You cannot be happy when the rest of mankind is unhappy. You are an organic part of the human community. Share your prosperity with others. Strive to alleviate the sufferings of others. That is your duty." (SS34)

Dr. George talked a lot about happiness and continuously exhorted his students to be happy under any circumstances. He taught this over and over by showing us how to do any job and by happy doing it.

"You may never be rich, you may never be famous, but you <u>will</u> be happy if you stay with the path of Self-realization and meditation." (Dr. George looked me in the eye and told me this at The Farm in the summer of 1964.)

"You can have everything, but unless you can experience God within when you meditate, you will never have lasting happiness. You may be up for a little while, but then you will have a corresponding sorrow or defeat." (Dr. George gave us a little reality talk in a Sunday sermon at The Farm in August, 1973.)

"God is joy, joy, joy." (Simple words in October, 1971 at The Farm.)

Yogananda said the following in his talk in Los Angeles in May of 1944:

"The secret of happiness is consciousness of God's presence."

I can attest to the reader that Master George's promise to me is valid and has been fulfilled.

It is so sad that in the United States, where we have such unbelievable wealth compared to the rest of the world, where the great majority of the planet makes less in one year than we make in a week, and where there are a huge number of people who do not have a car or a telephone compared to one of us. We have five percent of the world's population and we use 43% of the resources used in one year. Yet, there are millions of people who have such depression and unhappiness that they are on drugs to alter their moods, and we have a vast amount of addicted people, whether it is smoking, drinking, or dope. We seem to have everything, but are not happy. Maybe it is time that we listen to Yogananda and Sai Baba.

Heaven/Hell

Swami Rama said the following about heaven/hell to Dr. O'Brien:

"These concepts are substitutes for understanding human fulfillment; they are a creation by misguided minds, which have been enforced by clergy to control people over the centuries." (13)

Sai Baba said the following words on this topic:

"You must see to it that the heart does not contain dust and lust. Lust is the worst quality. It is the number one enemy of those who are going along the spiritual path. If you want to go to heaven, you must develop a pure heart. All your thoughts must be turned towards God." (SS32)

"Remember: Spiritual elation is heavenly, despondency is hell." (SS26)

"Heaven is not a supra-terrestrial region of perpetual spring. It is an inner experience, a state of supreme bliss. Hell is a place of the mind, a mental state in which there is much worry and suffering. It is an after-death state. Sai is here to guide his devotees so that they do not fall into that state." (SS3)

Master George said the following:

"There is no such place and heaven or hell. All we have is *our consciousness* and our deeds. Hell is a state of separation from God because of our desires and delusions. You need to be in heaven right now, in your heart, otherwise you will not be 'in heaven' when you die." (He told this to a group of us at The Farm in May, 1972.)

"If you do not have heaven in your heart right now, it won't matter what happens when you die." (Sermon, April, 1968, church.)

"You create your own hell by your ego, delusion, desires, and the harm you cause others resulting from those things." (Sermon, The Farm, March, 1970.)

Another time, while driving in the car a long distance with him, he said the following, which I am summarizing from my memory. The notes of this talk have disappeared, but I remember it clearly:

"There are many, many worlds, life on many, many planets. These human bodies fit this earth, but would not work on other planets; however, life goes on there, but in different forms. Likewise, the physical universe is just a small speck compared to the astral universes and the causal worlds. There are many dimensions and worlds and planets and places to go. I will tell you of a few."

"When people do very bad wrongs, they often go to a place which is not too different from what John Bunyan talked about in *Pilgrim's Progress,* except it is not eternal. The 'sins' are burned off, literally, and then the soul has a choice of how to deal with the mathematical law of karma and how to pay back. Unfortunately, often, the soul goes back into a human form and does more harm, and the process repeats. Eventually, slowly, the soul learns and improves. Sometimes, a soul must regress to animal bodies and be killed over and over until the debt is paid. That is the choice of the soul.

"There are places where great artists and musicians go. They hang out and learn from each other. There never was a period of better art than the 1400-1600 when all the great masters came. Most of them were very advanced beings and they agreed on the other side to come together to assist and inspire mankind. Likewise, Mozart, Bach, Beethoven, etc., came together to inspire mankind to higher goals."

"There are places where you can think of what you want and it comes. You think of anything or anyone and they are there. You must qualify and be accepted.

"Dr. George then chuckled and said, "They do not allow any meat eaters, dopers or smokers there!"

"There is no sex on the other side, because there is no need for procreation. You merge your energies with loved ones.

"You meet any one whom you have harmed. You must work it out with them, or you must reincarnate to pay it back.

"You have a chance to review your lives and your deeds and your thoughts. There are no secrets. Every thought and deed is a matter of record. It is called the *Akashic Record*.

"There is even a place like that program you like on television (in those days, I really liked

"Dean Martin Roasts," because I love comedy and love to laugh). You join with many other souls and review each other's lives. You watch your life like a movie and everyone laughs and teases you, and you laugh and tease the others when their lives come up. It is a great learning experience and souls learn quickly that they are literally playing their lives like a movie role on this planet with a heavenly audience.

"Your sister was very close to God, but she had been royalty as you know and she was very courageous. She saw her karma clearly on the other side and she did not want to spend too much time on the Earth, which is why she *chose* to come in the form she did (i.e., deaf and going blind). Yogananda and I helped her go fast. She will never be required to return to this Earth. She is in a very high place; it is more beautiful than you could ever imagine."

My Experiences with Heaven/Hell

As I have written about in this book, in 1968 I fell from 12 feet and landed on my head on concrete. I was in a coma for 35 days. Ostensibly, I was dead, but came back. I specifically remember a searing white light of incredible joy, infinite in nature, beyond description. Since that experience, I have never had any fear of after death states.

In 2002, while living in Denver, Colorado, I foolishly agreed to take prescription for slightly high blood pressure (which I later cured with diet and exercise). I had an allergic reaction to this medication and my neck, face, arms, etc. swelled up. I was fifteen minutes from dying and was brought to the hospital in time. I was out for about five days. The great doctors in the hospital in Aurora, Colorado saved me with heavy duty whatever medications.

However, I was conscious on the Other Side when I was out. I remember hanging out with my mom, my dad, my sister, Yogananda, and Master George. I remember very clearly standing with Dr. George watching the Universe; it was very inspiring. I saw many past lives: I saw myself digging in dirt, dying in battle, bearing children as a mother. I saw myself having many tough times with an occasional bright spot.

At the time I was out, the World Series of 2002 was starting on Earth. The Giants were playing the Angels. I was really looking forward to seeing it. While I was out and standing with Dr. George, I thought about missing the World Series, and, as he did on earth, responded to my thoughts, and said, "Don't worry Sam. As long as there is a desire for it, they will have baseball in the heavenly worlds!"

In that "Other Side" experience, I saw many of my past lives as hard, hard, hard, like I was digging in brown hard rocky dirt. Then, Dr. George and Yogananda seemed to "paint" it all over with a beautiful green, softening and coloring the formerly hard brown rock. I do not know what that meant, but I am open to any interpretations.

Inner Voice and Inner Vision

Jesus said simply in Luke, "God is Spirit, and they that worship Him must worship Him in Spirit and in truth."

Sai Baba has stated the following on this subject:

"There are three stages in concentration. In the first stage, you receive My messages in the form of thought waves. In the second stage, you can hear My own voice. In the third stage, you can hear my voice as well as see me. With successful purification of the mind, you will be able to progress from stage to stage." (SS23)

"The knowledge that we acquire from the study of physics, Botany, chemistry, etc., is only artificial knowledge, but no wisdom born of inner vision. The knowledge born of inner enquiry and inner vision is true knowledge and the rest is only ignorance." (SS14)

"The body is the temple of God. In everybody, God is installed, whether the owner of the body recognizes it or not. It is God that inspires you to good acts, that warns you against the bad. Listen to that Voice. Obey that Voice and you will not come to any harm." (SS28)

Dr. George said the following about Inner Vision:

"There are two ways of seeing things: Outwardly, with your eyes and senses, and inwardly, with intuition and love. It is wise to look at things from your inner vision. Many things and people which appear good on the outer are not, and many things which appear bad, are very good." (He told me this in November, 1974 at The Farm.)

"Ask Divine Mother for guidance and to see clearly. She will show you." (He told me this in 1965 related to a major problem I had at that time. Acting on Dr. George's advice, I started chanting to Divine Mother at 9 p.m. on a Sunday evening and did not stop until 6 a.m. the next morning, when I got a wondrous vision from Divine Mother and got the guidance and answers I needed for the circumstances, which then worked out very well for me.)

"When you are working with someone, try to feel who they really are by contacting your own inner divinity." (He gave me these instructions in 1976 when he made me a minister of his church.)

Yogananda described an experience in Cosmic Consciousness, every devotees goal of inner vision:

"Sri Yukteswar [Yogananda's Guru] seldom indulged in riddles. He struck gently on my chest above the heart. My breath became immovably rooted. Breath was drawn out of my lungs as if by some huge magnet. Sound and mind instantly lost their physical bondage, and streamed out like a fluid piercing light from my every pore. The flesh was as though dead, yet in my intense awareness I knew that never before had I been fully alive. My sense of identity was no longer narrowly confined to a body, but embraced the circumambient atoms, People on distant streets seemed to be moving gently over my own remote periphery. The roots of plants and trees appeared through a dim transparency of the soil. I discerned the flow of their sap."

"The whole vicinity lay bare before me. My ordinary frontal vision was now changed to a vast spherical sight, simultaneously all-perceptive. Through the back of my head, I saw men strolling far down the Rai Ghat Road, and noticed also a white cow who was leisurely approaching. When she reached the space in front of the open ashram gate. I observed the brick wall. I saw her clearly still."

All objects within my panoramic gaze trembled and vibrated like quick motion pictures. My body, Master's, the pillared courtyard, the furniture and floor, the trees and sunshine, occasionally became violently agitated, until all melted into a luminescent sea, even as sugar crystals, thrown into a glass of water, dissolve after being shaken. The unifying light alternated with materializations of form, the metamorphoses revealing the law of cause and effect in creation. An oceanic joy broke upon calm endless shores of my soul. The Spirit of God, I realized, is exhaustless Bliss. His body is countless tissues of light. A swelling glory within me began to envelop towns, continents, the earth, solar and stellar systems, tenuous nebulae, and floating universes. The entire cosmos, gently luminous, like a city seen afar at night, glimmered within the infinitude of my being. The sharply etched global outlines faded somewhat at the farthest edges; there I could see a mellow radiance, ever-undiminished. It was indescribably subtle; the planetary pictures were formed of a grosser light.

"The divine dispersion of rays poured form an Eternal Source, blazing into galaxies, transfigured with ineffable auras. Again and again, I saw the creative beams condense into constellations, then resolve into sheets of transparent flame. By rhythmic reversion, sextillion worlds passed into diaphanous luster; fire became firmament.

"I cognized the center of the empyrean as a point of intuitive perception in my heart. Irradiating splendor issued from my nucleus to every part of the universal structure. Blissful amrita, the nectar of immortality, pulsed through me with a quicksilver-like fluidity. The creative voice of God I heard resounding as AUM, the vibration of the Cosmic Motor.

"Suddenly, the breath returned to my lungs. With a disappointment almost unbearable, I realized that my infinite immensity was lost. Once more, I was limited to the humiliating cage of a body, not easily accommodative to the Spirit. Like a prodigal child, I had run away from my macroscopic home and imprisoned myself in a narrow microcosm." (1)

Karma

Swami Rama stated the following on this topic to Dr. O'Brien:

"You cannot live without it. On this earth, all humans must act and produce consequences. Thus, the trick is to stay honest, unselfish, and perform all actions with love. In that way, you won't get entangled in consequences which lead you endlessly to more and more [karma]" and "Desirelessness is impossible living in the world, so you must purify your desires and ask The Lord and guru to guide your desires, and do your best to release the attachments to the results." (14)

Sai Baba has said the following about Karma:

"When one dies, the only items taken with one are one's good deeds and bad deeds." (SS14)

"There are three types of karma: past, present, and future. Present karma must continue. It is like the carriage behind which is a trail of dust. If the carriage stops, the dust will settle on it. A doubt might be that the carriage cannot forever continue so as to be ahead of its dust. The highway is equivalent to the grace of God. There is a difference between the benefit of grace and the benefit of Bhakti, of devotion. A patient with a pain is given a sedative which dulls the pain, but grace is an operation that entirely does away with the karma." (SS11)

"Regarding the question why is a certain person born to certain parents: Karmic debt is the reason for that. Your actions and *samskaras* [the diverse rites of passage of a human being from conception to cremation, signifying milestones in an individual's journey of life] make you beholden to certain people. You are indebted to them and this debt has to be repaid at sometime or the other. The debt does not have to be merely financial. It could be that you did something to a certain person or he(she) did something to you. The damage has to be repaired and the debt has to be canceled. It is left unrepaired or uncancelled in this birth, it has to be set right in the next. This is what is meant by karmic debt."

Dr. George said the following about karma:

"It is virtually impossible to obtain freedom from your past karma without the help of a Guru." (He told this to a small group of us at The Farm in June, 1967.)

"In working out your karma, when you are really on the Path, you do 25% of the work, the Guru does 25%, and God does the rest." (He told me this in January, 1966.)

"The only way Jesus can 'save you' from your karma is if you actually follow his teachings. That is, loving God with all your heart, all your mind, and all your soul; and loving your neighbor as thyself; and forgiving seventy times seven." (He told us this informally at The Farm in August, 1976.)

"If they find a cure for cancer, the Lord will just find another disease. The doctors can't cure karma." (He told me this while we were watching the news on TV in September, 1974.)

Jesus said the following in Matthew: "Blessed are they which do hunger and thirst after righteousness, for they shall be fulfilled."
I have had a lot of karma to work out this lifetime from the past. I asked Dr. George , Yogananda, and Sai Baba to help me work it out so I did not have to reincarnate on this earth, except to help others. I have seen countless times when my karma has come back to me, good or bad. I work on releasing my evaluation of good or bad karma and take it as it comes.

Knowledge

Sathya Sai Baba has formed a complete educational system out of nothing over the years. He has instituted grade schools, high schools, and universities. Besides top-flight academics, these schools stress ethics, moral values, and "human values." The United Nations has given great respect and honor to Baba's schools. Likewise, the Prime Minister of India once said that these schools of Baba's should be the model for education in all of India.

Further, Sai Baba has said the following about this topic:

"The knowledge that you are the Divine Spark, encased in the sheaths of bliss, intelligence, feelings, sensations, and organic substances; this knowledge is the Light. You must light your own lamp. Earn this knowledge yourself. Even knowing it is no enough; you must experience it." (SS18)

"Seek the gem of Divine Knowledge within you, just as precious stones have to be sought in the bowels of the earth. Now, what you seek and know is trivial. Go deeper within you, where the treasure is stored!" (SS23)

"There are certain qualities which are necessary to acquire Atmic knowledge. One should adhere to truth, right conduct and have a spirit of selfless service. You should have the attitude of caring only for the welfare of humanity and strive to make them happy by serving them." (SS19)

Dr. George basically taught that inner divine experience, actually feeling God within, was reality. Just reading and saying the words meant little. He said this in many ways and in many different words. In fact, he stated often that mere book knowledge or memorizing scriptures meant very little and was often harmful to the soul and others, if said reader took himself too seriously in that pursuit.

On the other hand, Swami Rama said the following to Dr. O'Brien: "No knowledge, no freedom, no society" and went out of his way to encourage formal learning. He was relentless in enforcing higher education in his students.

Love

Jesus said simply in Luke: "These things I command: That you love one another."

This topic is probably the topic most often spoken about by Sai Baba:

"There are different forms of love: love for family and love for money, but love for God is devotion. The most important thing you have to develop is love as devotion to God; if you develop that, you do not have to develop anything else." (SS9)

"The central part of my teachings in regards to living in the world is to see in other people that essential quality which is God, and to love that quality and not be bothered by all the other actions, qualities, misbehavior, or characteristics of the person. The love of God in the person with whom one is dealing is Spiritual love and not physical conditional love." (SS55)

"There is only one religion: the religion of Love." (SS45)

"You must cultivate love towards everyone, regardless of what they are like or what they do. You have no right to judge whether a person is good or bad, or whether an action of his is good or bad. Leave the judgement to God. He is the only Judge of persons, things, and actions. Your job is to love others." (SS29)

Swami has said many, many times: "True love is the recognition of brotherhood and sisterhood of all people and all nations."

Dr. George represented Divine Love, unconditional love, and had the following things to say on the subject:

"Even tigers love their family; true love is the recognition of brotherhood and sisterhood of all people and all nations. (He said this to a small group of us at The Farm at Christmas, 1967).

"Jesus said to love your enemies, and you cannot graduate from this Earth and go on unless you can do that. Your anger and resentments will keep you in bondage and reincarnating on this earth until you can forgive and love unconditionally." (He told me this in October, 1965 in a restaurant in Milwaukee.)

"Love that is not Unconditional, love that puts conditions and terms and demands is not love; it is something else. Real love asks for nothing in return; it is rare." (He told me this working at The Farm in September, 1969.)

They called Yogananda an "Incarnation of Love." Even though I did not meet him in the body, I feel his love every day. I feel Yogananda's total caring for me from every dimension and every facet.

There has hardly ever been a love on earth like the love of Swami Vishwananda. I do not know how to describe it in words. If must be felt and experienced. I will give you an experiment: Go online and find his picture (Vishwananda.org or Vishwananda.US.), then sit still and focus on his picture and ask him to come and visit you spiritually and ask him to help you feel his love. If I told you what an orange tasted like, it wouldn't mean too much until you ate it yourself. This love of the Great Beings is unlike any other love ever. Try it.

I sing many of Yogananda's songs, including these two:

"Thou art my life, thou art my love,
thou art the sweetness which I do seek
In the thought, by my love brought
I taste thy name, so sweet, so sweet
Devotee knows, how sweet you are
He knows, whom you let know"

And

"How sweet the sound of Om,
It's Master's voice I hear
In all pervading silence

He whispers, 'I am here'
My heart is all a'glowing,
It seems eternally
There is no other love like
My Master's love for me"

I have experienced many types of love in my life, but there is no love like the love of God and the love of The Guru. Normal "love" is conditional and wants something in return for something. God's love is forever and unconditional, as is the love of a true Master.

How to experience this love? The first and best way is to consciously practice giving unconditional love. Try loving folks without expecting anything in return. Look for the divinity and the good things within them. Do not judge others and do not focus on their faults. Start with your family and close friends and then expand to the whole planet.

As I have studied the lives of the Masters, if I could summarize it all into one word, it would be Love. The unbelievable and superhuman love these folks exhibited in their lives is a spiritual gauntlet in the face challenge to all of us.

When you think of Mother Therese, St. Francis, Sai Baba, Lord Krishna, Jesus, and their peers, it expands your soul and cheers you up about the potential of mankind. Even in these days of selfishness, war, greed, cruelty, egotism, arrogance, and ignorance, still there appear these giant souls who live the highest spiritual truths every minute, every hour, every thought of their lives. We can do the same.

Mantras

In my research, one of my favorite mantra teachings was that given by Swami Rama to his disciple, Dr. Justin O'Brien, later Swami Jaidev. This occurred in 1971 during Justin's very first days with Swami Rama, spoken in Justin's words.

"Swami Rama told me to come back and see him and he would teach me the art of meditation. He told me to make an appointment downstairs and then said, 'But first, you need a Mantra.' I asked him, 'What's a mantra?' Without answering, Swami Rama walked over to me, cupped his hand around my right ear, and chanted a few Sanskrit syllables. I listened intently. He then asked me to join him in repeating the mantra sounds so that he could check my pronunciation. 'What's this about?' I thought. It made little sense to me, but I began repeating the words.

"'Oh, you've got the rhythm well,' he said, pleased. Then he quickly wrote out on a pad of paper the personal qualities characterized by the mantra that would develop in me over time. 'The mantra's vibration will bring forth these qualities in you. It is time now for you to move ahead [i.e., spiritually],' the Swami insisted."

Sai Baba has recommended mantras as a way of keeping the mind on God. In many ways, many talks, and many instructions to devotees, he gave a universal mantra: *Om Sai Ram*. This mantra is for everyone to use and it means, "The sacred part of your heart where the Lord abides." Sai Baba told Jack Hislop (who repeated these words to us in many of his talks) that the early Christians would use the mantra, "Lord Jesus have mercy on us." Jack further said that Swami told him to repeat "Om Sai Ram" over and over in his mind and picture God inwardly. Jack said in many of his talks that it took him three years before his mind continuously and irrevocably repeated that mantra and he felt God all the time within!

Sai Baba also has said the following about Mantras:

"Of the various sadhanas, repetition of the name of God is the most effective." (SS33)

"Even Westerners who experiment with the Gayatri Mantra find it has power." (SS19)

"Mantra means 'potent formula.' Man makes y*antras* (machines), mantra makes man! The maker of yantras is called a scientist, the maker of mantras is called a saint." (SS7)

Dr. George said that it was good to keep your mind on God as much as you could, given the circumstances of your work and your responsibilities. He said that any mantra is good and to use one that made you feel good. He told some folks to say, "God, Christ, Gurus." He told me personally to always visualize the form of the Guru as I did the mantra.

Dr. Hislop, as I have mentioned, gave us all a great gift of simplicity: He told thousands of Sai devotees for many years all over the world, Swami's simple instruction to him:

"All you need in this age on the path is to constantly chant the name of the Lord within yourself, and use this mantra: '*Om Sai Ram.*' Chant this every waking minute as long as your mind is not engaged in necessary duties. When you can, visualize your dearest form of divinity or your guru at the same time."

Meditation

Jesus said in Matthew "Blessed are the pure in heart, for they shall see God." And: "And as Moses lifted the serpent in the wilderness, so must the Son of Man be lifted up." (Note: Dr. George told me that this statement and the earlier statement about Moses in the Old Testament referred to Moses "raising the kundalini, or shakti up the spine in advanced meditation. In Hinduism, the serpent is a symbol for the energies that go up and down the spinal column of humans, which is why, Dr. George also had an alternative view of the crucifixion of Jesus, i.e., he said that Jesus did not die, but went into the advanced yogi breathless state and appeared dead. After he was taken down, he recovered his consciousness and his close ones helped him heal himself with herbs and prayers, then he left for Kashmir.)

And: "The light of the body is the eye; if therefore thine eye be single, thy body shall be full of light." (Most yogis and meditators interpret this passage as a description of the Spiritual Eye, the Single Eye, on which you focus when you meditate. Great Yogis can transmute the cells of their bodies into light by this technique. This is how Jesus could walk on water, i.e., by turning his body into light so it had no mass.)

Sai Baba had a lot to say about meditation:

"Meditation, for its proper practice, should be at the same place, at the same time. In that way, it surely will be successful. If one is away from home in travel, in his mind, he can go to the accustomed place no matter where he is." (SS34)

"It is not practical to attempt to concentrate on that which has no form. To concentrate on the *jyoti* (flame) is an illustration. The object of concentration can be sound, form, the jyoti, a Master or Guru, etc. It needs to be something concrete. It is not easy to fix the mind on the abstract." (SS27)

"The Atma is everywhere, but for the purpose of meditation, the life principle can be considered as being ten inches above the navel and at the center of the chest." (SS13)

"Chanting God's names and meditation are means by which you can compel the manifestation of divine grace." (SS10)

Dr. George encouraged all his devotees to meditate regularly to get close to God within:

"You should meditate, but do not ignore your responsibilities. Work and service are just as important as meditation." (He said this or similar statements often to all of us.)

"When you meditate, release all desires except to experience God." (He told me this the first night I met him in 1964.)

"In the silence of your soul, there you will find all things." (I will never forget him telling me this in July, 1964 at The Farm.)

Yogananda spent his entire life teaching folks to meditate. In one of his lectures in 1944, he stated firmly the following:

"…but greater than activity, devotion, or reason, is meditation. To meditate truly is to concentrate solely on Spirit. This is esoteric meditation. It is the highest form of activity that man can perform, and it is the most balanced way to find God. If you work all the time, you may become mechanical and lose Him in pre-occupation with your duties; and if you seek Him only through discriminative thoughts, you may lose Him in the labyrinths of endless reasoning, and if you cultivate only devotion for God, your development may become merely emotional. But meditation combines and balances all these approaches."

In a talk at the SRF Temple in Encinitas in November of 1938, Yogananda said,

"Without self-analysis, people lead robotlike lives. Millions of people never analyze themselves. Mentally, they are the mechanical products of the factory of their environment, preoccupied with breakfast, lunch, and dinner, working and sleeping, and going here and there to be entertained. They do not know what or why they are seeking, nor why they never realize complete happiness and lasting satisfaction. By evading self-analysis, people go on being robots, conditioned by their environment."

I can tell you that meditation is the greatest blessing of my life.

Miracles

Sai Baba, who arguably has done more "miracles" than any other human being in history, doing hundreds of documented miracles per day, has said the following on the topic:

"You elaborate in your lectures the unique powers of Sai, the incidents that are described as 'miracles' in books written about me by some persons. Do not exaggerate their significance. The most important power is my *prema* (grace) and my *sahana* (fortitude). I may turn the sky into earth or earth into sky, but that is not the sign of Divine Might. It is the prema, effective, universal, ever-present, that is the unique sign." (SS24)

"Besides being spontaneous tokens of my love, my so-called miracles are to plant the seed of faith in the minds of unbelievers and to foster humanity and veneration towards a Higher Power." (SS5)

"The manifestation of Divine Power must not be interpreted in terms of magic. Remember: there is nothing that Divine Power cannot accomplish. It can transmute earth into sky and sky into earth. The human 'magic' is the Divine's logic." (SS15)

"My miracles are part of the unlimited power of God and are in no sense the product of yogic powers, which are acquired. They are natural and uncontrived. There are no invisible beings helping me. My divine will brings the object in a moment. I am everywhere." (SS21, in response to a question about Sai materializing matter from nothing.)

Dr. George did a lot of miracles but didn't talk a lot about them. Here are a few things he said:

"Miracles are not really 'miracles,' they are only the use of higher laws that most people are not aware of at this time." (He said this at the dinner table at The Farm in October, 1965.)

"Sometimes people want miracles or healings, but it wouldn't be right for them if it happened." (In answer to a student's question at The Farm in November, 1972.)

"Yogananda told me to keep very secret and 'never let them know who you are.'" (He told me this at his house on 20th Street in June, 1965.)

"Yogananda did a lot of public miracles until 1931, then he said that he didn't want to be a sideshow, he only wanted those who only wanted God." (He told me this in the car in October, 1970.)

Swami Rama stated that, "Belief in miracles is due to ignorance of our own divinity" and "Belief in miracles is lazy thinking."

I have related many miracles in my personal experience already. I can tell you a few more:

A man named Jack Collins, who was in his eighties, lived in the Veteran's Hospital in Milwaukee. I used to pick him up and bring him to church once in a while and sometimes took him up to The Farm on the weekend. Jack was born in Australia and was an orphan. He had one older brother, his only kin. When his brother reached the age of 12, he was assigned to be a cabin boy on a merchant ship. Two years later, Jack was similarly assigned to a merchant ship. The two never saw each other again for many years. In fact, by the 1930's, Jack had totally lost track of his brother.

Jack told me that he joined Dr. George's church (i.e., the one with the dirt floor and home-made log pews, complete with splinters) in the early 1930's. He said that he knew of George's miraculous powers and asked him in 1936 if he could help him find his long-lost brother. He said that Dr. George paused for a while and told Jack that it would be a tough one, but that he would work on it.

Seven years passed. Jack worked for many years on the railroad. The railroad workers left Milwaukee and traveled to Seattle and back. When they reached Seattle, the workers had a few days off and usually went to movies. One night at the movies, the works filed in down the left aisle, led by Jack, who slid into a row and moved over to the middle to accommodate the remainder of the men. While he was thus sitting, another group of men came down the right aisle. They were led by a man who slid into the row that was occupied by Jack and his men. That man came in and sat next to Jack. They looked at each other and knew: It was his brother! They forgot about the movie and went outside. Jack's brother was still on the ships and currently was on one which docked in Seattle. Their relationship restored, they met another few times before his brother passed away.

I was in Denver in March, 2003, living in a townhouse. I entered through the garage, which was always locked. I used the garage door opener to open the garage door, drove in, closed the garage door, and came into the kitchen. Thereupon, being very absent-minded, I would set my keys on the counter next to the refrigerator. Then, I would lock the inner door to the garage as well. There was a small living room on that level, but I was mainly in the two bedrooms and office upstairs.

I called my good friend, Judy Boss, the remarkable clairvoyant, in St. Paul, Minnesota. We talked for a while and I asked her if she had any words of guidance from Dr. George for me. (Note: She is a very accurate medium and channeler for certain Great Beings on the Other Side, as well as specific guides and loved ones; we had been doing this together for years, because of her gift and my receptivity from a lifetime of meditation.) We got quiet, she in St. Paul, me in Denver, on the phone. Soon, Dr. George was there, with my mother. Judy said that they were smiling at me and giving me encouragement. Then she said in surprise, "I see Dr. George with a big Alpine Horn in his hands, stretching out on the ground in front of him. He seems to be blowing on this horn." Just then, to my total shock, the security horn on my car, sitting below in the locked garage, with the keys on the counter, went off! That car horn honked and honked. I had to put Judy on hold, go downstairs, get my keys, start up my car, and get the horn to go off. I went back up. Judy and I were laughing, then she told me that Dr. George had some more words: "See? I can still toot my horn!" Judy went on to say that my mom was standing there on the other side laughing at this little metaphysical joke from the

"Other Side." (Reminder: Dr. George had passed away in 1978.)

The Mind

Sai Baba has said the following about Mind:

"When the mind is not engaged in any particular work, its attention should be kept between the eyebrows. That is the eye of wisdom, of Shiva." (SS6)

"In every man, there is mind, Super Mind, Higher Mind, Illuminated Mind, and Over Mind. All these are in man. Therefore, he is Divine. You have a very broad heart in spite of the size of your body. The galaxy of stars twinkle in the sky. You can visualize them in a mirror. In the same way, our heart is a mirror. You can visualize the whole universe in it. So, there is nothing greater than your heart and therefore there is no God superior to yourself. It you think you are small, you will continue to be small. You should think 'I am God' and this truth will bestow on you the Divine Aspect which you should contemplate upon." (SS24)

"To mankind, God gave the sword of the mind. In the beginning of time, the one who trains the mind and trains it well flourishes in the world. But he who is enslaved by the mind can never enjoy peace and comfort even in the realm of dream." (SSI19)

"From the identification of 'I' with the body, all troubles and complications arise. Since it is the mind that has woven this web of identification with the body, it is the mind that must now turn and seek one's true nature through discrimination, renunciation, and enquiry. Both ego and intelligence must be included in the word 'mind.'" (SS36)

Dr. George had a little different description of the Mind. He was a little more metaphysical about the Mind and contrasted it with the Intellect. He said that one of the big problems with religion was that it was encased by the intellect and left no potential for the infinite divine to be experienced in the mind. One day, he told me, "God is just beyond the fringe of your mind." I thought about that for a long time. I meditated on those words. He answered my thoughts one day without me even asking, "I speak of the Mind as the 'higher mind.' You are thinking of 'mind' as your everyday thoughts. You have to meditate and rise into joy and bliss to be in the 'Higher mind.' If you keep meditating and doing your spiritual practices, you will experience the 'Higher Mind.'"

He also said the following to me at different times:

"Keep your mind on God all the time, except when you have to do your required and necessary duties on this Earth."

"The mind can be stretched to infinity and back again; always try experience your own omnipresence."

I have spent much time and effort trying to break through the befuddlement and confusion of my thoughts to get to the infinite within me. What was very helpful to me was Dr. George's statement to me, "Yogananda said, 'God is just beyond the fringe of your mind.'"

Using Kriya, control your breath and thereby control your mind so you can get into your higher mind."

Music

Sai Baba, who possibly is the most prolific songwriter of all times, having written countless devotional songs to God and all the various forms of God, has said the following about music:

"God loves music." (SC, May, 1996)

"Music as a vehicle of peace is universally popular. Men, women, and children of all lands are amenable to its subtle influence. Even animals and plants are susceptible to music. The Lord has said, 'Where my devotees sing, there I am.'" (SS37)

Dr. George said the following about music:

"When you play your music, Yogananda and I will be right there with you; you just have to show up. Those who feel and benefit from the vibrations will stay and those who don't will leave. It's not up to you." (He told me this inwardly in 1981, after he had passed from the body.)

"God loves you when you sing to Him."
(Sermon, The Farm, April, 1969.)

"Elvis Presley was very close to God. He is
a good boy. When he sang, people's chakras were
opened. That is why they loved him so much. He
helped them feel God within for a few minutes and
brought them joy." (He told me that in August,
1977, after Elvis died.)
        "When Neil Diamond wrote the music for
'Jonathan Livingston Seagull,' he meditated for a
long time and tuned into his Higher Self. That is
why that music is so good." (He told me why he
often liked us to play that record in church.)

        Music is my gift from God. My mom put me
on stage when I was five years old and I won three
dollars in a singing contest. I picked up the sax, the
guitar, and the five-string banjo. I love folk music. I
had my first professional gig when I was 17. I have
played music ever since and was in the business for
many years. I have traveled in all fifty states. My
Martin guitar has been in 48 states. Now, I mostly
play spiritual music and love to get folks together to
chant and sing to God. One of my best memories is
playing music over in India at Sai Baba's ashram. I
always wanted to play for Swami so much.
        In 1995, we went to India for Sai Baba's
birthday. Through a remarkable and fortuitous set of
happenings, I got to join a group to play and sing
for Swami at his huge birthday celebration. That
was the year when he fed 1.2 million peasants free
for ten days. We got to sit up front and play right in

front of him. Except for the minor fact that I got unbelievably sick just before the songs started and I couldn't get up and leave, and that Brian form Australia had to almost carry me back to my room, and that I was out for three days and got better just in time to play our second round of music at the closing ceremonies, thanks to a strong antibiotic.

I guess I did have a little slice of heaven in 1975 when for a good stretch, I was able to play music in Steamboat Springs, Colorado at a place called "The Cantina" in downtown Steamboat. I got good pay, condo up by the lift, and free meals. I was able to ski every day and play music in the evening. Sometimes, even a banjo-picker lands on his feet.

I also did school assembly programs all over the Western United States. I developed a program called "History of American Folk Music." Mostly, I played very small towns and Indian Reservations. Often, I stood on the gymnasium floor and had grades K-12 up on the seats all together and I entertained them.

I was very lucky and blessed to be able to play music. Thanks, Divine Mother.

Nirvana/Liberation

Sai Baba said the following about Nirvana/liberation:

"Liberation (*moksha*) is when you have lasting joy and lasting peace. If only men knew the path to permanent joy and peace, they would not wander distracted among the bye-lanes of sensual pleasure." (SS2)

"Liberation means that birth is finished with. There is no more birth again." (SS45)

"If a person who is trying to get liberation is killed, he has to be born again after some time as a human being and start his trial afresh. Thus the date of his liberation is postponed. By not attempting to get liberated, one may do wrong things and be reborn as an animal. Thus, his date of liberation is also postponed. Therefore, refraining from attempts to get liberation is equated with the act of killing a person who is attempting to get liberation." (SS30)

"Without surrender, there can be no liberation." (SS20)

"Liberation will not come through meditation or penance. Love is the only means. When you render service with Love, it will become meditation, penance, and all else." (SS6)

Dr. George spoke about liberation, calling it the "state of nirbikalpa samadhi." He said that the most critical thing about attaining liberation was the release of desires. He said that continually surrendering to the will of God, and continual release of our spurious desires was essential. He said that desires and attractions would bring us back to the body again. He also stated that dislike of something would attract it to us. He told us over and over to be even-minded about all circumstances. He laughingly told us about the past lives of families wherein certain family members were bitter enemies and that hate had brought them back together again until they resolved it with either love, forgiveness, or neutrality.

Dr. George said the following:

"Nirvana is the same essential state of consciousness as samadhi, liberation, oneness with God, divine bliss, etc. They are the same; only the words are different." (Sermon, July, 1969, The Farm.)

"When you ask yourself, 'Who am I' and continue to seek the answer, when it comes, you will be in nirvana." (He told me this and it puzzled me in November, 1965.)

He told me one time, when I was reading a book on Buddhism, "Nirvana is the same state of consciousness that Jesus referred to as 'The Kingdom of Heaven'" and "No matter what path you trod, you will eventually come to the same consciousness." And then I had a brief experience in omnipresence. I felt all creation as part of God.

Swami Rama stated: "Nirvana is a synonym for 'Samadhi,' just a different tradition (i.e., Buddhism)." (13)

Every once in a while, I have had brief experiences with this state. Obviously, I am always striving for more. However, I remember Dr. George's admonition to me, at The Farm in October, 1971:

"If you attain the state of nirbikalpa samadhi and are not totally prepared, you will not be able to stay in your body. It would be like too much voltage going into a low-watt bulb. It is better to slowly and persistently prepare your atoms and cells to receive this incredible experience."

OM (Aum or Soham or Amen)
Sai Baba said the following on this topic:

"AUM is a name of God which can find universal acceptance. The Christians say 'amen' in their prayers every day. It is only a different form of 'aum.' AUM has universal relevance and applicability. It cuts across all barriers of time, place, religion and culture and can be uttered by all men. The entire universe is vibrant with the sound of AUM. Remember that you should merge in God even as the bubble of water merges in the water whence it comes from, and chant the AUM within you repeatedly." (SS4)

"If you have the inner ear attuned, you can hear OM announcing God's presence in every sound. All of the five elements produce this sound of OM. The bell in the temple is intended to convey the OM as the symbol of the omnipresent God. When the bell sounds, you will awaken and you will be aware of His presence." (SS7)

"It is not possible for anyone to fully cognize or even describe the form of the sacred word 'AUM.' It is an integral word that stands for the Divine. It is divinely precious and should be recognized as the Name of God." (SS10)

Dr. George told us to chant the Om often. When you were with him and were quiet, you could hear the Om vibration very loud right within you. Also, when you came into his church in Milwaukee or his little chapel at The Farm, you could hear the Aum ringing in your ears.

Lord Krishna is always depicted in statues and pictures playing his flute. Krishna's flute is the Aum vibration. When you tune into that sound within, surrender to it, merge with it, you will be guided to the joy and bliss and love of God within you.

When I come into a spiritual place, sometimes the Aum is very loud within me. This is also true when I am alone up on the mountains. Some of the loudest "Aum" places I have been are the following: wherever Sai Baba is; all of Yogananda's SRF centers; the Song of the Morning Ranch in Michigan; Dr. George's old church in Milwaukee; The Farm; Dr. Justin O'Brien's Swami Rama ashram in St. Paul, Minnesota; Holy Hill, the Catholic monastery in West Bend, Wisconsin; Rocky Mountain National Park near Estes Park, Colorado; the Hare Krishna temple in Santa Monica, California; the "Avenue of the Giants" big redwood trees south of Eureka, California; Mount Shasta; Lake Tahoe, by myself up in the mountains above it; anyplace quiet along the Pacific Ocean; sitting by Lake Geneva in Switzerland; the big cathedrals in London; St. Anne's in Montreal, Quebec; Voyageurs National Park in Minnesota and Canada; Yosemite National Park; Yellowstone National Park; many other places in Colorado; and wherever Swami Vishwananda is.

Patience

I can attest that being around Sai Baba demands patience. For many, many years, Swami walked through the masses every morning and every afternoon. However, you had to line up at about 4 a.m. and sit there patiently waiting for the head of your line to pick a numbered chit to determine the seating arrangements inside the *mandir* (temple). Likewise, in the afternoon, you had to wait many hours in the hot sun for Swami to appear. It demanded determination and patience. Many times, all of us had many urgent matters in our lives to ask Swami's help about. Countless patient hours have been spent by hundreds of thousands of devotees over many years waiting for the opportunity to be near or have access to Swami. I, myself, have spent many, many hours waiting many days in India. I have been extremely lucky. I have had three interviews over the years and have been with Swami up close. We all assume the time we spent waiting was of great purification for us and of great spiritual benefit.

Swami has said the following about this topic:

"The quality of patience is a most important quality. Of all the good qualities a person can have, patience and forbearance rank at the very top." (SS42)

"Patience is all the strength a man needs." (This was on a sign at the Ashram.)

"The Lord is the Sun and when His rays fall upon your heart, unimpeded by the clouds of egoism, the lotus bud blooms and the petals unfold. Remember, only the buds that are ready will bloom, the rest will have to wait patiently." (SS60)

Dr. George said the following on patience:

"Your biggest challenge this lifetime is patience. Do not be in too much of a hurry. Calm down and let God do the work through you." (He told me this in May of 1968, recognizing one of my big faults.)

"You can outwait God." (He said this to me in October of 1964, and I have found it to be true, i.e., when you ask God a question, if you determine rock-hard within yourself that you will wait for His answer until death, then you will get it.)

"He who waits, also serves." (He told all of us this many times.)

I have found that one "leverage" you have with God is patient persistence. If you are impatient, you will only be delayed and frustrated. So, if you are asking God for something, I have found that the only way is to have total patient determination, and say to God, "I will keep persisting until I die and then keep on going then." You have to really mean it. If you do, you will get an answer from God or Guru or Great One. For example, if you say to Jesus, "I really would like to meet you and see you in the Spirit. Please come to me." Well, one little prayer won't do it. You have to keep asking and keep meditating and waiting patiently for Him to come to you. He will, he told us to ask and we would receive and knock and the door would be opened.

Pineal Gland and Medulla Oblongata

Sai Baba said the following about the pineal gland:

"The speaker emphasized the importance of the pineal gland in the brain which is the pacemaker and timekeeper. The ancient rishis grasped the wisdom of keeping the alignment of the intricate molecular system of the body and maintaining the biological clock in good order. By meditation and diet control, taking only fruits and vegetables, the ancient Rishis maintained the system in perfect condition. Lacto-oval vegetarian diet (milk, vegetables, and fruits) is the best to adopt. The ancients were not afraid of death and they were happy. They established communion with bliss within themselves." (SS18)

Dr. George talked about the pineal gland a lot; unfortunately, I didn't understand most of what he said at the time:

"God's life energy comes in through the medulla oblongata. We should be able to live without eating, by deriving the energy form God coming through, which Jesus referred to as 'The Word of God.'" (He told me this in May of 1971.)

Yogananda said the following:

"Man's body is not sustained by gross food alone, but by the vibratory cosmic energy (AUM). The invisible power flows into the human body through the gate of the medulla oblongata. This is also the sixth chakra and is located at the back of the neck at the top of the five spinal chakras. The medulla is the principal entrance for the body's supply of universal life force and is directly connected with man's power of will, concentrated in the seventh chakra or Christ Consciousness in the third eye between the eyebrows. The bible invariably refers to AUM as the "Holy Ghost" or invisible life force which divinely upholds all creation. 'What, know ye not that your body is the temple of the Holy Ghost which is in you, which ye have of God, and ye are not your own?'" (1)

Politics

Dr. George said the following things about politics:

"The dark forces control all the money and all the politics in the world." (He told me this in June of 1966 while driving with him.)

"Sam, Yogananda said, 'Do not go into politics.'" (He told me this many, many times, and I realized that he was working on getting that desire from my soul, and I realized that I had done a lot of politics and military in past lives.)

Sai Baba said the following:

"From the prime minister down to the beggar, all ask for peace and aspire for peace. But peace cannot be purchased at the bazaar, nor can it be manufactured by industrial undertakings. It can be secured only by acts and activities charged with love. This is a holy place because you pay sincere attention to the proper development of the children under your care and devote your efforts to transmute them into sublime individuals and worth sons and daughters of this sacred land [India]. This is the only means by which we can ensure the welfare and prosperity of this country. Politics is powerless. In cannot save us. Machines and machinations cannot rescue us. Only by installing in our hearts the sacred ideals of Indian culture and marching forward toward those goals can peace be attained." (SS56)

Jesus said, "Render unto Caesar's that which is Caesar's and to God, that which belongs to Him." I have to constantly remind myself to get detached and keep on trying to change myself. I vote and shoot my mouth off about issues and situations and problems in the public sphere. I know that Dr. George and Yogananda do not want me to get too involved. They have told me pretty strongly, so I go along with it.

Reincarnation

On the subject of reincarnation, Jesus said the following things:

In Matthew 17:10-13, he answered his disciples as they asked him, "Why to the scriptures say that before you were to come, Elijah was to come?"

"Elijah truly shall first come and restore all things. But I say unto you, that Elijah has come already, and they knew him not, but have done with him whatsoever they wanted. Likewise shall also the Son of Man suffer of them." Then the disciples understood that he was speaking to them of John the Baptist." Note: Most metaphysical Christians, yogis, and Buddhists believe that John the Baptist was the reincarnation of Elijah and had to have his head cut off because of the bad karma he incurred as Elijah when he not only defeated the 400 prophets of Ba'al, but had their throats slit as well! Also, Yogananda, Dr. George, Swami Rama and others stated that Jesus was Elisha in a past life, the disciple of Elijah, and called for his guru while on the cross.

In Mark, 11:11-13

The disciples came to Jesus and said, "Why say the scribes that Elijah must come first [i.e., before the Christ]? Jesus said, "Elijah verily cometh first and restoreth all things, and how it is written that the Son of Man that he must suffer many things and be set at nought. But, I say unto you, that Elijah is indeed come and they have done unto him whatsoever they listed as it is written of him."

And in Luke, Jesus said, "Verily I say unto you, except a man be born again, he cannot see the Kingdom of God" and Nicodemus said, 'How can a man be born when he is old? Can he enter the womb a second time and be born?' Jesus answered, "Verily I say to you, except a man be born of the water and of the Spirit, he cannot enter into the Kingdom of heaven. That which is born of the flesh is flesh and that which is born of spirit is spirit. Marvel not that I said unto you, that you must be born again."

In a private conversation with a few close devotees in 1949, Swami Kriyananda herein recounts his guru, Paramahansa Yogananda telling them about some past incarnations of famous people:

"Sometimes he (Yogananda) intrigued us with references, always casual, to the past lives of certain well-known public figures. 'Winston Churchill,' he told us, 'was Napoleon Bonaparte. Napoleon wanted to conquer England. Churchill, as England's Prime Minister, has fulfilled that ambition. Napoleon wanted to destroy England. As

Churchill, he has had to preside over the disintegration of the British Empire (which of course included freedom for India in 1947). 'Napoleon was sent into exile, then returned again to power. Churchill, similarly, was sent out of politics, then after some time came back to power again.'

"'Hitler,' Master continued, 'was Alexander the Great.' (An interesting point of comparison here is that in warfare, both Alexander and Hitler employed the strategy of lightning attack, blitzkrieg, as Hitler called it. In the Orient, of course, where Alexander's conquests were responsible for the destruction of great civilizations, his appellation 'The Great' is quoted sarcastically).

"Master had hoped to reawaken in Hitler Alexander's interest in the teachings of India, and thereby to steer the dictator's ambitions to more spiritual goals. Master actually attempted to see Hitler in 1935, but his request for an interview was denied."

"Mussolini, Master said, was Marc Antony, Kaiser Wilhelm was Julius Caesar, and Stalin was Ghengis Khan."

"I inquired, 'Who was Roosevelt?' Master replied with a wry smile, 'I've never told anybody. I was afraid I'd get into trouble!'

'Abraham Lincoln,' he said, 'had been a yogi in the Himalayas, who died with a desire to help bring about racial equality. His birth as Lincoln was for the purpose of fulfilling that desire. 'He has come back again in this century,' Master said, 'as Charles Lindbergh.'"

"It is interesting to note that the public acclaim that was denied Lincoln, though so richly deserved, came almost effortlessly to Lindbergh. Lindbergh was interested in Indian Philosophy. Perhaps, one wonders, if he will once again in his next life become a yogi.

"Of more saintly people, Master said that Therese Neumann, the Catholic stigmatist of Konnersrueth, Germany, was Mary Magdalene. 'That,' he explained to me, 'is why she was granted those visions of Christ's crucifixion.'" (15)

On the subject of reincarnation, Sai Baba has spoken often. Here are some of his words:

"You feel happy and elated when the result is good. You feel unhappy and dejected when the result is bad. These emotional responses set off further desires and impulses which inflate or deflate the ego. This in turn leads to more action, and action results in reaction, and thus a never-ending chain of action-reaction and rebirth is produced. The desires and impulses remain with you even after death. They are so strong that you are born into this world again and again in order to fulfill them. As long as desires remain, rebirth is unavoidable. So, if you wish to avoid rebirth, you should get rid of worldly desires. They are binding on you. They are like magnets which attract you again and again into this world. Critical to release of desires is to change your attitude toward the result or fruits of your actions." (SS36)

"Whatever things we do with this body are leading to a rebirth of this body. Any actions, good or bad, can be compared to seeds. In order not to sow seeds, we should do all actions without desire. All actions should be done in and only for the pleasure of God. If you sweep a place, think that you are doing that for cleaning the heart, the shrine of God. When you help others, think that you are doing it for yourselves. Then, you will never let yourself harm anyone else." (SS13)

"Infinite years ago, we were all part of that single Almighty God enjoying Bliss. However, we separated from Him, being surrounded by ignorance and became atomic life. Since then, we took countless number of bodies from the microscopic to the macroscopic sizes, went through plant and animal lives and at last were born as men. Even the human body, we changed innumerable times. We lived in the Old Stone Age, The New Stone Age, times of Rama, Times of Krishna, Zarathustra, Buddha, Jesus, and Mohammed in different parts of the world, wearing different bodies. We were wicked in some lives and passed through the terrible path of *yama* (death) and the hells in the interlife subsequent to those lives. We acquired merit by doing good deeds and developed devotion to God in some lives and traversed the pleasant path of *dharma deva* (heavens) in the interlives subsequent to those lives. After passing through these innumerable lives, we have at last been born again in a blessed time when the God from whom we were originally separated from has taken a body like our own, and the name, Sai Baba, to show us the further way to proceed to the blissful state which will be obtained after merging in Him." (SS18)

"Your rebirth is determined by the type of death you get. If you want a good rebirth and a good life in the next birth, you must also desire a good death. We should not devote our life to fulfilling meaningless and sensory desires." (SS14)

Dr. George said the following things about reincarnation:

I asked him if I had known him in any previous incarnations, and he said yes, quite a few. When I asked him about one of them, he said the following: "It was 325 B.C. and you were in India." I said, "Was I Hindu?" "No, you were Greek; you were with Alexander the Great's army." He chuckled and laughed and went on: "You got your face full. You were captured and held for ransom by one of the India generals. You became friends with him and stayed there the rest of your life." I said, "Who were you in that lifetime?" He wouldn't say and I knew by then that when he didn't answer, it had a lot to do with deep humility, so I asked the question differently, "Were you a holy man then and did you become my guru?" He smiled and nodded, and said, "You were a very hard case. I kept you from being executed and you became a student of the Vedas and began to meditate."

I asked him, "Was I ever a woman in past lives?" He laughed, and said, "Many times. In France, you were a big fat woman and had about 11 kids. You lived on a farm and were pretty happy."

I asked him, "What about gay people? Why are they gay?" He said, "It is s transition lifetime. Often, a male gay was a woman for a number of lifetimes in a row and identified very strongly with the female form. Likewise, with a female gay person; she had been a man many lifetimes in a row and got attached to that form. As part of his/her evolution, they are now transitioning over to opposite outer form for a while. The first such lifetime is very difficult. It is not good that people are cruel to other people who are a little different. Sam, you should always go out of your way to be kind and good to folks who are different. We are all God's children. Everyone you see on the street was gay in some lifetimes and so were you."

"General Rommel was Hannibal in a past life and General George Patton was his younger brother. Their love was why they never faced each other on the battlefield."

To me, specifically, he said: "You have spent many, many lifetimes as a soldier. This lifetime, you had to come unarmed. You must learn to forgive, totally forgive and release all wrongs to you."

To me, he said one day at The Farm while having coffee, "If you meditate, practice Kriya yoga, and forgive and help others, you will greatly hasten your evolution and not have to spend too many more lifetimes on this earth."

He told me that my sister, Gail, was Marie of Denmark, who married the Czar Alexander II of Russia and was thereby the Queen of Russia. That is why she was born totally deaf and going blind. He explained to me that she *chose* to work out her final karma in that method. He explained that this was her last required lifetime.

Since I first started meditating, I started to remember certain past lifetimes. Here are some of the lifetimes I have remembered:

- I was a mountain man and cowboy and guide in the west back in the early 1800's. I think that is why I love westerns and the west.

- I was a large peasant woman in France with ten or 11 kids. I was on a big farm and kind of ran the place. It was a happy life.

- I was an American Indian warrior. I was strong and full of my strength and courage.
- I was an American Indian slave woman, enslaved by another tribe. I was beaten,

raped, and brutalized. I was literally worked to death by the time I was 18. Worked out a lot of karma.

- I was a Buddhist monk in an oriental country. I was thin and had a shaved head and loincloth. I later ran the monastery and was a real jerk. I was outwardly pious and made everyone follow all the rules, but had little inner realization. After that life, I said to myself, "Oh boy, do I need to expand."

- I was a woman actress and entertainer. I do not know the details

- I was a composer and musician in the 1700's sometime.

- I was a very wealthy patron of the arts in Italy in the 1600's. I think I was gay that lifetime.

- I was a soldier many times. When I saw the movie "Braveheart," by Mel Gibson, I was struck to the bottom of my soul, because I truly remembered fighting just like that. Real tough stuff.
- I was in China and India a number of times.

Repentance

Sai Baba has said the following about repentance:

"If you do wrong, then pray repeatedly for intelligence not to repeat it. Beyond that, it depends on His Grace whether he punishes and protects or pardons and corrects." (SS2)

Dear Reader: Please take note of the next two statements by Baba. They seem to be contradictory. Maybe it was to whom he was speaking at the time. Who knows?

"However much we repent towards the end of our life, it is very difficult for us to realize that such repentance comes to us in a manner in which it cannot atone for our sins. After indulging in sins and doing bad things all through one's life, even if one repents towards the very end, that repentance is not of much value. Alas, repentance always comes much after the event and too late to do any good to anyone." (SS9)

"Even the most heinous sinner can quickly cleanse his heart and become pure by surrendering to the Lord in anguished repentance." (SS39)

"A person may realize his mistakes, and that what he has been doing is wrong. He is overcome by remorse, sincerely repents for his past misdeeds and tries to atone for them. In that case, he will make his payment in the same birth itself.

Repentance, atonement, spiritual practices – all these can mitigate or reduce the suffering caused by past karmas. They cannot cancel out the karma. You can dilute your suffering with the help of sadhana, japa, dhyana, bhajan, namsmarana, etc. They cannot completely wipe out past karma because the consequences of karma have to be faced." (SS48)

Dr. George said the following about repentance:

"A man smokes, drinks, eats meat, hurts others, and then as he is getting near to dying, he suddenly gives his life to Jesus and says, 'Save me!' And Jesus will tell him, 'Where were you in your youth?'" He told my mother and I this one day in the car in August, 1972.

"God will forgive you and release you if you truly repent and change, but you have to forgive others. If you ask God to forgive you and then blame and criticize and hold anger for others, the Lord will spit you out." (Sermon, church, September, 1967.)

"Folks always look for faults in others. That is real stupid. That does nothing but hurt you! What you need to do is be very vigilant, looking for your own faults and mistakes, and repent and change yourself! Stop trying to change others. Jesus didn't say, 'Try to change others.' He said, 'Love one another as I have loved you.'" (Sermon, church, January, 1966.)

It is very therapeutic to meditate and examine oneself. I have had great benefits from repentance and penance.

Self-Realization

Sai Baba has stated the following about this topic:

"When the soul attains complete realization, it has full wisdom, beauty, splendor, power, fame and fortune. One's nature is then full existence, full knowledge, full bliss." (SS15)

"Until realization of God, the name can be used. The idea of separation will end only with merger, not before that. Do not waver or doubt once you are convinced as to the effectiveness of this method." (SS3)

"There is no need to retire into a forest or cave to know you inner Reality and to conquer your lower nature. Win the battle of life by being in the world, but free from attachments. That is a victory for which you can be congratulated." (SS12)

"Mankind is steeped in illusion, and he cannot free himself from this illusion. He forgets his origin and he does not understand the Universal Absolute. However, if this situation did not exist, there is no reason why the Overself should come as an avatar at all. What exists as reality is only one, but what we see is manifold. What is real is the

Supreme Light. This Supreme Light is the Splendor of the Self." (SS7)

"Search for existence, that which suffers no change." (SS2)

Dr. George said the following about Self-realization:

"If there are enough people of Self-realization in America, it will be spared much of its bad karma. It is not good to fight wars like this one (Viet Nam); all the money could be spent to help people, and the men, women, and children we kill over there. That's bad karma for us." (He told me this in the kitchen at The Farm in December, 1971.)

"Mankind's first and foremost duty is to attain Self-realization." (He said this many, many times over the years.)

Self-realization is a synonym for "God-realization," "being one with God," attaining nirbikalpa samadhi or nirvana, or Christ Consciousness. It is the awareness of one's Self as divinity. Even the beginning meditator gets little glimmers of this regularly. The object of spiritual practice is to extend those glimmers and make them longer and longer until permanent.

Lahiri Mahasaya said the following:
"He only is wise who devotes himself to realizing, not reading only, the ancient revelations.

Solve all your problems through meditation. Exchange unprofitable religious speculations for actual God-contact. Clear you mind of dogmatic theological debris. Let in the fresh healing waters of direct perception of God. Attune yourself to the active inner Guidance. The Divine Voice has the answers to every dilemma of life. Though man's ingenuity for getting himself into trouble appears endless, the Infinite Succor is no less resourceful."

Sending Love

Sai Baba has stated the following on this topic:

"The *ananda* (bliss) that can be derived by unselfish scattering of Love is a rare elevating experience. It is a very valuable *sadhana* (spiritual discipline)." (SS26)

"Love is the natural state and all other contrary emotions are unnatural. Therefore, when you send a wave of spontaneous love to a person, it is bound to strike some chord in him or her. When you go on showering love, it will slowly begin to cleanse and purify, and soon the undesirable traits will be weeded out and goodness will shine through." (SS26)

Dr. George said the following on this topic:

"When someone does you wrong, send them love and forgive them." (He said this many, many times in different words.)

"Instead of wasting your thoughts and minds worrying and being angry, try sending love to other people. It will really make you happy. It takes practice. Just try it and keep trying it. The minute you start worrying or start blaming others, start praying for others and send them love. If you cannot pray for your enemies, then start praying and sending love to your friends." (Sermon, The Farm, November, 1977.)

"God likes you when you get your mind off of yourself and send love to others." (Sermon, The Farm, September, 1964.)

I had a remarkable proof of the power of this one time. It was 1976 and I was on a date with a pretty actress one Saturday night. We went to this place in Calabassas that had great music. This night, a few of the Beach Boys were jamming with some pretty good musicians. We were really enjoying it. Then, suddenly, this very big and very nasty drunk guy came over, sat across from us, and started calling me every dirty name in the book. I remained calm and did not say a word. I called on my Guru and proceeded to look him in the eye and send him love. I just kept sending him love. Finally, he sputtered to a stop, looked at me quizzically and walked back to his place at the bar.

My date was shocked. She suggested we get out of there. We did. We went down the road to another place. We were sitting there. She was totally shook up. She said, "What did you do?" I told her that I had just sent him love. I told her that I was a yogi and meditated. I told her that my philosophy was not to fight, but to send love.

Well, I did have a proof of the power of sending love, but the actress was shocked by my explanation. This business of sending love to an enemy was a lot more scary to her than some guy threatening me and trying to start a fight or something. That was my first and last date with her. Oh, well; the right one would have understood and agreed with me.

Later, when I saw Dr. George, I told him about this experience. He chuckled and was happy that I had done that. He really laughed when I asked him the final question: I said, "Dr. George, I have to confess. I was sending him love and was very calm. I did not respond to his insults. However, I had my hands under the heavy wood table and if he had made a move, I was fully prepared to push the table over on top of him and run out the door. Was that OK and allowable?" He chuckled and said, "Yes. Sometimes you do have to defend yourself but, most of the time, God will protect you. You did well. I *was* with you."

Another time, after we started working with the Sai Baba people, I found some very tough folks with strong egos and no sense of humor. There was one older Indian lady who ran that Sai Center with an iron fist. She tolerated no interference in her dominion over that group. She did not like me because I was a possible threat to her authority. Since we had to deal with her, it was a puzzle to me. I meditated and asked Sai Baba to give me guidance. I kept asking, and one day, he came to me in meditation with a big smile, and looked dreamily and said, "Love, Love, Love." So, thereupon, every time I saw her or thought of her, I sent her "Love, Love, Love." I, myself was totally shocked, because she became one of my best friends in the Sai organization. We became good buddies. Her husband was amazed that we got along so well as were other Hindu ladies in the group. I just kept sending her love.

Tolerance

Jesus said the following in Matthew: "Judge not that you not be judged, for with what judgement you judge, you shall be judged, and with what measure you mete, it shall be measured to you again." He also said, "Why is it that you see the speck in your brother's eye and you cannot see the beam in your own?"

Sai Baba said the following on tolerance:

"First, be fixed in the consciousness that you are the immortal soul, which is indestructible, which is holy, which is pure and divine. That will give you unshakable courage and strength. Then, you must develop mutual love and respect. Tolerate all kinds of persons and various opinions, all attitudes and peculiarities. The school, the home, and the society are all training grounds for tolerance." (SS2)

Dr. George said the following about tolerance:

"The Lord and the Great Ones just shake their heads in sorrow when people claim to have the one and only religion and hurt other people in the name of that religion. You should be kind and understanding about all religions." (Sermon, The Farm, October, 1965.)

"The essence of civilization is tolerance. America was formed for tolerance of everyone. Selfish and greedy people want to make differences and have you look down at people who are a little different. We are all God within. All beings, all life is God. When you are intolerant of others, you are intolerant of yourself!" (Sermon, The Farm, October, 1972.)

"Just be kind." (He said this often.)

"What difference does it make to you what someone else believes in? That's not your problem. People do not like it when someone else believes something else because that makes them uneasy about their own beliefs. If you meditate and base your beliefs on actual inner experience, you will be secure in your own identity as sprit." (Sermon, March, 1965, The Farm.)

Yogananda replied when asked about civil rights, "God does not like to be insulted when he is wearing his dark suits." (Dr. George told me that he heard his guru say this in the late 1930's. I believe it was also stated later by Swami Kriyananda.)

Yogananda, Sai Baba, and Dr. George all started churches and/or organizations recommending tolerance and respect for all religions.

Related to me, don't even get me started on this topic. Nothing on earth ticks me off more than intolerance. I am totally intolerant of intolerance. I just do not have any idea why someone cannot respect or at least be neutral about someone who is a little different. It boggles my mind. I enjoy someone who is different than me. I am tired of me, most of the time. I like a little spice here and there and like to learn new things. I have never met anyone on this Earth that I couldn't learn something from.

Unity

Sai Baba has stated the following on this topic:

"In this cosmic university, all are students. Hence, everyone should render social service to the extent of one's capacity and spread Swami's ideals among all. There is nothing selfish in Swami's message. Hence, anyone can spread it selflessly. Sow the seed of love in your hearts and it will grow in due course into a big tree. God is one. Do not entertain any differences of creed or caste. Carry the message of unity to every home." (SS6)

"On the fathomless ocean, countless waves arise. Though the waves appear as different from each other, the ocean is one. Likewise, though living beings appear in the Universe in a myriad of forms, all of them are waves that have emerged from the ocean of *sat-chit-ananda* (being-awareness-bliss)." (SS11)

"There are today few who recognize unity in diversity, though there are any number of intellectuals who are engaged in promoting divisions and differences. The world today needs righteous men who will promote unity." (Same as previous statement.)

"India today is in a crisis created by a myriad of difficult problems. However, *Bharat* (India) is not alone; all countries are also facing similar crises. What is the reason? It is the total failure to remember the spiritual oneness of mankind. Only the sense of spiritual unity will generate universal love. That love alone will bind men together in unity. This love principle should emanate from the heart. Only then, true unity will emerge." (SS5)

"To unite all mankind into one caste or family in the establishment of unity, that is Atmic realization, in every man and woman, which is the basis on which the entire cosmic design rests. Once this is realized, the common divine heritage that binds man to man and man to God will be apparent and love shall prevail as the guiding light in the universe." (SS7)

"The universe is the body of God. Every particle in it is filled with God, His Glory, His Might, His inscrutability. Believe that God is the inner Truth in everything and being. He is Eternal. Be humble before the evidences of His power and majesty." (SS8)

Dr. George said the following about Unity:

"Yogananda was sent by the Great Ones to show the unity of the Christian and Hindu scriptures and religions. Remember, Yogananda always said, 'The word Krishna is the same word as the word Christ.' The words mean, 'The consciousness that is in every atom of creation.' You should remember that you, too, are on your way to become 'Christs.' The only difference between you and Jesus or Krishna is *time*. Expand your consciousness now and identify with all creation; experience yourself as every atom of creation. That is who you really are. You are now deluded into thinking that you are Bob or Paul or Sandy, a little person here in Wisconsin. You are the eternal spirit! You are made in God's image. God is big. You are big. You are infinite within." (Sermon, The Farm, October, 1974.)

"You must see and experience God within all beings. It will be very difficult to do that if you kill animals and eat them." (Informal talk at the dinner table, The Farm, May, 1971.)

"It is very important now that mankind recognizes the unity of all religions." (He told me this in February, 1969 at The Farm.)

In the Gospel of Mark, here is a statement by Jesus: The disciple John said to Jesus that they saw a fellow casting out devils in Master's name and did not follow the disciples, and we forbade him from doing his thing because he did not follow them. And Jesus said: "Forbid him not, for there is no man which shall do a miracle in my name that can lightly speak evil of me, for he that is not against us is on our side."

It is my opinion that we must come together on this planet or else we will perish. We must realize that God is within all life and all beings. There is no reason we cannot get together and solve the world's problems. Only greed, selfishness, and narrow-mindedness prevent it. The first step is blessing someone who does not agree with you.

Lahiri Mahasaya was a great example of unity. Yogananda described his guru's guru as follows:

"A significant feature of Lahiri Mahasay's life was his gift of Kriya yoga initiation to those of every faith. Not Hindus only, but Moslems and Christians were among is foremost disciples.

Monists and dualists, those of all faiths or of no established faith, were impartially received and instructed by the universal guru. One of his highly-advanced disciples was Abdul Gufoor Khan, a Mohammedan. It shows a great courage on the part of Lahiri Mahasaya that, although a high-caste Brahmin, he tried his utmost to dissolve the rigid caste bigotry of his time. Those from every walk of life found shelter under the Master's omnipresent wings. Like all God-inspired prophets, Lahiri Mahasaya gave new hope to the outcastes and downtrodden of society." (1)

Vegetarianism

Sai Baba has always strongly recommended a vegetarian diet for all of his devotees:

"It is a fact that plants also have life like animals. But animals are endowed with mind and nervous systems like humans. Plants do not possess the same. The animals cry and weep when they are being killed. It is not the case with plants. Trying to equate killing of animals and eating plants is faulty logic. Further, the killing and eating of animals leads to the creeping or dissemination of the animal qualities and behavior in the person who kills or eats them, meaning that the eater acquires the beastly qualities by eating animal flesh." (SS32)

"With meat, people say that the body will get the proteins, but mental proteins will not be there. If you are keen on spiritual life, eating meat is not worthwhile. Also, when you kill an animal, you give him suffering, pain, and harm. God is in every creature, so how can you give such pain? Animals did not come for the purpose of supplying food to human beings." (SS19)

"Keeping in mind that man has risen from the stone to the plant, and from the plant to the animal, and eventually to his present life form as a human. We should remind ourselves of our struggle to achieve human birth, which according to the Vedas, is the most difficult to attain. Realizing this, it is totally wrong to take the life of an animal for almost any reason except self-defense or to save the life of another human." (SS13)

Dr. George strongly recommended that all of his students become vegetarians. He said dairy and eggs were okay, but did not have any problems with some devotees becoming vegans. He said the following:

"There will not be an end to war until mankind stops killing and eating animals." (He said this to me and others many times.)

"Because of your body type, it would be advisable for you to eat a little fish regularly." (He told me this the second day I knew him in 1964.)

"It is nearly impossible to meditate well if you eat meat." (He told all of this many, many times over the years.)

"If you eat meat, you will pick up the vibrations of anger and fear the animal emitted when he was killed. It doesn't matter if someone else did the killing." (He said this in many talks over the years.)

I have felt so good physically since I became a vegetarian. I truly recommend it to everyone. You will be happier and healthier if you stop eating meat. You may think you need it, but after a while, it grosses you out.

It would be better for the entire planet if we didn't eat meat.

Wisdom

Sai Baba said the following on this topic:

"The man of wisdom sees everything as the Divine Substance. The man of devotion sees everything as the play and drama of God. The man of action sees everything (i.e., all actions) as service to God." (SS10)

"The wise persons who do not have pride and delusion, who have conquered the evil of attachment, who always remain in the thoughts of soul, who are away from sensual desires and who are free from the opposites known as pleasure and pain go to that imperishable state (liberation)." (SS5)

"The wise are those who know the Atma. When the wise man experiences the Atma, he is endowed with Supreme Bliss. It is sheer waste if a person has no such experience but has pored over mountains of spiritual texts or earned fame as a deep scholar and does not feel God, the Atma within." (SS62)

Dr. George always differentiated between knowledge and wisdom. He revered the ancient wisdom of the Rishis of the Himalayas. He was a walking wisdom purveyor, and he looked at things differently than most of us do. For example, one time I was horrified by some scenes from World War II on a television program we were watching, and Dr. George chuckled and said brightly, "Well, it sure did work out a lot of karma in a very short time. Many souls made great advancements during those years." Needless to say, I have pondered those words ever since. I still do not quite grasp it, however.

Swami Rama definitely encouraged many of his devotees to get top education from good universities. He, himself, was very well educated and no stranger to the halls of academia and centers of science. His great devotee, Dr. Justin O'Brien, for example, has two PhD's. It could be that he wanted such devotees to be respected by their worldly counterparts, knowing how difficult it is for mystics to just exist on this earth. I truly remember so many years of meditating and being a vegetarian when it seemed there was no one with whom I could talk about it, and being viewed as totally whacko by many "normal" people. However, Swami Rama pressed his devotees very hard on to practice his teachings, i.e., meditate, meditate, meditate; do the *pranayams* (life-force control); change the thoughts, etc.

Yogananda, on the other hand, was more of a mix of Dr. George and Swami Rama. He met the famous and wealthy people of his day on equal terms. His disciples were a very high quality of spiritual *and* worldly people. Though he stressed seeking God inwardly, morning, noon, and night, he also taught very specific strategies and systems for his folks to make their ways successfully in the outer, as well.

The story goes that Socrates was told that he was the wisest man on Earth. He said, "No, no, not really." Then, he went to a conference of sages and came back and said, "Well, I changed my mind; I am the wisest man on earth because I am the only one who knows he doesn't know anything!"

I have found that after all my years of meditating, I know a lot less than I did when I started. I do *experience* a lot more.

The Word of God

Jesus said (Matthew 4:4), "It is written, 'Man shall not live by bread alone, but by every word that proceedeith out of the mouth of God.'"

Metaphysical Christians and Yogis interpret this as the Aum vibration coming from the medulla oblongata.

Sai Baba has said the following:

"It is God's word that if you have devotion to God, He will look after your future. He will look after all the welfare that is due to you." (SS5)

Dr. George said often that the Christian religion (and other religions) get caught up in legalistic interpretations of scriptures. They memorize scriptures and talk about "believing in the *literal* words of the scriptures." In this way, they greatly resemble the Pharisees and Scribes which Jesus railed often about. George went on to say that what Jesus specifically meant by the "word" of God was the Om vibration that you can hear when you are meditating. This comes into the human body through the medulla oblongata and brings the life force. He taught me how to use that energy to reduce the need for food. In fact, when he passed away, it was discovered that Dr. George *did not have a stomach*. He had always said, "There will come a time when mankind will not need the stomach, because he will learn to live on the energy direct from God through the medulla oblongata." We looked back and realized that he truly hadn't eaten much in many years and spit up much of the mostly liquids that he ingested. I do not remember him eating anything solid for at least seven years before he passed away. Others say the same thing.

This topic is of great interest for me. I have tried fasting many times, and I still have not got the hang of this technique. Maybe, one of these days, I will have a breakthrough.

Thoughts

Sai Baba has said the following about thoughts:

"Everything is based on man's thoughts, which find expression in external forms, a reflection of his inner being. Thoughts lead to action. There can be no action without thoughts. Hence, it is essential to entertain sacred thoughts. Everyone should realize that all the sorrows and miseries of modern man are due to his bad thoughts. Every man thinks that someone else is responsible for his troubles. This is not so. You alone are responsible for the good and evil that befalls you. You blame others because of your weakness." (SS27)

"There is no use in resisting or fighting thoughts. If suppressed, they are always ready to spring forth at weak moments, like snakes in a basket. If the cover gets loose or is removed, the snakes spring forth. The way to overcome bad thoughts and impulses is by having thoughts of serving the Lord, good conversations with wise people, good actions, and words. The weight of good acts and thoughts will bury the seeds of bad actions and thoughts. Both good and bad thoughts and impulses are like seeds in the mind. If buried too deeply in the earth, seeds rot and waste away. Good thoughts and deeds bury bad seeds so deeply that they rot and pass away and are no longer ready to spring forth." (SS56)

"Thoughts constitute the very basis of one's life. It is the mind that lends life, sustains it, and ultimately brings it to an end. Mind is the cause for creation, sustenance, and dissolution." (SS3)

Dr. George had some wry comments on Thoughts:
"Mosquitoes are the product of mankind's bad thoughts." (He said this as we were working on a building one especially-bad mosquito day at The Farm in 1967.)

"Why would I want to?" spoken in answer to a student's question in 1972, January. The student asked Dr. George if he could read people's thoughts, noting that he had apparently demonstrated this ability quite often with her, personally.

"It doesn't do any good to be nice to someone when you have bad thoughts about them. You need to change your thoughts to love and forgiveness. You need to know that if you see a flaw in someone else, you have the seeds of the same flaw within you." (He told us this in a talk at The Farm in July, 1965.)

Yogananda said the following in his talk at SRF Encinitas in November, 1938: "Thought produces everything in the universe." In 1926, in an informal talk, he said the following: "In the Yoga philosophy, the universe is spoken of as God's dream. Matter and mind, the cosmos with its stars and planets, the gross surface waves and the subtle undercurrents of the material creation; the human powers of feeling, will, and consciousness; and the states of life and death, day and night, health and disease, success and failure are realities according to the law of relativity governing this dream of God's." and "Only the superman, who has learned to expand and transfer his consciousness to the Infinite, can realize creation as a dream of God's. He alone can say with true knowledge that matter has no existence."

Yogananda said the following in a talk in December, 1937 in Los Angeles: "Everything on earth had its birth in the factory of the mind, either in God's mind or in man's mind. Actually, man cannot think an 'original' thought. He can only borrow God's thoughts and become an instrument to materialize them. Experiment with your thoughts. Try out your strongest on your body. See if you cannot overcome undesirable habits and persistent ailments When you are successful, you may apply your thought to make changes in the world around you.

"The relationship between thought and matter is very subtle. Suppose you see a wooden pillar and try, by the power of thought, to remove the pillar. You cannot do that. In spite of what you think, the pillar is still there. It is a materialization of someone's previous thought. It will not go away merely by your thinking it is not there. Only when you *realize* it is a materialization of thought may you dematerialize it to your consciousness. As you learn by experimenting with overcoming habits, pain, and so on, you will begin to understand that the entire design of the body and all its processes are controlled by thought."

I have really worked my whole life on controlling my thoughts. I do not like negative thoughts. I absolutely refuse to hold a grudge. I forgive real quickly and get it out of my mind. I also do not like worrying. I truly try to give all my problems to God and let him or one of the Great Ones deal with them. They seem to do a better job than I do anyway.

I have had a lot of trouble with this stuff they call "the law of attraction." This subject is popular right now, but I just do not get into it. I prefer just to keep my thoughts on God and love all the time, and surrender to God what is mine and what I will attract. I think that the "Law of Aversion" is just as powerful. I think that if you are on the spiritual path and there is something that bothers you, it seems that you get that in spades until you learn to love it, forgive it, or it doesn't bother you anymore. Then, it seems to go away.

Jesus Lived in India or Alternative Views of Jesus

What we have to account for the traditional religious point of view on the life and death and resurrection of Jesus are four short books which have a dubious and questionable history and origin. Even what is written in those four "books" in the bible is suspect. The words have been altered over the centuries. The original Bible was formed by the Roman Emperor Constantine during a process that many potential scriptures were thrown out.

Over the years, I have heard some say that 95% of the early Christian writings were burned or destroyed, or discredited by Constantine and his people in the process of forming a religion whose purpose was not Truth, but was political stability at a tough time in the Roman Empire.

This is by no means to diminish Jesus. I fully state that he was a Divine Incarnation and was one with God. I totally believe that he did all the miracles they have described in the Bible and a whole lot more. However, never once did he say, even in the manipulated Bible, that he was the only Son of God and he didn't say that he was dying for the sins of mankind. These were concepts already done in many prior cultures and countries in pagan traditions, which Constantine compiled, threw Jesus in with it, and made it Christianity. The birth date, December 25 came from paganism. What Constantine's moves did, however, was to unify paganism and Christianity under the same church banner and thus stabilizing the Empire – actually not a bad move on his part.

Given this background, I feel that I have the right to offer alternative views of the life and work of one of the most important humans who ever lived, if not the most important. So, in this section, I will be briefly summarizing my findings in this area.

I have read many books by psychics, clairvoyants and channelers dealing with this subject. Since I have been in the metaphysical field for 56 years, and since I also have been in the entertainment, mining, and oil businesses, I feel that I have a PhD in recognizing questionable data, and have a well-trained sense of what is real and what is not. Relying on that (shaky) expertise, I will first briefly summarize from a number of these books. (I have listed these in the bibliography as "Psychic Writers."):

Metaphysicians and yogis widely state that Jesus lived in India for most of the time between ages 13-30. It is also said that the Three Wise Men were his gurus and came to protect the Great One at his birth and that at age 13, Jesus and his father, Joseph went to India in a caravan. It is further said that Joseph left that body in the Himalayas in the company of the Great Master Babaji. (Note: However, Sai Baba has a slightly dissenting point of view, stating in SS, January, 1996, P.2-3, "His father passed away when Jesus was only ten.") It is also said that the Brahmins drove him out of India because He taught that there was only one caste, the caste of humanity. (Apparently, he couldn't get a break from organized religion; Dr. George said with a slight tongue in his cheek and in a laughing manner, "If Jesus came back today, the Christian Church would possibly kill him faster than the Romans did then.")
There is some practical evidence of this, which includes three basic things: 1) the miracles

he did were "yogi" miracles, i.e., miracles that had been done and are still being done by yogi Masters from India; 2) the place he is most likely to have been was in the Kashmir sector of the Himalayas, and the garb he wore was Kashmiri; 3) there is a grave in Kashmir to this day of his mother, Mary, and the town thereof is called "Mar"; 4) his disciple and brother Thomas was martyred in Puri, India; 5) his hairstyle was Kashmiri; 6) there is still some physical, narrative, archeological, and folk history evidence of his life in India.

In fact, in my opinion, there is much more evidence supporting this hypothesis than anything the organized Christian religion can put up for any contravening point of view.

Here is what some Masters have said about this:

Swami Rama

"There was a manuscript written in the Tibetan language preserved in a monastery situated at the height of 14,000 feet in the Himalayas. It was later translated by a Russian writer and then into English and published as "The Unknown life of Jesus Christ." Swami Rama goes on to say that there was a special spiritual cave on a mount which was sacred because it is averred that Jesus meditated there. Near there, Swami Rama came to an ashram to stay for a while. A swami at the ashram told Swami Rama that there was a young roving adept (master) who visited the sacred shrine every summer, but no one knew where the adept lived permanently. People coming from Ladakh saw him treading the mountain paths all alone.

I wanted very badly to meet this adept. Of all those I have met in my life, three were very impressive and left deep imprints in the bed of my memory. That adept was one of them. I stayed with him for seven days, just fifty yards away from the shrine. He visited this cave shrine practically every year. He was about twenty years of age, was very handsome, and the luster of his cheeks was like that of cherries. He was a *bramacharya* (yogi renunciate) who wore only a loincloth and possessed nothing. He was so acclimated to high altitudes that, with the help of yoga practices, he could travel barefoot and live at elevations of 10,000 to 12,000 feet. He was insensitive to cold.

Living with him was an enlightening experience to me. He was perfect and full of yoga wisdom and serenity. People called this young adept *Bal Bhagavan* (Child-God Incarnate), but he always kept himself above such praises and constantly traveled in the Himalayas. He already knew my name and had lived in our cave monasteries. He asked about several students who were then practicing meditation with my master. He spoke briefly in gentle sentences, but I could feel that he was not pleased when my guide started bowing, touching his feet, and running around in emotional devotion. This great adept became an example for me. I had never before seen a man who could sit still without blinking his eyelids for eight to ten hours, but this adept was very unusual. He levitated two and a half feet during his meditations. We measured this with a string which was later measured by a foot rule.

I asked him a question about the highest state of the enlightenment. He muttered a mantra from the Upanishads, and stated, "When the senses are well-controlled and withdrawn from contact with the objects of the world, then sense perceptions no longer create images in the mind. The mind is then trained in one-pointedness. When the mind no longer recalls thought-patterns from the unconscious, a balanced state of mind leads to a higher state of consciousness. A perfect state of serenity established in *sattwa* (divine peace) is the highest state of enlightenment. The practice of meditation and non-attachment are the two keynotes. A very firm conviction is essential for establishing a definite philosophy of life. Intellect intervenes and blind emotion misguides. Though both are great powers, they should be known first, analyzed, and then directed toward the source of intuition. Intuition is the only source of true knowledge. All this, whatever you see in the world is unreal because of its constantly changing nature. Reality is hidden beneath all these changes."

Swami Rama put this story into a chapter in LWHM that is entitled, "Jesus in India." Master George told me that Jesus still lived in the Himalayas and worked for the evolution of mankind. Those previous words are very similar to the biblical admonitions of Jesus where he told folks to not build up treasures on Earth or build their houses on sand, rather, go to what was unchangeable, the Kingdom of Heaven within.

Dr. George

Dr. George stated clearly that "Jesus was in bliss when he was on the cross" and "Jesus lived to be over 120 years old in that body." Dr. George told a few of us this information in informal talks here and there. He went on to say that Jesus had gone into the breathless state and appeared dead, which is why his ally, Joseph of Arimathea was able to bribe the guards and get Jesus down. Dr. George said that Jesus was healed by his friends, herbs and his own powers, he said his wife, Mary and mother, Mary were the key healers.

Archeological Research

Dr. Helmut Kersten, a German researcher, wrote a remarkable book called *Jesus Lived in India*. In this book, he compiled a lot of the data which has been accumulated against all odds on this subject.

Sai Baba on Jesus

In his Christmas discourse of 1978, Sai Baba said the following about Jesus: "Jesus was a master born with a purpose, the mission of restoring Love, Charity, and Compassion in the heart of man. He had no attachment to the self, nor paid any heed to joy or sorrow, loss or gain. He had a heart that responded to the call of anguish, and he went about the land preaching the lesson of love. His life was a libation for the upliftment of humanity.

"Like most seekers, he first searched for the Divine in the objective world, but he soon realized that the world is a kaleidoscopic picture created by one's own imagination, and sought to find God within himself. His stay in the Himalayan monasteries in Kashmir and in other centers of Eastern asceticism and philosophical inquiry, gave him greater awareness.

"From the attitude of being a 'messenger' of God, he developed in those monasteries the realization that he was beloved by God and was now considered a 'Son of God.' The 'I' was no more some distant light or entity. The Light became a part of 'I.' With the body-consciousness predominate, he was a 'messenger' of God, With the heart-consciousness in the ascendant, he felt a greater nearness and dearness, and so the son-father bond seemed natural at this stage. Later, as the Atman-consciousness was established, Jesus could declare, 'I and my Father are one.' The three stages may be described as 'I was in the Light,' 'The Light was in me,' and 'I am the Light.' The final stage is the one when all duality has been shed. This is the essence of all religious disciplines and teachings.

Jesus was honored by the populace as Christ, for they found in his thoughts, words, and deeds no trace of ego. He had no envy or hatred, and was full of love and charity, humility and sympathy. Jesus' original name was Isa. In the Tibetan monastery where he spent some years, his name is written as Issa, which means the 'Lord of all living beings.'"

In his New Year's speech in 1978, Sai Baba said the following:

"Jesus was the embodiment of compassion and love. His heart melted in sympathy when he saw any one suffering. His entire life was dedicated to service. In the interest of truth, he laid down his own life. Such persons are revered in the world, however much times may change" and "Christ spent all his life in the service of mankind. He spent twelve years alone, promoting the inner vision and realizing God. Thereafter, Christ spent five years in the Himalayan region of Bharath (India). He settled in Kashmir and met many exponents and practitioners of the *adwaitha* system of thought, which declares that there is only One God. He realized the One-ness beneath all diversity and then He spread the Truth that 'I and my Father are One.'"

In the 1979 Christmas discourse by Swami, he said the following:

"There are various theories about the date of birth of Jesus, based on the bright star that appeared on His birth. It is visible once in 800 years, it is said. Some say that He was born on September fifteenth, but he was born at 3:15 A.M. on December 28th, 1980 years ago. It was Sunday. The star that appeared that day appears only once in 800 years. It had nothing to do with the birth of Jesus. There is no rule that when Divine Energy or Divine Incarnation descends on Earth, a star has to appear. That is the opinion of devotees only. But Jesus was a *Star of Infinite Value*, spreading brilliance of infinite dimension. Why posit another less brilliant glow?" and "The Jews held the rituals and regulations laid down by the prophets in the scriptural texts as valid for all time and so they held the teachings of Jesus to be wrong. They were not moved from their personal hatred of Jesus. This problem arises in every age, the conflict between the letter and the spirit, the doctrines that are held to be holy, the various do's and don'ts that have to be scrupulously followed versus the Underlying Truth. In the Vedic Faith (i.e., Hinduism), one can find this conflict between the upholders of ancient tradition and the promoters of deeper understanding."

In the 1972 Christmas discourse, Swami probably said some of the most compelling things:

"The Great Teachers belong to mankind. It is wrong to believe that Jesus belongs to the Christians and that Christmas is a Holy Festival for the West only. To accept One of them as one's own and discard the rest as belonging to others is a sign of pettiness. Christ, Rama, Krishna, they are for all men everywhere. The various limbs and organs together form a body; various States and communities together form the world, the sustenance given by Divine Grace circulates in every part of the Body, helping it to function in unison. The sustenance of Love, endowed by Divine Grace, has to circulate in every State and community to make the World live in Peace and Joy. If this truth is realized, there will arise no idea of difference" and "There is one point that I cannot but bring to your special notice today. At the moment when Jesus was emerging in the Supreme Principle of Divinity (i.e., after his resurrection), He communicated some news to his followers, which has been interpreted in a variety of ways by commentators and those who relish the piling of writings on writings and meanings upon meanings, until it all swells up into a huge mess. The statement itself has been manipulated and tangled into a conundrum. The statement of Christ is simple: 'He who sent me among you will come again!' and he pointed to a lamb. The lamb is merely a symbol, a sign. It stands for the voice, 'Ba-ba.' The announcement was the Advent of Baba, 'His name will be Truth,' said Christ. Sathya means Truth. 'He will wear a robe of red, a blood-red robe.' (Here, Baba pointed to the robe he was wearing!) 'He will be short, with a crown (of hair).' The Lamb is the sign and symbol of Love. Christ did not declare that he will come again; he said, 'He who went me will come again.' That Ba-ba is THIS Baba, and Sai the short-curly-hair-crowned red-robed Baba is come. He is not only in this form, but he is in every one of you, as the Dweller in the Heart. He is there, short, with a robe of the color of the blood that fills it."

Over the years, Baba has materialized pictures of Jesus at various stages in His life. At the Christmas discourse in 1996, Swami did an amazing thing, which was witnessed by thousands of people and videotaped as well, which anyone can see in slow motion, i.e., after stating that there was a conference held in England to go over all the data known on Jesus, in the 16th Century, a book was created, the Russians made a very small copy, and secreted it in a monastery in Armenia, and then it found its way to a museum. Baba waved his hand and apported it to the stage in front of thousands of witnesses and being videotaped. He showed many people this very tiny book and stated that it was from the museum but told the real story of the life of Jesus. Then, he said he had to get it back there before the guards knew it was gone! (Note: Not to worry: no thieves could ever duplicate this technique because to attain such mastery over time, space, and matter requires some significant spiritual advancement!)

Even though I was raised in the Presbyterian Church, and still do like the church, nonetheless, I never really knew Jesus until I started meditating. Then, I could feel him within me. He is always very joyful when he comes to me. I have never experienced him sad. I do not like the pictures that make him sad. He is one with the Infinite. He is major league cool to me. I am ashamed sometimes for what his supposed followers do in His name. I personally believe that Jesus went into the breathless state on the cross, survived and moved to Kashmir for a long life. I also believe he has come back and is helping man's evolution.

Bibliography and Sources

The following books about Sai Baba are published by the Sri Sathya Sai Books and Publications Trust in India. These are the resources I used for most of the teachings and some of the miracles of Sai Baba in my work. I have put the dates with each individual work, when they are available. All of the books in this section have the same publisher, same address, and same city:

Sri Sathya Sai Books and Publications Trust, Prashanthi Nilayam, Pin – 515 134, Anantapur District, Andhra Pradesh, India

The Vaahinis Series (books written by Bhagavan Sri Sathya Sai Baba. This collection of volumes contains the wisdom prevailed throughout the ages.)

SS1 *Bhagavatha Vaahini* (The story of the Glory of the Lord)
SS2 *Dharma Vaahini* (The Path of Virtue)
SS3 *Dhyana Vaahini* (Practice of Meditation)
SS4 *Geetha Vaahini* (The Divine Gospel)
SS5 *Jnana Vaahini* (The Stream of Eternal Wisdom)
SS6 *Leela Kaivalya Vaahini* (The Cosmic Play of God)
SS7 *Prashanthi Vaahini* (The Supreme Bliss of the Divine)
SS8 *Prasnothara Vaahini* (Answers to Spiritual Questions)
SS9 *Prema Vaahini* (The Stream of Divine Love)

SS10 *Rama Katha Rasa Vaahini* (Part I) (The Sweet Story of Rama's Glory)

SS11 *Rama Katha Rasa Vaahini* (Part II) (The Sweet Story of Rama's Glory)

SS12 *Sandeha Nivarini* (Clearance of Spiritual Doubts)

SS13 *Sathya Sai Vaahini* (Spiritual Message of Sri Sathya Sai)

SS14 *Sutra Vaahini* (Analytical Aphorisms on Supreme Reality)

SS15 *Upanishad Vaahini* (Essence of Vedic Knowledge)

SS16 *Vidya Vaahini* (Flow of Spiritual Knowledge Which Illuminates)

Sathya Sai Speaks Series: Four Decades of Discourses by Bhagavan Sri Sathya Sai Baba

SS17 Sathya Sai *Speaks Volume – I (Years 1953 to 1960)*

SS18 *Sathya Sai Speaks* Volume *– II (Years 1961 to 1962)*

SS19 *Sathya Sai Speaks Volume – III (Year 1963)*

SS20 *Sathya Sai Speaks Volume – IV (Year 1964)*

SS21 *Sathya Sai Speaks Volume – V (Year 1965)*

SS22 *Sathya Sai Speaks Volume – VI (Year 1966)*

SS23 *Sathya Sai Speaks Volume – VII (Year 1967)*

SS24 *Sathya Sai Speaks Volume – VIII (Year 1968)*

SS25 *Sathya Sai Speaks Volume – IX (Year 1969)*

SS26 *Sathya Sai Speaks Volume – X (Year 1970)*

SS27 Sathya Sai Speaks Volume – XI (Years 1971 to 1972)

SS28 Sathya Sai Speaks Volume – XII (Years 1973 to 1974)
SS29 Sathya Sai Speaks Volume – XIII (Years 1975 to 1977)
SS30 Sathya Sai Speaks Volume – XIV (Years 1978 to 1980)
SS31 Sathya Sai Speaks Volume – XV (Years 1981 to 1982)
SS32 Sathya Sai Speaks Volume – XVI (Year 1983)
SS33 Sathya Sai Speaks Volume – XVII (Year 1984)
SS34 Sathya Sai Speaks Volume – XVIII (Year 1985)
SS35 Sathya Sai Speaks Volume – XIX (Year 1986)
SS36 Sathya Sai Speaks Volume – XX (Year 1987)
SS37 Sathya Sai Speaks Volume – XXI (Year 1988)
SS38 Sathya Sai Speaks Volume – XXII (Year 1989)
SS39 Sathya Sai Speaks Volume – XXIII (Year 1990)
SS40 Sathya Sai Speaks Volume – XXIV (Year 1991)
SS41 Sathya Sai Speaks Volume – XXV (Year 1992)
SS42 Sathya Sai Speaks Volume – XXVI (Year 1993)
SS43 Sathya Sai Speaks Volume – XXVII (Year 1994)
SS44 Sathya Sai Speaks Volume – XXVIII (Year 1995)
SS45 Sathya Sai Speaks Volume – XXIX (Year 1996)

Sathyam Sivan Sundaram Series, author: Kasturi

SS46 (Life Story of Bhagavan Sri Sathya Sai Baba)

SS47 Sathyam Sivan Sundaram Part I (Birth to 1962)
SS48 Sathyam Sivam Sundaram Part II (Years 1962 to 1968)
SS49 Sathyam Sivam Sundaram Part III (Years 1969 to 1972)
SS50 Sathyam Sivam Sundaram Part IV (Years 1973 to 1979)

Summer Shower Series (discourses on Indian culture and spirituality by Bhagavan Sri Sathya Sai Baba.)

SS51 Summer Showers in Brindavan 1972
SS52 Summer Showers in Brindavan 1973
SS53 Summer Showers in Brindavan 1974
SS54 Summer Showers on the Blue Mountains (Ooty) 1976
SS55 Summer Showers in Brindavan 1977
SS56 Summer Showers in Brindavan 1978
SS57 Summer Showers in Brindavan 1979
SS58 Summer Showers in Brindavan 1990
SS59 Summer Showers in Brindavan 1993
SS60 Summer Showers in Brindavan 1996

Other Publications of the Sri Sathya Sai Baba Book and Publications Trust

SS61 *Conversations with Bhagavan Sri Sathya Sai Baba* by John S. Hislop (1976)

SS62 *Finding God* – by Charles Penn (1971)

SS63 *Garland of 108 Precious Gem* (108 Holy Names of Bhagavan) (1982)

SS64 *Gems of Wisdom* (1979)

SS65 *Loving God* – by N. Kasturi (1965)

SS66 *My Baba and I* by Dr. John S. Hislop (1974)

SS67 *Sadhana – The Inward Path* (1983)

SS68 *Sai Baba – The Holy Man and the Psychiatrist* – by Dr. Samuel Sandweiss (1973)

SS69 Divine Memories – by Diana Baskin (1990)

SS70 Transformation of the Heart – by Judy Warner (1984)

Books by Howard Murphet

SS71 *Sai Baba Avatar*: Macmillan India Limited, 1978.

SS72 *Sai Baba Invitation to Glory*: Macmillan India Limited, 1982.

Other Works

1) Yogananda, Paramahansa, *Autobiography of a Yogi*. Los Angeles, CA: Self-Realization Fellowship, 1971 (originally written in 1946).

This is one of the most amazing autobiographies ever written! It is an in-depth account of the great yogi, Paramahansa Yogananda's life and details his growing up in India and meeting his guru, Sri Yukteswar. The book is full of wonderful accounts of the saints and sages of India including stories of Mahavatar Babaji, Lahiri Mahasaya, and other great souls. Yogananda had visions of traveling to America to do a work there and his teacher, Sri Yukteswar encouraged him in this. The book leads the reader to America where Yogananda brings the science of yoga and Kriya to thousands of people. He establishes Self-Realization Fellowship in California, writes books, and teaches many about spirituality. His great mission, to bring the Eastern wisdom to the West, was accomplished and the reader celebrates with him. Throughout the book are wonderful photographs of Yogananda's life and encounters with others. The book is dedicated to Luther Burbank, the great horticulturist, who Yogananda called "An American Saint." Yogananda, throughout the book, marvels about the accomplishments of others, their sainthood, their innate goodness and yet, he, himself accomplished much and brought the love of God to all who would listen. Whoever is fortunate enough to read this book is greatly blessed.

2) Witt, R.E., *Isis in the Ancient World*. Baltimore, MD: The John Hopkins University Press, 1971.

This is a scholarly study of the Cult of Isis
with an emphasis on the historical and
archaeological aspects of her. Witt follows Isis
throughout her expansion from Egypt into the
Graeco-Roman world as well as Europe and in
particular, has an interest and focus on how the
worship of Isis fed into the development of
Christianity. He believes that archaeological
findings do and will bear out the existence of the
cult of Isis and that Western culture really has some
of its roots from Isis because she, in turn, informed
the Graeco-Roman world and Christianity. Thus,
instead of thinking Ancient Egypt as a remote and
different world from the Western one, he believes
there is a direct connection between them.

3) Harvey, Andrew, *Songs of Kabir*. Boston, MA:
Weiser Books, 2002.

Although the translation of Kabir's
poems/songs were done by the great Indian poet and
writer, Rabindranath Tagore, the lengthy
introduction to this book was written by Andrew
Harvey. Andrew Harvey is well known for his own
books on Jesus and other great souls, as well as his
own spiritual journey with his gurus, and has
translated mystical texts. Andrew Harvey is also
known for his passion and love for the heart of the
mystical experience and so is well suited to analyze
Kabir's poetry. Kabir, who was a poet of the heart,
is introduced by Andrew Harvey to the reader, in a
very thorough way. The introduction offers the
reader a context with which to better appreciate and

understand Kabir's philosophy as demonstrated in his poetry.

4) Bryan, Magee. *The Story of Philosophy, The Essential Guide to the History of Western Philosophy.* New York, NY: DK Publishing, Inc, 1998.

This is a beautifully illustrated compendium of the main western philosophers with an introduction to western philosophy. It covers the Greek philosophers such as Plato and Aristotle, then moves into Christianity explaining how it was informed by the Greek philosophers. Next it examines how modern science had its beginnings in the 16th and 17th century. The book also examines the Rationalists, Empiricists, the French philosophers, German philosophy, early American philosophers and finally 20th century philosophy. It also includes a helpful comparison between Eastern and Western philosophical thought. This is an easy book to use for reference, giving brief, yet detailed descriptions of the philosophers and their philosophies. Drawings, photographs, and illustrated sidebars make it easy for the reader to engage the book.

5) Murphet, Howard. *Sai Baba: Man of Miracles.* York Beach, ME: Samuel Weiser, Inc., 1973.

Howard Murphet, who has just recently died (2004), has written many fine books about his teacher, Satya Sai Bai, of India. This book is a fascinating and detailed account of the life of Satya Sai Baba. It is filled with personal stories and Murphet's own experiences with Sai Baba. So it is both a first-hand account of being a devotee of Sai Baba's as well as an objective reporting of Sai Baba's life, his mission, his teachings, and his countless miracles. Murphet's style draws the reader in and his narrative often reads like a good novel. There are many, many books written about Sai Baba, but in my experience, this book is one of the most thorough and detailed accounts of this great being. Murphet wrote that this book is meant to introduce people to Sai Baba and is meant to be objective in its narrative. Because of the nature of this great teacher, Sai Baba, it is a fascinating read and will help someone who has never heard or read about Sai Baba, to really begin to understand the enormity of who he is. Highly recommended!

6) Starbird, Margaret. *The Woman with the Alabaster Jar*: *Mary Magdalen and the Holy Grail*, Rochester, VT: Bear and Co., 1993.

Margaret Starbird has written several books about the restoration of the forgotten feminine. She had an awakening after reading *Holy Blood, Holy Grail*, which postulates that Jesus Christ was married to Mary Magdalene. Having been trained and studied in the Judeo-Christian scriptures, this came, as she admits, as a complete shock to her. So began her deep quest into history, symbolism, art, psychology, the Bible and even the meaning behind the sacred numerology of the Bible, to uncover and begin to understand what the Church has hidden. This book focuses on Mary Magdalene, who she was historically as well as symbolically and why she has remained under wraps for so many years. In her own words, "Doctrines I had believed on faith had to be uprooted and discarded, and new beliefs had to be sown and allowed to take root. The entire Roman Catholic framework of my childhood had to be dismantled to uncover the dangerous fault in the foundation and then the belief system carefully rebuilt when the fissure had been sealed." This took her seven years to accomplish. Her quest with this book and others is to find the "Holy Grail," the deeper meaning of it as well as what is actually is.

7) Leslie-Chaden, Charlene, *A Compendium of the Teachings of Sathya Sai Baba.* Parsanthi Nilayam, AP, India: Sai Towers Publishing, 1996.

8) Yogananda, Paramahansa, *The Divine Romance.* Los Angeles, CA: Self-Realization Fellowship, 1986.

9) Isherwood, Christopher, *Ramakrishna and His Disciples.* Hollywood, CA: Vedanta Press, 1965.

10) Vandananda, Swami, *The Complete Works of Swami Vivekananda.* Pithoragarh, Himalayas, India: public domain, 1976.

11) Walters, J. Donald, *The Path.* Nevada City, CA: Crystal Clarity Publishers, 1977.

12) Yogananda, Paramahansa, *Man's Eternal Quest.* Los Angeles, CA: Self-Realization Fellowship, 1982.

13) Rama, Swami, *Living with the Himalayan Masters.* Honesdale, PA: Himalayan Institute Press, 1978.

14) O'Brien, Dr. Justin, *Walking with a Himalayan Master.* Honesdale, PA: Himalayan Institute Press, 1998.

15) Evans-Wentz, W.Y., editor, *Tibet's Great Yogi Milarepa.* New York, NY: Oxford University Press, 1973.

    This edited version of the biography of the Tibetan yogi, Milarepa, is probably the most well-known and regarded book about this incredible saint. Even though Evans-Wentz edited the book in 1928, this rendition was a second edition published first in 1950. Evans-Wentz first received this biography from his own Tibetan guru, the late Lama Kazi Dawa-Samdup, who was the translator. Evans-Wentz traveled to India and met Himalayan and Indian yogis who shared much of the ancient wisdom with him. In his original preface, he quotes his guru, "That this translation of the life-history of Milarepa might contribute a little to help to make him as well known and esteemed in other lands as he is already in his own was the one wish which impelled me as I worked at my task, and remains my ardent prayer as I lay down my pen." (xvii) So, you could say, in a sense, this book was really handed down from teacher to student, preserving a kind of lineage.

Besides its thorough description of the life and teachings of Milarepa, it also gives the reader a "vivid record of the social conditions which prevailed in the Tibet of the eleventh and twelfth century of the Christian Era." (1, introduction). Tibet then was actually quite developed philosophically and spiritually compared to other places on earth. This book is considered a gospel of the Kargyutpa sect of Buddhism of which Milarepa was initiated into by his guru, Marpa.

This is not an easy book to read as it is full of references, unfamiliar terms to the lay person, numerous footnotes of explanation and is an older translation. The reader can delve in and find precious gems of wisdom, but must be willing to wade through difficult and not very accessible language.

Meditation Centers:

- Yogananda: www.yogananda-srf.org

- Kriyananda: www.onlinewithananda.org

- Swami Rama: www.himalayaninstitute.org

- Sathya Sai Baba: http://us.sathyasai.org

- Dr. George Gaye:
  www.SelfRealizationWisconsin.com

About the Author

Sam Podany is an author, musician, composer, business consultant, and long-time disciple of Dr. George and Sai Baba. He lives in Ft. Collins, Colorado. Contact him at banjosam99@gmail.com

Services Available for You
Your Words in Print

You have a valuable, valid perspective that needs to be shared. Whether it is a story, an idea, a how-to, or a memoir, we help materialize your book.

Richard A. Bowen has written, edited, and published more than 15 books. He knows from first-hand experience the process of materializing a book, and the thrill and gratification of seeing *Your Words in Print*. It's incomparable.

Karen A. Bowen has 20 years' experience helping individuals remove the obstacles to their success and offers business coaching to first-time authors.

If you are at the "idea" stage, *Your Words in Print* helps you organize and clarify your ideas so you can begin to write. If you already have written material (a manuscript), *Your Words in Print* edits the manuscript to get it ready for distribution. We then work with you to make the book available in both print and e-book versions.

FREE ESTIMATE

Your Words in Print offers a FREE ESTIMATE of how much time and effort it would require to bring your manuscript into a form so you can make it available to your audience. See www.YourWordsInPrint.com for more information.

Made in the USA
San Bernardino, CA
17 July 2017